RELATIONAL PARTNERSHIPS FOR MISSIONS MOBILIZATION

Enoch Wan & Joshua Paxton

Relational Paradigm Series of CDRR

Relational Partnerships for Missions Mobilization

Copyright 2022 © Western Academic Publishers

Enoch Wan & Joshua Paxton

Cover designed by Mark Benec

ISBN: 978-1-954692-14-5

CDRR (Center of Diaspora & Relational Research) @ https://www.westernseminary.edu/outreach/center-diaspora-relational-research

Western Academic
Publishers

FORWARD

As I write this Forward the hottest movie showing in theaters is "Top Gun: Maverick." The film is so popular you may have watched it yourself. Worldwide, ticket sales have crossed well over the $1 billion mark. The movie is an action-packed drama that centers on a raid made by four F/A 18 Super Hornets launched off the deck of the USS Theodore Roosevelt. The objective is to bomb a well-concealed nuclear processing plant hidden deep in the towering mountains of Iran that threatens national security.

You may be wondering, "What does that movie have to do with this book?" Actually, plenty!

When it comes to the importance of partnership and synergy this movie illustrates these principles best. In a review of the movie, Alvin Townely astutely observed that there are two passing scenes depicting the carrier's crew that most people would miss. Townely points out that those crew members huddled together in a shot next to the departing jets are wearing different color uniforms. Those wearing purple shirts have fueled up the jets; red shirts have armed them. Green shirts have maintained the engines and readied the catapults and arresting cables. Blue shirts run the ship's massive elevators, unchain the aircraft, and clear the chocks. Yellow shirts lock the aircraft into the catapults and send the aviators and their backseat flight officers rocketing off the deck. Each brown shirt serves as a plane captain, shouldering responsibility for ensuring their $70-million jet is ready. Townely adds:

> Everyone loves the sunglasses-wearing figures in flight suits; they're just the tip of a long spear, however. Each man and woman aboard Theodore Roosevelt makes it possible for these aviators to drop ordinance on a target and accomplish the ship's collective mission of advancing national security.[1]

That is what this book is all about – synergy. In this case it relates to the synergy needed to successfully launch well-mentored and trained missionaries into cross-cultural service. This book makes clear the partnership and synergy needed among three entities in the preparation of missionaries: the theological schools, the mission agencies, and local churches. Paxton shows how the three are equally necessary to bring balance to that preparation process.

---

[1] Alvin Townley, "The Most important 'Top Gun: Maverick' Moment Nearly Every Moviegoer Missed." Fox News, July 9, 2022.

The advantages of partnership and collaboration are certainly not new. Three thousand years ago wise King Solomon said this in Ecclesiastes 4:9-12:

> Two are better than one, because they have a good return for their work:
> If one falls down, his friend can help him up.
> But pity the man who falls and has no one to help him up!
> Also, if two lie down together, they will keep warm. But how can one keep warm alone?
> Though one may be overpowered, two can defend themselves.
> A cord of three strands is not quickly broken. (NIV)

This nugget of wisdom speaks to an enviable relationship. It contains the beauty of unity, equality, and harmony. But let's be realistic. Partnerships can be both magnificent and messy at the same time. Conferring and working together may not be easier, but it is better! In this short passage Solomon delineates why working in synergy is beneficial.

First is the benefit of a better chance of success (verse 9): "… have a good return for their work:" Put another way, there is the advantage of a better yield. More can be accomplished when done by many working in harmony. There are more persons to shoulder the workload, and each can focus on the specific aspect of the work of which they have expertise. In so doing, there is a better chance of what we all want – "a good return."

Second is the benefit of better stability (verse 10): "If one falls down, his friend can help him up." This is the advantage of mutual assistance by those who are in partnership. If one lags behind, others can rally round to take up the slack to help assure progress.

Third is the benefit of a better chance of survival (verse 11): "… they will keep warm." Remember this was written before central heating. Here is a picture of a husband and wife huddling together on a cold winter night under the warmth of the blankets – for survival. Two or three entities working together keep the mission viable and alive.

Last is the benefit of better security (verse 12): "A cord of three strands is not quickly broken."
This refers to the advantage of safety and on-going viability. It is the reason why fighter jets fly in pairs consisting of a lead jet and a wingman. It is why warriors fight in pairs, and why countries forge alliances with other countries. Together they are all more secure. They are not easily broken.

Success, stability, survival, security. Every forward-looking organization and institution values these benefits. This book was written to bring to the fore the benefits of synergy to the missionary preparation process. The cord of three strands comprised of the theological school, the mission agency, and a local church, working in partnership makes this synergy possible.

Dr. Marvin J. Newell
Executive Director
Alliance for the Unreached/A Third of Us

TABLE OF CONTENTS

LIST OF TABLES

LIST OF FIGURES

CHAPTER 1

INTRODUCTION

Introduction

Following the reformation, Protestant churches were slow to get onboard with taking the gospel to unreached peoples. Several factors contributed to this; the isolation of Protestant countries from missions lands, difficulty of travel, and in-fighting between Catholics and Protestants. The greatest barrier of all was a theological position that was best reflected in the words of J.R. Ryland to William Carey, "Young Man, sit down, when God pleases to save the heathen, He will do it without your help or mine."[2] A statement which is in direct opposition to Romans 10:14, 15. Perhaps the simplest reason for the slow advance of Protestant churches into the missions endeavor was merely that they lacked the resources to send and support missionaries.

Gradually and with great effort, William Carey and others overcame these challenges eventually resulting in the founding of the first Protestant missions organization, *The Particular Baptist Society for the Propagation of the Gospel to the Heathen* (founded 1792). Subsequently, many more mission organizations would be founded, including the first American foreign mission board, the *American Board of Commissioners for Foreign Missions* (founded 1810). Others would follow closely behind, *American Baptist Foreign Mission Society* (1814), *China Inland Mission* (1865), and *Africa Inland Mission* (1895).

Today the world is filled with mission agencies. Just some of the partners that we have at Calvary University are *Avant, Crossworld, SEND, Ethnos 360, Midwest Church Extension, Village Missions* and many more. Historically, mission agencies arose to come alongside Protestant churches and denominations and help them to fulfill their responsibility in global missions. However, over time this relationship became an unhealthy one of churches abrogating the responsibility for missions to the mission agency by sending their people and their money and then largely taking a hands-off approach to missionary care and support. The support and care of the missionary on the field was viewed as the agency's job. The mindset of many churches became, "pay, pray, and stay out of the way." Unfortunately, many agencies were all too happy with this relationship. In the past 10-15 years however, a shift has been

---

[2] C. Gordon Olson, *What in the World is God Doing?: The Essentials of Global Missions*, 7th Ed. (Lynchburg: Global Gospel Publishers, 2013), 119.

happening in the relationship between churches and mission agencies. Churches have been asking for more control over their missionaries and caring for them on the field and agencies have been seeking to get churches more directly involved in the mobilizing and equipping and caring process of their missionaries.

Agencies such as Avant have begun leading the way through their Joint Venture program. A cooperative program between the church and agency that aims to see the local church take more of the initiative and responsibility for sending teams to the mission field.[3] Missio Nexus, an organization committed to the networking of missions agencies, has launched their Mobilization Ideation program, around the question of how agencies can work more cooperatively with churches in mobilizing people for the mission field.[4] Biblical Ministries Worldwide has begun having church/agency think tanks in order to encourage churches to take more responsibility for raising up and sending out their people.[5] As represented in the book *Pipeline: Engaging the Church in Missionary Mobilization*[6] a shift is coming in how the Western church raises up, equips and sends missionaries.

While much of the current discussion surrounds the relationship between agencies and churches, there is also a third player that needs to be included in this conversation and so far, has been largely left out of it. Within the rise of the Modern Missions Movement through the 19th century there was another phenomenon that was taking place. The Bible Institute Movement began primarily with three schools, the founding of NYACK college in 1882, Moody Bible Institute in 1886, and Tyndale University in 1894 represented a paradigm shift in how pastors and missionaries were trained for their ministries.[7] From this beginning with these three organizations; many Bible colleges, Bible institutes, universities and theological schools would rise to fill the need of well taught, well-trained pastors and missionaries. From these schools would come most of the missionaries throughout the 20th century.

However, two recent trends demonstrate a shift away from 4-year colleges and universities as training centers for missionary candidates. The first is the

---

3 "Churches," Avant Ministries, accessed October 28, 2019, https://avantministries.org/churches.

4 "Mobilization Ideation," Missio Nexus, accessed November 7, 2019, https://missionexus.org/mobilization-ideation/.

5 Paul Seger, "Why Would A Church NOT Want to Send Missionaries from their Congregation?" *latest*, accessed November 7, 2019, https://www.biblicalministries.org/see/blog/2019/06/03/why-would-a-church-not-want-to-send-missionaries-from-their-congregation/.

6 David and Lorene Wilson, *Pipeline: Engaging the Church in Missionary Mobilization*, (Pasadena: William Carey Publishing, 2018).

7 Lem Morgan, *Introduction to Missions*, (Calvary Bible College: unpublished course notes, 2002), 38.

closing of many of these educational institutions. Christian universities face many challenges in today's politically charged educational environment and many have been unable to survive.[8] The second is a shift away from Christian colleges as a primary source for missionary recruits.[9] Biblical Ministries Worldwide reports that over the past decade the average age of believers joining their organization is 36 years old.[10] The looming question is what will be the role of these institutions in the future? David and Lorene Wilson's book *Pipeline* generally fails to consider the involvement of Christian colleges and universities in the training and sending of missionaries.[11]

The current reality in global missions is that today around 3.2 billion people still have little to no access to the gospel. These are people who stare into the grim blackness of a Christless eternity and have only separation from God to look forward to and yet they are not even aware of their plight. They are *A Third of Us*.[12] They have faces, they have names, they have stories, hope dreams, and fears. God has placed before His Church the call to reach them with the message of the gospel, the story of Christ's completed work and the only hope for salvation and yet our current efforts are not keeping pace with the population growth in the most unreached areas of the world. Something must change. More intentional effort is needed on the part of the Universal Church to join together to raise up and launch more workers to the harvest.

The Background of this Book

The story of this book and the relational partnerships created through the Synergy process comes against the backdrop of Calvary University. Calvary University, located in Kansas City, MO, was originally founded in 1932 as Kansas City Bible College. The school underwent several mergers and name changes from 1961 to 1987 when it became Calvary Bible College and Theological Seminary. The name was formally changed to Calvary University in 2016 following the appointment in late 2015 of former President, Dr. Christopher Cone.[13] The current president, Dr. Alexander Granados was

---

[8] William Anderson, "The Coming Crises for Christian Colleges," The James G. Martin Center for Academic Renewal, accessed October 4, 2019, https://www.jamesgmartin.center/2019/01/the-coming-crises-for-christian-colleges/.

[9] Clark Macaulay, "Recruiting Missionaries," Biblical Ministries Worldwide, accessed July 20, 2021, https://www.biblicalministries.org/see/blog/2014/10/30/recruiting-missionaries/.

[10] Biblical Ministries Worldwide, "Senders Think Tank." (Biblical Ministries Worldwide, unpublished handout, 2019).

[11] Wilson, *Pipeline: Engaging the Church in Missionary Mobilization*. I have spoken with David at length about this and it appears the fault is not his own but rather the unresponsiveness of schools and professors he asked to participate in his book.

[12] Marvin J. Newell, *A Third of Us: What it Takes to Reach the Unreached*. (Littleton: William Carey Publishing, 2021).

[13] *Calvary University Catalog 2017-2019*, (Kansas City: Calvary University, 2017), 18-19.

appointed on October 1, 2021. Throughout its existence, Calvary has maintained a commitment to the Bible as the sole authority for faith and practice. This is evidenced throughout the school but especially in its mission statement and by-laws. The mission of Calvary University is to "prepare Christians to live and serve in the church and the world according to the biblical worldview."[14] The author of this book is a faculty member at Calvary University.

Calvary has long enjoyed close working relationships with many mission agencies. Faculty and staff have served on mission agency boards, agency staff have served on Calvary's board and several faculty and staff members have served on the mission field in cross-cultural locations. The University's annual Conference on Global Engagement in January easily draws over forty missions' representatives, missionaries, agency presidents and executive directors from thirty or more agencies. All this activity frequently becomes overwhelming to our approximate 150 on-campus students.[15] For a relatively small school we enjoy many great relationships with these organizations.

Of these, there are fifteen that form a closer group to which graduates tend to serve with following completion of their degree. They are represented by having their names on the chapel wall. Five of these fifteen are then part of a select group through which we have formed a partnership through the Synergy process. These five are Crossworld, Biblical Ministries Worldwide, Ethnos 360, Midwest Church Extension and Village Missions. Midwest Church Extension and Village Missions as nationally focused church planting/revitalization ministries are in a separate student track from the other three and, as such, they were not included in the research upon which this book is based. Even so, the conclusions can be equally applied to those two organizations.

This book is the result of Joshua Paxton's dissertation research, a study which outlined an understanding of the roles of the local church, the university,[16] and mission agency in the mobilizing and equipping of the next generation of missionaries. It examines a practical solution through the creation of relational partnerships in the Synergy process at Calvary University. Traditionally, this level of cooperation is only seen among denominations that maintain control of all three entities. However, the unity we share in Christ (Eph. 4:4-6) requires greater cooperation for reaching the lost. The research was concluded, and the dissertation written in Spring of 2022. Enoch Wan was Josh's academic advisor and dissertation chair. Marv Newell, Director of the Alliance for the Unreached and former Vice-President

---

[14] *Calvary University Catalog*, 10.

[15] Calvary had a total 2019 enrollment of 434.

[16] Throughout this paper "university" is used to refer mainly to private Christian colleges, universities, or theological schools offering 4-year undergraduate degrees.

of Missio Nexus served as second reader. After Josh finished the EdD program, the three men collaborated together on this book project, utilizing the data collected and interpretation found in the dissertation. More information on the research design and process can be found in the Appendices.

The Purpose of This Book

Traditionally, organizations involved in mission mobilization have operated in their own silos. Relationships and partnerships are created but no single non-denominational process exists for mobilizing missionaries which includes the involvement of all stakeholders. An intentional process is needed to mobilize the next generation for reaching the remaining peoples of the world with the gospel with the involvement of the local church, theological school, and mission agency. The purpose of this book is to introduce the reader to the Synergy process at Calvary University as a way of understanding how relational partnerships (between the local church, Christian university, and mission agency) are formed and operated for the mobilizing and equipping of the next generation for Christian mission. Along the way the reader will also be introduced to a model of relational partnerships. Partnerships which are based not on MOU's or articulation agreements (which can be important) but on shared relationship. This relational basis for partnership is especially relevant for believers in Christ who share the Holy Spirit and are united into one body (1 Corinthians 12).

The Authors

Enoch Wan has served on the faculty at Western Seminary for twenty-one years, leading two doctoral programs in intercultural studies and intercultural education. He served for two terms as president of the Evangelical Missiological Society and as vice president in various capacities for two decades. Enoch began his research on the two paradigms (i.e., relational realism and diaspora missiology) during his sabbatical as scholar-in-residence at Yale Divinity School two decades ago. Since then, he has published many articles and dozens of books on these two themes.

Joshua Paxton graduated from Calvary Bible College in 2004 with a Bachelor of Science in Biblical Counseling, and Calvary Theological Seminary in 2009 with a Master of Divinity in Pastoral Studies. Both institutions are now under the umbrella of Calvary University. He and his wife served briefly as part of a church planting team to Verona, Italy with Avant Ministries and then five months in Juneau, Alaska as camp pastor of Echo Ranch Bible Camp. He served as Missionary in Residence for Calvary during the 2011-2012 school year and was subsequently hired by the school to oversee the

Intercultural Studies Program. The Burnham Center for Global Engagement and Synergy were created in 2017 under his guidance. In 2022 Joshua graduated from Western Seminary with a Doctor of Education in Intercultural Education. Currently he serves as the Director of the Burnham Center for Global Engagement and is Associate Professor of Intercultural Studies at Calvary University.

Definition of Key Terms

Participatory Action Research: "Action research is a systematic approach to investigation that enables people to find effective solutions to problems they confront in their everyday lives."[17] It is considered "participatory" when all stakeholders are involved in the research process.[18]

Relational Realism: "Ontologically, 'relational realism' is to be defined as 'the systematic understanding that 'reality' is primarily based on the 'vertical relationship' between God and created order and secondarily 'horizontal relationship' within the created order."[19]

Christian Mission: "a process by which Christians (individuals) and the Church (institutional) continue on and carry out the *missio Dei* of the Triune God ("mission") at both individual and institutional levels spiritually (saving souls) and socially (ushering in *shalom**) for redemption, reconciliation, and transformation ("missions") *'*shalom*' is the context of total wellness in which created humanity can reach his/her full potential and properly respond to God and His message relationally (Jer. 29:7, 1 Tim. 2:1-5)."[20]

Missions: "ways and means of accomplishing 'the mission" which has been entrusted by the Triune God to the Church and Christians."[21]

Mobilization for Christian Missions: mobilization is a term frequently used in missions to refer to the total process of recruiting, equipping, and launching prospective missionaries to their field of service.

Ethnographic Profile: As used in this study refers to the completed qualitative and/or quantitative description of a particular group of people., noting specific characteristics, traits, and values which are important to their decision-making processes.

Culture: "The context/consequence of patterned interaction of personal Beings/beings, in contrast to popular usage of culture applying to the presumed closed system of Homo sapiens. This definition of culture can

---

[17] Ernest T. Stringer, *Action Research*, 4th ed. (Los Angeles: Sage, 2014), 1.

[18] Stringer, *Action Research*, 14-15.

[19] Enoch Wan, "The Paradigm of 'Relational Realism.'" *Occasional Bulletin*. (2006), 1.

[20] Enoch Wan, ed. *Diaspora Missions to International Students*, (Portland: Western Seminary Press, 2019), 10.

[21] Enoch Wan, "Rethinking Missiological Research Methodology: Exploring a New Direction." *Global Missiology*, October 2003b, www.GlobalMissiology.org.

freely be applied or referred to angelic (fallen or good) beings of the angel-culture and the dynamic interaction of the Three Persons of the Triune God in theo-culture"[22]

Intercultural Education: The multidimensional process of relational interaction of Beings/beings: students, and educational community (teacher, mentor, pastor, peer); towards spiritual and intercultural development (being, knowing, doing). Intercultural education has two areas of focus: 1) education across cultures in which the teacher is of one cultural background and the students another or multiple, and 2) education for interculturality*: where the focus is preparing the student for intercultural work/ministry. *Interculturality is the quality of being culturally sensitive in situations involving people from multiple cultures.

Synergy: Refers to the Synergy process[23] at Calvary University, described in Chapter 2.

Who Should Read this Book?

This book is intended for anyone who is passionate about fulfilling Jesus' final command to reach the lost.[24] As I[25] write this, fully 3.2 billion people remain unreached with the message of the gospel. They have no churches, no Bibles, no songs, no Christian coffee shops or radio stations. They have little to no testimony of the person of Christ. Those of us living in the West can scarcely imagine what it means to be born, live, and die, heading to a Christless eternity having never even heard of His existence. Our current efforts to reach the unreached are sadly poor. While many are invested in this work, including our brothers and sisters around the world, the job remains unfinished, and so long as it remains unfinished it remains our task to complete.[26] To that end this book is written to the Church, if only to be one more voice calling for us to wake up and complete the task the Lord gave us.[27]

This book is intended for pastors of local churches. It dives deep into the biblical and theological basis for mission and demonstrates its primacy in the operation of the local church. The local church is the visible manifestation of the Universal Church and as such it bears responsibility for fulling Jesus' final command to make disciples. While the Universal Church is a multifaceted and

---

[22] Enoch Wan, "A Critique of Charles Kraft's Use/Misuse of Communication and Social Sciences in Biblical Interpretation and Missiological Formulation," *Global Missiology*, October 2004, www.globalmissiology.org.

[23] "process" is used because Synergy cannot accurately be described as an academic "program." The term "program" defines an academic degree.

[24] Matthew 28:18-20, Mark 16:15, Luke 24:46-49, John 20:21, 2 Corinthians 5:18-21.

[25] The pronoun "I" is used throughout the book for ease of reading with a personal touch.

[26] See the literature review in Appendix II for a discussion of the task of missions and the local church's responsibility to accomplish it.

[27] Matthew 28:18-20; Mark 16:15; Luke 24:47-40; John 20:21; Acts 1:8; 2 Cor. 5:18-21

complex organism made of all believers who organize themselves in many ways, scripturally, missions remains the responsibility of the local church. It is clearly demonstrated in Acts 13:1-4 through the calling of Paul and Barnabus to their first missionary journey and subsequently through the reports they make at the end of the first (Acts 14:24-28) and second (Acts 18:22-23) missionary journeys. Missions is not optional for the local church, nor is involvement of small churches with limited resources particularly easy. Read this as a call to be involved, but also as an arm reaching out to help, because you are not alone. There is help to be found in the other arms of the Body of Christ.

This book is also intended for the leaders of mission agencies and other mobilizing organizations. You are passionate about missions and rightly so, as you have studied the scriptures and seen clearly the call to get involved. However, you don't have to go alone. You especially don't need to mobilize alone. Agencies spend a wealth of resources every year on mobilizing new workers for the field, resources that could be better utilized on the field itself. How would partnerships with universities and local churches help you create a ready supply of Christians raised up and ready for the field? How might partnerships enable you to better serve and send resources to the field by placing more of the responsibility for mobilizing with the church and the university?

Finally, this book is intended for Christian university professors and administration as an encouragement toward forming Kingdom partnerships. Universities exist for their students. Those students come to study any number of disciplines in preparation for their career. However, for Christian universities a higher calling and a higher responsibility exists then simple career training or granting of credentials. Our goal is to biblically equip students for life and service to the King of Kings, who has left a very important command to His followers: the command to spread the message of the gospel to the farthest corners of this world. Careers and credentials are important but inconsequential next to knowing Christ (Phil. 3:8). As you read this book, ask yourself, "how is my institution forming intentional pathways to raise up, equip, and launch the next generation to the mission field?"

The authors speak as one of you, professors at Christian institutions of higher learning. Higher Education has come under intense scrutiny in recent years with mounting costs, student debt, and a shrinking job market. How will we continue to fulfill our calling in this environment? Partnerships which draw direct links for our students to ministries and jobs where they can utilize their training are essential. Read this book with a mind to how you can connect your students to areas of ministry and service following graduation.

Organization of the Book

This book is the result of dissertation research conducted by Joshua Paxton under the supervision of Enoch Wan. To keep the book more readable the relevant research and literature review information have been moved to the appendices. Each chapter concludes with questions for discussion as you consider working with others in creating relational partnerships for your own context. Chapter two explains the Synergy model as it has been created and put into place by Calvary University. It also lays out the educational foundation for the program and the context for transformational learning through partnership. Finally, it establishes the theological foundation for Synergy through an understanding of the Trinity, the Universal Church and the roles of the local church, mission agency, and university; each as organizational members of the Body of Christ. This is placed in the context of the relational paradigm.

Chapter three takes a deeper dive into the practical outworking of the Synergy process. Included in this chapter is a discussion of how the process works for each of our Synergy partners. While Village Missions and Midwest Church Extension where not part of the original study, this chapter includes an explanation of how the process works with them as nationally focused church planting and church revitalization agencies. Including them demonstrates the high degree of flexibility that is possible with this process.

Chapter four is a discussion of the missiological, ecclesiological, and educational implications of the research conducted. The creation of Synergy and the research that went into improvements in its design have demonstrated several areas for consideration by churches, agencies, and schools. Unsurprisingly, the biggest implication is simply the significance of relational partnerships in ministry. These partnerships are built upon a solid foundation of relationship through shared vision, conviction, and goals which outlast all manner of formal contracts. Chapter four concludes with recommendations for further research into relational partnerships.

Finally, the largest section of this book is the appendices. The literature review for the study as well as the methodology behind the research has been included here. This information has been moved to the appendices to facilitate the readability of the book. Readers who plan to implement partnerships are highly encouraged to review the rich material and benefit from the resources. The literature review contains important theological and theoretical information for the development of relational partnerships.

Questions for Discussion

1. All ministry is contextually dependent. Consider first what is the context of your ministry, who are the major players and potential partners, who are you trying to reach?

2. An old adage states, "to begin with the end in mind." As you consider your context, think also about your end goals. What are you trying to accomplish? How will you measure success? A good exercise would be to think through the following steps:
   - What are your outcomes? What is the desired result of your ministry partnership?
   - After determining your outcomes think of two or three measurable standards for each one.
   - Finally, what are the benchmarks which will help you to know if you have met those standards?
3. Now that you know your context and where you are going, ask yourself how you will get there and who needs to be involved in the process.

CHAPTER 2

THE SYNERGY MODEL AND EDUCATIONAL PROGRAM

Introduction to Synergy

The Cambridge dictionary defines "synergy" as "the combined power of a group of things when they are working together that is greater than the total power achieved by each working separately."[28] Synergy is a cooperative effort available to Calvary University students through the Burnham Center for Global Engagement. Through Synergy, students can progress immediately to the mission field following graduation by taking specific coursework at Calvary in conjunction with the mission agency's existing training program. Twelve hours of coursework are available to be earned through this program.[29]

Synergy was 'soft launched' in December of 2017. The initiating factors were ongoing discussions between then President of Calvary University, Dr. Christopher Cone, Paul Mattson, International Director for Crossworld, and Joshua Paxton, Director of the Burnham Center for Global Engagement. Crossworld was the first of Calvary's Synergy partners and this explanation of the process will focus on them. As the first partner in Synergy, Crossworld is the ideal example and "best of both worlds" as it was initially designed with them in mind. Synergy lines up very well with Crossworld's existing member orientation and pre-field orientation.

Located in Kansas City, MO, just a 30-minute drive North of Calvary's campus, Crossworld's main mission is engaging the world's least reached marketplaces through business as mission strategies.[30] Crossworld focuses on placing professionals in the international marketplace who can both work and reach the lost through a focus on discipleship. Their location and historical relationship make them an ideal partner in Calvary's Synergy process. In addition, Crossworld's opportunities make them the ideal choice for students interested in a business-as-missions model of ministry. Crossworld is our premier partner for Teaching English as a Second Language (TESOL) opportunities, including an opportunity in Thailand that students can progress to immediately following graduation.

---

[28] "synergy," *Cambridge Dictionary*, accessed June 2. 2022, https://dictionary.cambridge.org/us/dictionary/english/synergy.

[29] Joshua Paxton, "Synergy Handbook," (Kansas City: Calvary University, unpublished, 2022).

[30] "About," *Crossworld*, Accessed June 2, 2022, https://crossworld.org/about.

A student who wishes to be involved in Synergy will begin by filling out the Synergy application, available online at Calvary's website.[31] The application includes a pastoral reference form to be sure that the student's home church is aware of the direction they are undertaking.[32] Having applied to the program itself the student will be directed to complete the organization's application process. For Crossworld, this involves an initial enquiry to the mobilization team online after which they will send a link to the application. This application must be completed by February of the spring semester of the student's sophomore year.[33] This requires students to be forward thinking in determining their educational goals and direction following graduation. For that reason, not all students will take advantage of this program as many are unsure of where they want to serve after they graduate.[34] This merely serves to emphasize the importance that the local church plays in discipling its young people to have a missions mindset upon entering school. I have personally witnessed everything from students who enter university with a strong foundation and a clear goal for their education that they never waver from, to students who don't know what they want to do even following graduation. The partnership of the local church and families within the local church is essential in promoting mission mindedness early on!

Synergy is also incredibly flexible. The college credit is designed to slot into the open electives of a student's planner. This allows students of any major to benefit from the process while preparing for a variety of professional options. It is also possible for a student to complete the Synergy process and the training and yet not join the agency, either because they or the agency does not believe them to be a good fit. However, the student still retains the credit for the coursework and can graduate as normal, they have everything to gain and nothing to lose. Even students who do not need the credit, because of their program or transferring in many hours that take up their open electives can still benefit from the process or being trained by the agency and developing the necessary relationships while still in school. Once a student is accepted by Crossworld, or another agency, they begin the coursework and training, which is summarized in the table below.

---

[31] "Synergy," *Calvary University*, Accessed June 2, 2022, https://www.calvary.edu/synergy/.

[32] This reference form serves as the introduction of a local church not previously aware of Calvary or Synergy to the partnership model.

[33] This is the ideal timeline; exceptions can be made and there is possibility for students to join the program later in the academic career depending on their unique program and schedule for completion.

[34] This lack of direction serves to further highlight the necessary involvement of the local church in guiding and directing students early in life towards a life of being on mission for God.

Table 1. Synergy Crossworld Completion Timeline[35]

Year	Calvary Course	Crossworld Training
Sophomore		
Fall	Introduced to Synergy	
Spring	Complete Application Process	
Summer	IC361	Pre-Candidate Orientation Sessions
Junior		
Fall	IC362	Weeklong Candidate Orientation
Spring		Post Candidate Orientation
Summer	IC363	Pre-Departure Orientation
	Internship*	Vision Trip
Senior		
Fall	IC364	Culture Bound
Spring	Graduate	
Summer	Finish support raising and deploy	

If required by the student's academic program

As the table above demonstrates, the process of joining and being trained by Crossworld can be worked right into the context of the student's four-year degree program. It requires the student to spend at least one week at Crossworld's International Headquarters and Training Center.[36] With the additional convenience of Calvary's blended course model, students can stay caught up in other coursework online while attending the training sessions at Crossworld. In addition, the recent Covid-19 pandemic has caused Crossworld to move much of its training online, increasing the flexibility for our students who may also be getting their education from Calvary online.

The Synergy process provides a completely unique opportunity for Calvary students to experience the practical outworking of integrated relational partnerships through several avenues. The first avenue relates to the fact that the relational partnership is maintained by Crossworld (and others) with Calvary University. The ability for these two separate organizations to cooperate under the umbrella of the Universal Church emphasizes Paul's words regarding the body of Christ in 1 Corinthians 12. While the direct application of this passage is for believers in fellowship in a local church, a

---

[35] This matrix is current as of Summer 2022, in an ever-shifting landscape it is important to keep up to date. Interested individuals can contact Calvary for current program details.

[36] Calvary University and Crossworld as well as Avant Ministries are only a 30-minute drive from one another, allowing a student easy access to both.

clear principle can be seen in the unique roles played by local churches, agencies, and the university.

The second avenue by which relational partnerships are experienced is found in the relationships that the student has with his local church (emphasized through the pastoral references and learning contracts), the theological school (through the taking of the four classes and overall enrollment in the program), and mission agency (through the training and process of becoming a member).

The last avenue of relational experience is the involvement of the triune God in the entire process, as God works in the life of the student and through believers in the local church, mission agency, and university.

As Synergy has been implemented over the past five years one thing has become increasingly clear, the greatest weakness to this process is in the relational ties to the local church. Synergy provides a framework for relationships between the theological school and mission agency. It also creates an environment for local church involvement and encourages local church ownership. However, greater investment is needed in involving the local church as a full-fledged partner in the process. To that end, Calvary is taking steps to connect with local churches and pastors to help solve this apparent weakness. Interviews conducted with pastors for the dissertation indicated a high degree of interest and involvement from pastors. However, more needs to be done to fully engage the local church as the initiator of missions mindedness with its people. The triunity of God and its accompanying reflection within the Universal Church provides a good background from which to build relational partnerships.

Unity in Diversity

The Triune God

The triunity of God provides the greatest scriptural foundation for partnership. The understanding of the nature of God as three-in-one is fundamental to the Christian faith, and the acknowledgement of the doctrine of the Trinity stands as one of the primary distinctions between an orthodox and unorthodox belief system.[37] The example of the Trinity provides an important illustration for the organizational diversity of the local church, missions organization, and university under the one unifying factor of the Universal Church.

The concept of the Trinity has a rocky history. Three incorrect views of the Trinity can be seen. Tri-theism placed too much emphasis on the diversity present in God at the expense of the unity. The result was a view that

---

[37] Paul Enns, *The Moody Handbook of Theology*, (Chicago: Moody Press, 1989), 198.

essentially resulted in three separate gods. Sabellianism, otherwise known as modalism, made the opposite mistake. Placing an over emphasis on the unity of God despite the diversity. This view stated that God exists as one person who can switch between the personalities of Father, Son, and Holy Spirit. The significant problem here was that He could only ever appear as one at a time. Tertullian placed undue emphasis on the submission of the Holy Spirit to the Son and the Son to the Father. Arias would take this to the extreme interpretation found in Arianism that the Father created the Son. The Council of Nicea in 325 A.D. condemned Arius' teaching.[38]

Paul Enns outlines an orthodox position on the Trinity in the *Moody Handbook of Theology*, emphasizing four important points: God is one in regard to essence, God is three with respect to persons, the three persons have distinct relationships, and the three persons are equal in authority.[39] I will deal with each of these aspects in turn for each one has theological implications for the formation of partnerships.

Figure 1. Triquetra, Celtic Symbol for the Trinity[40]

God is One in Regard to Essence

Represented by the circle in figure 1, this aspect of the Trinity speaks of its essential unity. This essential essence is reflected in the Shema found in Deuteronomy 6:4-9, "Hear O, Israel! The Lord our God, The Lord is one" (Deut. 6:4). The Israelites were distinctly monotheistic compared with their surrounding neighbors. The essence of God speaks directly to His being, that

---

[38] Enns, *The Moody Handbook of Theology*, 199.

[39] Enns, *The Moody Handbook of Theology*, 199-200.

[40] "Trinity Knot, The History of Triquetra," *Ireland Travel Guides*, accessed February 15, 2021, https://irelandtravelguides.com/trinity-knot-triquetra/.

while the "three persons possess the summation of God the essence of God is undivided."[41] James further stresses the unity of God in James 2:19 as something that even the demons acknowledge, "You believe that God is one; you do well. Even the demons believe – and shudder!" Jesus, the second person of the Trinity, repeatedly stressed to the Jews that the members of the Trinity do not act independently of each other, but are interdependent, (Cf. John 5:19; 8:28; 12:49; 14:10)[42] This interdependency of the members of the Trinity further reflects the character of their relationship with one another.

God is Three with Respect to Persons.

The statement that God is "three with respect to Persons" speaks to the essential diversity that is to be found in the Trinity. While God is one in essence, there are three distinct persons within the godhead: Father, Son, and Holy Spirit. Enns states that the word "persons" can be somewhat problematic as it implies greater separation at the expense of the unity of the Trinity. "Subsistences," along with "distinction," "relation," and "mode," are other terms that have been used to describe the uniqueness of each member of the Trinity.[43] The term "persons" is to be preferred, however, in that it emphasizes a unique manifestation of the one essence of God with a distinct personality for all three members.

Two key places in Scripture where we see all three members of the Trinity at work are in creation and in the baptism of Jesus. At the creation of man in Genesis 1:26 we have the declaration by God, "Let us make man…" The use of the qualitative imperfect plural "us" demonstrates that all three persons of the Trinity were involved in creation. Further, at Jesus' baptism we have all three persons present at the same moment in time. The recording of the event in Matthew 3:16-17 presents a clear picture as Jesus is in the water being baptized, the Spirit is visibly seen descending on Him, and the voice of the Father can be heard from heaven. On both occasions there is clear distinction in the persons of the Trinity. Both the unity and diversity of the persons of the Trinity are further seen in passages such as Isaiah 48:12-16 and 61:1 (which Jesus quotes as referring to Himself in Luke 4:18-21). These references emphasize both the equality and unity of the three persons as they relate specifically to Christ's mission.[44]

---

[41] Enns, *The Moody Handbook of Theology*, 200.
[42] Enns, *The Moody Handbook of Theology*, 200.
[43] Enns, *The Moody Handbook of Theology*, 200.
[44] Enns, *The Moody Handbook of Theology*, 200.

The Three Persons have Distinct Relationships.

The most relevant characteristic of the Trinity for our current discussion is the relationships between the members. These relationships have been misunderstood in the past, primarily through the words used to describe them, and they have been the source of many controversies in the early church as illustrated above. Several verses clarify the relationships within the Trinity.

The Son's relationship with the Father can be seen in John 1:18 (the Son makes the Father known); 3:16, 17 (the Father sent the Son); John 15:15 (the Son makes known what he hears from the Father); John 16:28 (the Son came from the Father); John 16:32 (the Father is with the Son); and 1 John 4:9 (the Father sent the Son). Many more verses, especially in the Gospel of John, spell out the unique relationship between the Father and the Son. Perhaps the most illustrative for the sake of the Trinity is John 14:11 in which Jesus states, "I am in the Father and the Father is in me…" This one statement speaks to the unity, the diversity, and the relationship that exists in the Trinity.

Chapters 14-16 of John's Gospel are also illustrative of the relationship that exists between the Father and the Spirit and likewise the Son and the Spirit. The relationship between the Father and Spirit can be seen in John 14:17, 26 (the Father sends the Spirit). However, it is not only the Father who sends the Spirit, but the Son is involved in this sending work as well. The Son asks the Father to send the Spirit (John 14:16); the Spirit is sent in the Son's name (John 14:26); the Son sends the Spirit from the Father (John 15:26); the Spirit bears witness to the Son (John 15:27); and the Son must leave so that the Spirit, 'helper', can come (John 16:7). Throughout these verses we can see both equality and submission within the Trinity. The Son does the will of the Father (John 14:10); the Spirit submits to the will of the Father and the Son (John 16:13).

The Three Persons are Equal in Authority.

It is vital to a proper understanding of the Trinity to note that all three Persons are equal in authority. It can be seen from the previous verses in John 14-16 that there is submission within the Trinity, the Son submits to the will of the Father (John 14:10), and the Spirit submits to the will of the Father and the Son (John 16:13). At the same time all three members of the Trinity are equally God. In 1 Corinthians 8:6 the Father and Son are viewed as equally authoritative. The Son is recognized as equally authoritative to the Father (John 5:21-23) and likewise the Spirit to the Father and Son (Matt. 12:31).[45]

This equality of authority is further demonstrated in seeing the deity of the

---

[45] Enns, *The Moody Handbook of Theology*, 200.

Son and the Spirit. The deity of the Son (Jesus) is well attested to in Scripture: Jesus is described as the eternally existent Word, (John 1:1, 2, 14); Jesus references the identity of God in calling himself the "I am" (John 8:58); Paul speaks to Jesus being "in the form of God" (Phil: 2:6); and Paul further speaks to the eternality of Jesus (Col. 1:15-17). These are but a few examples that demonstrate the equality that the Son has with the Father. The Holy Spirit is likewise seen to possess deity as well as equality with the Father and Son. The relationship between the Father and the Spirit is clearly illustrated in 1 Corinthians 2:10-13, which speaks of the revelatory work of the Spirit on God's behalf. Romans 8:9-11 is also particularly instructive of the Spirit's deity and relationship within the Trinity. The Holy Spirit is alternately called the "Spirit of God," "Spirit of Christ," and simply Spirit. The identity of this Spirit is given in verse 11 as the one "who dwells in you," making it clear that it is the Holy Spirit, third member of the Trinity, who is in view here since both Acts 2 and 10 give testimony to the Holy Spirit being the one who indwells believers.

These principles, laid out by Enns, speak to the theology of the Trinity. However, there have also been indications of the relationship that exists between Father, Son, and Holy Spirit. This integrated relationship is vital to the design of relational partnerships. As Enoch Wan stated in an article for the Occasional Bulletin of the Evangelical Missiological Society regarding the paradigm of relational realism, "Relationship is an essential nature within the Triune God (Father, Son, and H.S.) and among humanity (male and female)."[46] It is the unique qualities of this relationship which provide a strong foundation for the relationship between local churches, mission agencies, and universities. Let us briefly examine this considering the sending and submitting activity as outlined above.

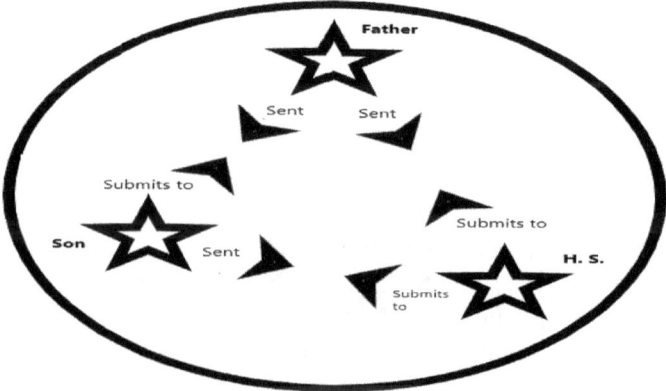

Figure 2. Sending and Submitting Relationships in the Trinity

---

[46] Wan, "The Paradigm of 'Relational Realism,'" 1.

From the above figure, the relationships within the Trinity pertaining to sending and submitting can be seen. The Father sends both the Son and the Spirit, the Son sends the Spirit and submits to the Father, and the Spirit submits to both the Father and Son. All three are equally God; however, they each also have unique roles to play in the redemption and reconciliation of God's relationship with man.[47]

Relational Realism

Enoch Wan proposed the relational realism paradigm as understanding of reality based on the Triune God's relationships both vertically and horizontally in an article first published in the Occasional Bulletin of the Evangelical Missiological Society.[48] In this article relational realism is proposed as an alternative to critical realism as embraced by Paul Hiebert.[49] The foundational aspects of relational realism are the vertical relationship between God and the created order and the horizontal relationship within the created order itself.[50] This distinction between God, as eternally existent, and the created order can be seen in Wan's figure below.[51]

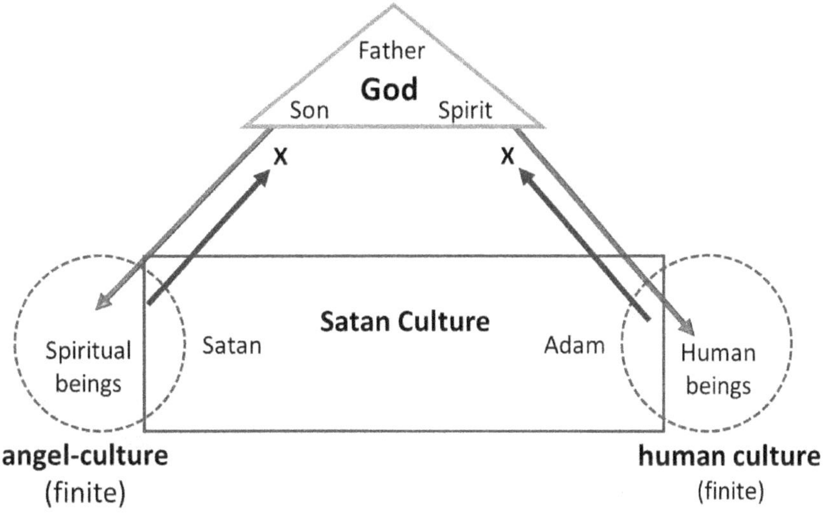

Figure 3. Creator and Creatures in Relation to Each Other

---

[47] See Appendix II, *Partnerships Within the Trinity,* 221.

[48] Wan, "The Paradigm of 'Relational Realism,'" 1.

[49] Paul Hiebert, *Missiological Implications of Epistemological Shifts,* (Harrisburg: Trinity Press International, 1999), 68-106.

[50] Wan, "The Paradigm of 'Relational Realism,'" 1.

[51] Enoch Wan, "Ethnohermeneutics; Its Necessity and Difficulty for All Christians of All Times," *Global Missiology*, January, 2004. globalmissiology.org.

The concept of the Trinity in understanding the relational characteristics of God is foundational to relational realism. Relationship undergirds every aspect of the Synergy process. Whether it is the relationships within the Trinity, between the triune God and teacher, student, missionary, and pastor or their relationships among each other.

The paradigm of relational realism has been further developed by Enoch Wan and Mark Hedinger in several articles and the recently released *Relational Missionary Training*.[52] The example seen in the relational framework of the Trinity provides a foundation to the relationships to be discussed later in the local church, mission agency, and university. The relationship inherent within the Trinity creates a natural environment for partnership, this same type of relational development and importance can also be seen scripturally in the Universal Church.

Relational Paradigm in the Universal Church

The Universal Church

The Church throughout all ages since Pentecost has both thrived and struggled to fulfill the calling which Christ has placed upon it to be "a chosen generation, a royal priesthood, a holy nation, His own special people..." (1 Peter 2:9). The Church has gone through strong times and rough times. It has been both persecuted and in power. Through it all, Christ's words in Matthew 16:18 that the gates of hell will not prevail against it have rung true and will continue to do so until the Church is removed from the world at the Rapture.

A sound ecclesiology is paramount to relational partnerships involving the Church because any attempt to bring Christians together in a common goal is fraught with peril. History is replete with examples of Christians fighting one another and even working to counter each other. While this book is no call to ecumenicalism or unity simply for the sake of unity, any attempt to build bridges of relationship between local churches, missions agencies, and theological schools must begin with what we have in common before moving on to the unique roles of each.

The Greek word for "church" is εκκλεσια. This same term is used of both local assemblies of believers as well as the universal Church. The εκκλεσια is not a uniquely Christian term, nor is it to be understood as having the literal meaning of "called-out ones."[53] Rather as noted by Louw and Nida, "The term εκκλεσια was in common usage for several hundred years before the Christian era and was used to refer to an assembly of persons constituted by well-

---

[52] Wan and Hedinger. *Relational Missionary Training.*

[53] Johannes P. Louw & Eugene A. Nida, ed., *Greek-English Lexicon of the New Testament Based on Semantic Domains*, (New York: United Bible Societies, 1989), 126.

defined membership."[54] The term itself does not provide a lot of insight into what exactly the Church is. Louw and Nida continue in their description to note that in the New Testament the meaning of the term is for "an assembly of God's people" and caution that never is it used to refer to a building as opposed to the gathering of the people themselves.[55] While this does provide clarity in our understanding of the Church as the gathering of believers rather than a particular organizational structure, it is to the New Testament usage of the word that we must turn in order to have an accurate understanding of what the Church is.

The first usage of the term, εκκλεσια, and first mention of the Church is when Jesus speaks of it in Matthew 16:18, "And I tell you, you are Peter, and on this rock, I will build my Church, and the gates of hell shall not prevail against it." Matthew uses the indicative future active, οἰκοδομήσω, to indicate that the action of building the Church is yet future. One of the most important concepts in understanding the Church is that it did not exist in the Old Testament. The Church is summarily described as the "body of Christ" (1 Cor. 12:12-27; Eph. 1:22-23, 4:15-16; Col. 2:19) and the "bride of Christ" (Eph. 5:32, 2 Cor. 11:2). In this, the Church has a unique relationship to Christ. Ephesians 1:22-23, 4:15-16, and Colossians 2:19 refer to Christ as the "head" of the Church. Of the members of the Trinity, Christ is in a unique relationship with the Church having purchased it with His blood (Acts 20:28).

Christ's relationship with the Church also defines its beginning. As Matthew 16:18 demonstrates, the Church did not exist in the Old Testament; it was to be a future creation of Christ. As can be seen through Scripture, the Church could not have existed until several events had taken place. First, as evidenced previously by Acts 20:28, Christ had to be crucified. It was by His death that the Church was purchased. Second, as Ephesians 2:5, 6 makes clear, Christ must be resurrected, as Paul further explains in 1 Corinthians 15:17, "And if Christ has not been raised, your faith is futile, and you are still in your sins." Third, Christ's ascension was essential to the founding of the Church. The ascension had three key factors tied into it that were essential for the birth of the Church. Christ had to be made head of the Church (Eph. 1:19-23), give the spiritual gifts (Eph. 4:7-12), and send the Holy Spirit (John 16:7, Acts 1:5). Finally, it was the arrival of the Holy Spirit that marked the beginning of the Church. Christ predicted it in Acts 1:5. In Acts 2 we have the actual occasion of the Holy Spirit baptizing and indwelling the Apostles and others gathered as evidenced by speaking in tongues. In response to the church in Jerusalem questioning him regarding his visit to Cornelius and eating with Gentiles Peter confirms that the Acts 2 event is the beginning of the Church

---

[54] Louw & Nida, *Greek-English Lexicon*, 126.
[55] Louw & Nida, *Greek-English Lexicon*, 126.

(Acts 11:15-16). From all of this, we see the Church as uniquely related to Christ and having a definite beginning with the arrival of the Holy Spirit at Pentecost.

The Church also has a definite ending. While views on the rapture vary,[56] it is evident that there will come a day when the Church is removed. Paul, in making his argument to the Thessalonians that the Day of the Lord has not yet come, provides a timeline of sorts for these events to comfort them. One of the key events that he describes is the removal of the one who restrains lawlessness (2 Thess. 2:7). Jesus describes one of the works of the Holy Spirit in John 16:8-11 as the convicting work of the Holy Spirit. The Holy Spirit is currently present on Earth through the indwelling of the saints (Eph. 1:13). His removal could be a reference to the Rapture of the Church. As Ephesians 1:13, 14 makes clear, He will be with the members of the Church until they acquire possession of their inheritance.

At this point we arrive at a definition for the Universal Church. The Universal Church is "That spiritual organism of which Christ is the Head and believers in Christ from Pentecost to the Rapture are members."[57] This definition includes several aspects that are rooted in Scripture as seen above and important for our consideration in this study. First, the Church is a "spiritual organism." The Church is not first and foremost an organization. While there are organizational aspects to local churches, the Church is the spiritual body of Christ. The Universal Church is also not defined by its location. Scripture presents the Church in two different ways, the Universal Church and local churches. While local churches, such as the churches of Ephesus (Eph. 1:1), Corinth (1 Cor. 1:2; 2 Cor. 1:2), and Thessalonica (1 Thess. 1:1), are a group of believers in a specific location, the Universal Church is much bigger than any one expression of it. The Universal Church is also spiritual in nature; it is bound together not by a constitution or by-laws but by membership in the Body of Christ through the indwelling work of the Holy Spirit (Eph. 1:13, 14). The Universal Church can be spoken of in both synchronic and diachronic terms. Synchronically, the Universal Church could be said to refer to all currently living members of Christ's Body at one point in time. Diachronically, it refers to every believer through its history from Pentecost to the Rapture. From this basis of the Universal Church, we will next consider local churches, mission agencies, and theological schools as expressions of it.

---

[56] Calvary University is theologically dispensational, premillennial, and pretribulation

[57] Lem Morgan, *Missions in the Local Church,* (Calvary Bible College: Unpublished Course Notes, 2002), 10.

The Local Church

Local churches can be viewed as local expressions of the Body of Christ in a specific location. Following Pentecost and the establishment of the Universal Church, we find the first local church in Jerusalem. Following Peter's sermon in Acts 2, three thousand who heard it are baptized and added to the number of believers. We are then given the first summary of the characteristics of the Jerusalem church in Acts 2:42-47. Several observations are noteworthy: they devoted themselves to the Apostles' teaching and fellowship (Acts 2:42), they ate together and prayed (2:42), the Apostles performed signs and wonders (2:43), they were together and shared their possessions (2:44, 45), there was frequent fellowship and rejoicing, and they were being praised by all the people (2:46, 47).

Following the arrest of Peter and John, Acts records another summary statement of the local church in Jerusalem. In Acts 4:32-37 we once again see the character of the church community in sharing their resources and giving testimony to Jesus' resurrection. Community, caring for one another, and giving bold witness to Christ were clearly characteristics of the early church in Jerusalem. Following the stoning of Stephen in Acts 7, the local church in Jerusalem is scattered (Acts 8:1), and many believers move throughout Judea and Samaria.

While several other events take place including the conversion of Saul, the next clear indication of a local church being formed is presented to us in Acts 11:19-30 with the church at Antioch. Notably, the church at Antioch is presented as the first multicultural local church (11:20) with a mixture of both Greeks and Jews. This church is where the believers gain their name of "Christians" (11:26), and it is also the church from which the Holy Spirit launches the first missionaries (Acts 13:1-4). From Acts 13 on, the book records the founding of numerous new local churches through the work of Paul and his team: Lystra and Iconium (14:23) and Ephesus (20:17), among others.

Outside of the book of Acts, there are several references to local churches in the New Testament, primarily in Paul's epistles to them. Interestingly, Paul does not call the believers in Rome a church in his greeting to them; however, he mentions several other churches at the end of the letter: Cenchreae (Rom. 16:1), churches of the Gentiles (16:4), and Prisca and Aquila's house church (16:5). Paul's typical style is to greet the local church to whom he is writing: Corinthians (1 Cor. 1:2; 2 Cor. 1:1), churches[58] of Galatia (Gal. 1:2), and Thessalonica (1 Thess. 1:1; 2 Thess. 1:1). Finally, one of the clearest indications of the plurality of local churches comes in the Lord's words to the

---

[58] Galatia was a region of Asia Minor, and the letter was to be passed around to multiple local churches.

seven churches in Revelation. Throughout Revelation 2, John records specific statements from Jesus to seven different local churches.

At this point we can arrive at a definition of the local church, "An assembly of professing believers in Christ in a specific location who are organized under biblical leadership to do God's will."[59] Breaking this definition down, we see three key concepts. First, the local church is made up of "professing believers." Especially relevant for this discussion is the reality that not everyone attending a local church is necessarily a true believer or necessarily saved and indwelt by the Holy Spirit. The account of Ananias and Saphira in Acts 5 potentially demonstrates the presence of unbelievers even within the early church in Jerusalem.[60] Second, local churches are in a "specific location," they are the manifestation of the Universal Church (which we cannot see) in a local way (which we can see). While the Universal Church is utterly spiritual and practically invisible, local churches can readily be seen, and their activity is observable by all. Finally, local churches are "organized under biblical leadership." Acts demonstrates this organization in multiple places: with the church in Jerusalem (Acts 6:1-7; 15:1-35) as well as Paul's establishing of elders on his journeys (Acts 14:23). The Letters to Timothy and Titus both lay out principles for biblical leadership in the local church (1 Timothy 3:1-13; Titus 1:5-6).

An important point to be recognized for this argument is the relationship between the Universal Church and local churches. While both are clearly portrayed in Scripture as noted above, there is also a clear distinction to be made. While the Universal Church is made up of all believers from Pentecost onward, local churches can be a mixture of both believers and unbelievers. It is naïve to argue that only genuine believers are to be found in local churches. Beyond Ananias and Saphira are also the Judaizers of Acts 15, the antichrists of 1 John 2:19, and the sheep and the goats in Matthew 25:31-46. Even church history and present experience demonstrate that not everyone who attends a local assembly is necessarily a genuine believer. To this end a distinction is necessary: local churches do not establish the Universal Church; the Universal Church establishes local churches.

---

[59] Morgan, *Missions in the Local Church*, 10.
[60] It is arguable that they may have been saved, Scripture is not entirely clear on their spiritual condition.

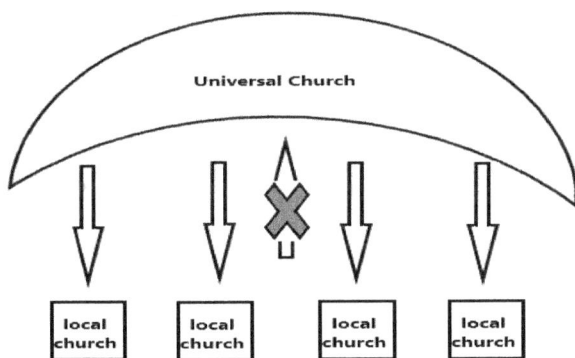

Figure 4. Universal and Local Church Relationship

The Universal Church, as the body of Christ, organizes itself into local representations in specific locations. These representations or expressions establish leadership based on biblical principles. They also organize themselves into culturally appropriate forms. Aside from the appointment of elders and deacons, very little in the way of a description is given in Scripture for how a local church is to be organized. Various principles for the character of local churches are found in the book of Acts, and Paul's instructions to local churches are also relevant. However, there is very little in terms of formal organization. What is important to recognize is the primacy of the Universal Church as presented in Scripture over any one local congregation. This in no way establishes a hierarchy akin to Catholicism or denominational control over local assemblies. Scripture also presents that local assemblies maintain their autonomy in leadership. The head of the church is Christ (Eph. 1:22), not the King, the Pope, nor the President of a denomination. However, the distinction is an important one, not the least for the recognition that there are no unbelievers in the Universal Church but for the relationship of local churches to one another and mission agencies and universities.

The Mission Agency

Mission agencies are largely a product of the Great Century of Western mission advance. [61] From the founding of William Carey's *Particular Baptist Society for the Propagation of the Gospel to the Heathen* in 1792[62] to more recent organizations being founded today, mission agencies have served to mobilize and equip Christians around the world for cross-cultural ministry. From their initial beginnings they were founded by gospel-minded Christians

---

[61] A term used to describe a period of history from 1800-1900 when colonial missions was at its highest.

[62] Olson, *What in The World is God Doing?*, 120.

to help send and support missionaries on the field.

However, scripture does not provide us with a clear picture of modern mission agencies, and to this end there are many today that would consider them unbiblical. While the modern mission agency does not exist in the pages of the Bible, there is a clear precedent set by the Apostle Paul throughout the book of Acts. Much like the precedent we see for the church's involvement in the missions endeavor (Acts 13:1-4), the account of Paul's missionary team is largely descriptive rather than prescriptive.[63] However, just as with the role of the local church, we can also draw principles that help us understand the role of the mission agency.

Paul's mission team, sometimes referred to as the "Pauline Band," provides us with a biblical precedent for the mission agency.[64] Ralph Winter writes, "Paul's team may certainly be considered a structure. While it's design and form is not made concrete for us on the basis of remaining documents, neither, of course, is the structure of a New Testament congregation defined concretely for us in the pages of the New Testament."[65] Paul's mission team was first initiated by the Holy Spirit in Acts 13:1-4. As the leaders of the Antioch church were gathered in ministry and prayer, it was the Holy Spirit who first spoke to them to set apart Barnabus and Saul for 'the work to which I have called them'. Only later do we get a greater indication of what this work was when in Acts 13:47 Paul refers to the Lord's command to take the gospel to the Gentiles. By Acts 13 the gospel had already gone out to Gentiles, and they were being included in the early church; however, no concerted effort had yet been made to reach them. This all changed with the first missionary journey. The Holy Spirit can also be said to be the primary sender in missions when in Acts 13:4 we see that Paul and Barnabus were sent out by the Holy Spirit. While the Holy Spirit initiated the first major outreach to Gentiles, the local church in Antioch was also very involved.

Several principles can be seen from Paul's relationship to his "sending church." First, Paul and Barnabus were delegated and sanctioned by the local church. In Acts 13:3 we see the church in Antioch laying hands on them and being very involved in the sending process, so much so that the local church and the Holy Spirit are co-senders of the missionaries (Acts 13:3, 4). Second, Paul maintained a position of delegated authority to the local church. We see this in Acts 14:27 and again in 18:22 were following both the first and second journeys, Paul returns to Antioch to report on the ministry. However, while Acts gives us a picture that Paul maintained a relationship with his local

---

[63] "What does it mean that a biblical passage is descriptive rather than prescriptive?" https://www.gotquestions.org/descriptive-vs-prescriptive.html, (Accessed June 8, 2022).

[64] Olson, *What in The World is God Doing?*, 296.

[65] Ralph D. Winter, "The Two Structures of God's Redemptive Mission," *Perspectives On The World Christian Movement*. 4th ed. (Pasadena: William Carey, 2009), 245.

church in Antioch, it also presents that Paul was directed in his ministry not by church leadership but by the Holy Spirit. One clear example is given in Acts 16:6-10. Often erroneously used as an example of a "call" to ministry, Paul is on his second missionary journey when the Holy Spirit directs him to go to Macedonia. It is telling that following his vision, Paul does not consult with church leadership in Antioch; rather, he "*immediately* sought to go into Macedonia" (Acts 16:10, emphasis mine).

Acts presents a picture that while Paul reported to his local church, he directed the ministry on his own under the guidance of the Holy Spirit. As Winter has stated, "Paul was 'sent off' not 'sent out' by the Antioch congregation. He may have reported back to it but did not take orders from it. His mission band (sodality) had all the autonomy and authority of a 'traveling congregation'."[66] While an argument from absence, we simply do not see Paul having a sense of needing to consult his local sending church before making ministry decisions. Ralph Winter's discussion of "The Two Structures of God's Redemptive Mission" is particularly relevant here. I will return to some of his key points in constructing a theology of theological schools.

Two more clear principles present themselves in Paul's ministry. As we have seen above, Paul was the clear leader of the pack. Not only do we see him directing the ministry in Acts 16, but repeatedly Paul is the one making the primary decisions for the group in Acts when he separates from Barnabus over Mark[67] (15:36-41), initiates the second journey (15:36), takes on Timothy (16:3), directs them to Macedonia (16:10), commands Silas and Timothy (17:15), and sets his sights on Jerusalem knowing what will happen (20:17-38). It is also no small significance that Paul is the main character from Acts 13 to the end of the book. Closely related to Paul's leadership in Acts is that we see him directing the ministry of others in many of his letters. In Philippians 2:19-30 Paul relates his desire to send both Timothy and Epaphroditus to the church in Philippi. In 1 Thessalonians 3:2 he speaks of sending Timothy to them, and Paul relates to Titus in Titus 1:5 the reason why he left him in Crete.

All of this presents us with a clear precedent for the work of the mission agency in today's global mission endeavor. Arthur Glasser states, "This mobile team was very much on its own. It was economically self-sufficient, although not unwilling to receive funds from local congregations. It recruited, trained, and on occasion disciplined its members."[68] Next, we turn our attention to a theological grounding for the college/university/theological school as a

---

[66] Winter, "The Two Structures of God's Redemptive Mission," 248.

[67] It is interesting to note that from this point on we never again hear about Barnabus or Mark in the book of Acts.

[68] Arthur F. Glasser, "The Apostle Paul and the Missionary Task,' *Perspectives on The World Christian Movement* 4th ed. (Pasadena: William Carey, 2009), 150.

training ground for today's missionaries.

The Theological School

To build a biblical theology for the theological school is an even more daunting prospect than for the mission agency. While mission agencies can find a precedent in Paul's missionary band, the closest that one can come to a structure for the theological school is within existing Jewish cultural structures of the first century. Obviously, establishing a school was not the early church's priority. Here a pathway is presented for developing a theology of the theological school in comparison with the early church's use of existing cultural structures, such as the synagogue as patterns for their own practice.

As previously mentioned, Ralph Winter laid much of the foundation for an understanding of the roll of parachurch organizations within the Universal Church. While primarily focusing on the modality of the local congregation and the sodality of the mission agency,[69] much of Winter's research points to the broader aspects of a theological basis for what have today become known as "parachurch" organizations. The term "parachurch" is in many ways an unfortunate label, defined as a ministry that "operates beside – and therefore outside – individual or affiliated church structures."[70] I label the term parachurch unfortunate because it implies that such ministries are not well founded in Scripture and indeed has been the basis for some to label them as unbiblical if not attached to a local congregation in some manner. In part, this comes from a poor definition of the Church which focuses only on the local expressions to the exclusion of the universal Body of Christ.[71]

Ralph Winter counters this mentality by pointing to the cultural origins of the local church within the Jewish synagogue and the agency within the existence of Jewish evangelists who went forth seeking proselytes.[72] Indeed, even Christ referenced the work of these Jewish evangelists in Matthew 23:15, though not in favorable terms. Winter continues his article tracing the historical path of both the local church and the mission agency from the first century through medieval times and the Reformation.[73] A key concept throughout is that the Church has always adapted its form to local contexts while preserving essential biblical functions, "to allow them to choose comparable indigenous structures in the countless new situations across

---

[69] Winter, "The Two Structures of God's Redemptive Mission," 248.

[70] Jon Bloom, "What is a Parachurch Ministry? Our Commitment to Love the Local Church," *Desiring God,* Accessed February 12, 2021, https://www.desiringgod.org/articles/what-is-a-parachurch-ministry.

[71] J. Mack Stiles, "Your Parachurch Ministry Isn't the Church," *Radical*, accessed February 12, 2021, https://radical.net/articles/your-parachurch-ministry-isnt-the-church/.

[72] Winter, "The Two Structures of God's Redemptive Mission," 244.

[73] Winter, "The Two Structures of God's Redemptive Mission," 244-246.

history and around the world – structures which will correspond faithfully to the *function* of patterns Paul employed, if not their *form*."[74] Winter's argument is compelling, and it is evident throughout that the term 'sodality' could apply equally to other ministries beyond just the missions or evangelistic organization. So, what about the theological school?

As Winter and others have indicated, the early church was patterned after the Jewish synagogue.[75] In the synagogue was a culturally and religiously familiar structure that the early Christians were accustomed to and could emulate in their own meetings.[76] Interestingly, James refers to a wealthy man entering the assembly of the believers, and yet the term he uses is not the more common εκκλεσια but συναγωγῇ, 'synagogue'. Indeed, it was common for the early believers to continue to attend the synagogue until such time as they were forced out (Acts 19:8-10). Alfred Edersheim (author and Jewish convert to Christianity) writes, "in turn, the synagogue seems as the model for the earliest Christian churches."[77] The synagogue, however, was not the only Jewish cultural and religious structure to serve as an example to early believers.

Bob Blincoe (President of Frontiers USA) recently commented on another cultural structure in Judaism, the "hevrah".[78] Blincoe draws direct parallels from the hevrah to Paul's missions team; however, the example of the hevrah could be equally applied to the theological school or even other parachurch ministries. Israel Goldman, (former Rabbi and Jewish scholar at the Chizuk Amuno Congregation in Baltimore, Maryland) wrote extensively on the practice of the hevrah among Jews.[79] Goldman writes, "In every Jewish community in past ages, the *hevrah* – a duly constituted society for the promotion of certain specific occupational, charitable, religious, or educational purposes – was the most significant unit of voluntary association"[80] He continues that there were hevrot[81] or "holy brotherhoods" of all kinds mentioning randomly tailors, woodchoppers, study of the Torah,

---

[74] Winter, "The Two Structures of God's Redemptive Mission," 246.

[75] Winter, "The Two Structures of God's Redemptive Mission,"244.

[76] "Religion: Christianity," *Jewish Virtual Library*, accessed February 24, 2021, https://www.jewishvirtuallibrary.org/christianity-2.

[77] Alfred Edersheim, *Sketches of Jewish Social Life in the Days of Christ*, (Independently published, 1876).

[78] Bob Blincoe, "The Task of Mission in Light of a Recent Discovery in the New Testament," Presentation given during Missio Nexus' Focus 2020, accessed September 24, 2020, https://missionexus.org/the-task-of-mission-in-light-of-a-recent-discovery-in-the-new-testament/.

[79] Israel M. Goldman, *Lifelong Learning Among Jews: Adult Education in Judaism from Biblical Times to The Twentieth Century*, (New York, KTAV Publishing House, Inc. 1975).

[80] Goldman, *Lifelong Learning Among Jews*, 173.

[81] hevrot is the plural of hevrah

visiting the sick, etc.[82] When exactly hevrot began is difficult to determine; however, Goldman indicates that they were in place during the Talmudic times.[83]A well-known example is the "Chevrah Kadisha" or "sacred society," a traditional organization first mentioned in the Talmud.[84] The Chevrah Kadisha was instituted to support families and communities at someone's time of death and continues this function in Jewish communities today.

There were also *hevrot* for learning. Goldman writes, "the crown of Jewish social life was the *hevrah* organized solely for purposes of *lehrnen* – learning and the pursuit of Jewish study."[85] hevrot were specifically devoted to lifelong learning and times of study on a concentrated and separate field of knowledge. While used primarily for study of the Mishnah, there were hevrot associated with the study of other topics as well.[86] Goldman references seven different categories of study as seen through the hevrot's *pinkasim* or "minute-books" including the Psalms, the Bible, the Bible and related literature, codes, moral and ethical literature, the Mishnah, and the Talmud.[87] Edersheim also speaks of a similar and related concept in the "Chabura," which was a fraternity or guild.[88] He speaks of the Pharisees as an example of this. The *hevrot* later found parallels in the Christian craft guilds.[89]

Blincoe also compares the Pharisees to a type of hevrah, and even Jesus and his disciples as a type of hevrah.[90] His conclusion is that this Jewish cultural structure provided Paul with a pattern for his missions team.[91] Goldman also writes about how the Pharisees would utilize the Synagogue as a means to spread their doctrines.[92] Paul simply continued what he was already familiar with as a Pharisee himself in taking the gospel to the Gentiles. Jesus even references the Pharisees' evangelistic activity in Matthew 23:15 as they, "travel across sea and land to make a single proselyte." While certainly there is little to commend the Pharisees in Scripture, they did serve as an example to Paul, the former Pharisee and now Apostle, as he began his ministry. The early church had no problem adopting the Jewish cultural structures of the day and utilizing them for Christian purposes.

To that end one more cultural structure of the Jews bears mentioning, In

---

82 Goldman, *Lifelong Learning Among Jews*, 173.

83 Goldman, *Lifelong Learning Among Jews*, 198.

84 "What is a *Chevrah Kadisha?" Gamaliel Institute*, Accessed February 24, 2021, https://www.jewish-funerals.org/chevrah-kadisha/.

85 Goldman, *Lifelong Learning Among Jews*, 197.

86 Goldman, *Lifelong Learning Among Jews*, 197.

87 Goldman, *Lifelong Learning Among Jews*, 210.

88 Edersheim, *Sketches of Jewish Social Life in the Days of Christ*, 92.,

89 Goldman, *Lifelong Learning Among Jews*, 175.

90 Bob Blincoe, "The Task of Mission in Light of a Recent Discovery in the New Testament."

91 Bob Blincoe, "The Task of Mission in Light of a Recent Discovery in the New Testament."

92 Goldman, *Lifelong Learning Among Jews*, 12.

addition to the synagogue and the hevrah was the "house of study", the "bet ha-midrash."[93] The earliest emergence of the bet ha-midrash is difficult to determine; however, rabbinical tradition has it as starting as far back as the patriarchal period.[94] Goldman indicates that it was specifically an "organized school of higher learning" for adults as opposed to the primary school for children, the "bet ha-seder".[95] There was additionally a separate structure on the Temple Mount called a bet ha-midrash; used primarily by members of the Sanhedrin, priests, and Levites, it was also likely open to others.[96] It is possible that this is the very structure in which Jesus' parents find him in Luke 2:46 speaking with the teachers. Subjects that were studied at the bet ha-midrash would have included the Mishnah, Midrash (Talmud), Halakhah, and Aggadah.[97] Finally, two groups were often associated as teachers in the bet ha-midrash, the scribes, and the rabbis. It is likely these are the same "scribes" and "teachers of the law" which we encounter numerous times throughout the Gospels (Matt. 2:4, 15:1; Mark 3:22, 7:1, 9:11, 14:1; Luke 6:7, 20:19; John 8:3).

The point in this discussion is not to draw a direct line from the hevrah of the bet ha-midrash to the theological school; that is simply not possible. Neither is there a direct equivalency from the hevrah to the modern mission agency. However, what we can see is that God has utilized various cultural structures throughout the history of His people. Within these cultural frameworks we can see parallels to the various ways in which the Universal Church manifests itself in local congregations (synagogues/churches), specialized ministries (hevrot/Paul's band/mission agencies), and educational institutions (bet ha-midrash/theological schools). It is now possible to draw some conclusions.

Unity Amidst Diversity

First, working backwards, we see how local churches are expressions of the Universal Church. The Universal Church, as all believers everywhere, establishes local assemblies in particular places. Mission agencies and theological schools (when made up of genuine believers) can also be expressions of the Universal Church working in culturally appropriate forms to fulfill biblical functions as seen below.

---

[93] Goldman, *Lifelong Learning Among Jews*, 23.
[94] Goldman, *Lifelong Learning Among Jews*, 23.
[95] Goldman, *Lifelong Learning Among Jews*, 24.
[96] Goldman, *Lifelong Learning Among Jews*, 25.
[97] Goldman, *Lifelong Learning Among Jews*, 27.

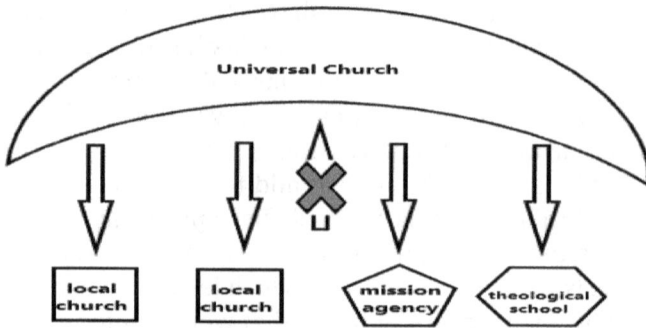

Figure 5. Modalities and Sodalities within the Universal Church

Second, in examining the diversity to be found in the tri-unity of God,[98] we can see a pattern (though not a direct equivalency) for the diversity within the Universal Church and various cultural structures.

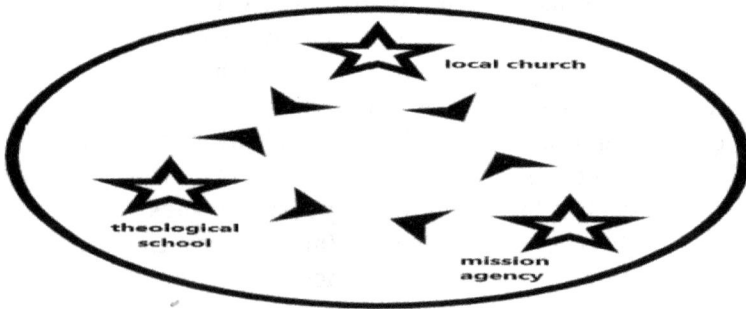

Figure 6. Local Church, Theological School, Mission Agency in Relationship

The arrows in the figure above are specifically undefined at this point as they indicate the relationship between members, discussed later. The point should also be driven home that no direct equivalency is being made between one member of the Trinity and each organization; the diagram is merely illustrative. However, within both the Trinity and the Universal Church can be seen a clear case for unity within diversity. The three persons of the Trinity are equally united in being God though they have different roles and purposes within creation and redemption. The three expressions of the Universal Church given here in local churches, mission agencies, and universities, while being united in being expressions of the Universal Church, have different roles and purposes in the growth and deployment of God's people on mission.

Three important clarifications should be mentioned here to avoid potential

---

[98] See page 110.

misunderstanding. First, an emphasis on the Universal Church and the unity of all believers is not meant to encourage ecumenicalism. While the fragmentation of the Body of Christ is to be avoided, so too is the kind of unity that comes from sacrificing doctrinal truth. This book encourages local churches, mission agencies, and universities to seek unity through their common bond of the personhood of God and the nature of Christ's body, the Universal Church. These connections and partnerships must still be made within the framework of agreement to sound doctrine. Churches, universities, and agencies must examine their statements of faith to determine their compatibility with one another.

Second, an emphasis on the Universal Church as a theological foundation for partnership should also not be taken as providing an argument for hierarchal church leadership structures such as found in some denominations or Catholicism. Scripture is clear that the Church has one head, Christ (Eph. 1:22, 23). There is only one mediator, Christ (1 Timothy 2:5). The spiritual unity of all believers in the Universal Church cannot be replicated through a hierarchal church structure on Earth.

Finally, while all believers share responsibility for being Christ's witnesses and we create many different, culturally, and biblically appropriate forms to achieve that function, Scripture clearly lays a foundation for the local church and local church leadership. The book of Acts displays the priority of local churches (Jerusalem, Acts 2:42-47, 11:1-18; Antioch, Acts 11:19-30, 13:1-4, 14:24-28; Paul's appointment of elders Acts 14:23; Ephesus, Acts 20:17). Paul's letters are addressed to individual churches (1 Cor. 1:2; 2 Cor. 1:1; Gal. 1:2; 1 Thess. 1:1). Qualifications for local church leadership are given in 1 Timothy 3 and Titus 1. To emphasize that partnership in missions be built on a theological foundation of the Universal Church is not to undermine the authority nor autonomy of local church leadership. For this reason, the above figure purposefully placed the local church on top as the primary partner.

"For just as the body is one and has many members, and all the members of the body, though many, are one body, so it is with Christ." With these words in 1 Corinthians 12:13, Paul begins to illustrate the necessity of the various gifts within the Church for the building up of the whole body. Within the Trinity there can be seen the unity of the godhead within the diversity of the three Persons. All three (Father, Son, and Spirit) are one God, and yet they each have different roles.[99] Within the nature of the Universal Church can be seen the unity of the Body and Bride of Christ; as Paul said, there is one Body. However, there are also many parts, different gifts, skills, and abilities; and each of these are to be used for the edification of the saints (Eph. 4:11-16). Local churches have a role and responsibilities to play in the mobilization of missionaries, as

---

[99] See pages 105 and following.

do universities and mission agencies. Next, I will move to a discussion of the various relationships involved.

Relationship within the Universal Church

The scriptural analysis of the Universal Church demonstrated the place that each partner (local church, university, mission agency) has within the universal Body of Christ. This cooperation can be illustrated with the figure below.

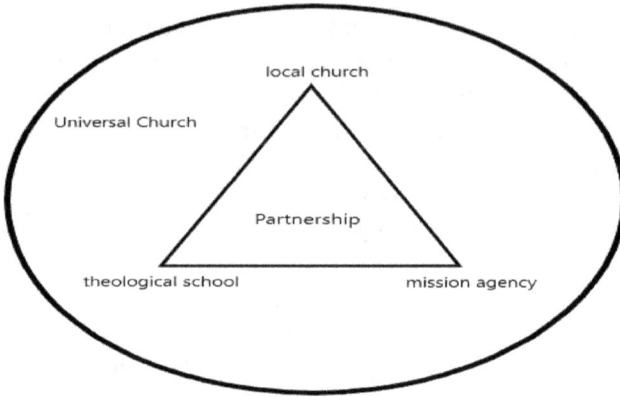

Figure 7. Relational Paradigm in the Universal Church

This figure is merely illustrative of the relationship between the three organizations in question within the Universal Church for the purpose of explaining the model being presented. The local church is intentionally placed on top as being seen as the primary partner.[100] As the model expands the location of the theological school and mission agency will become important as well. To further illustrate relational realism as the foundation the following figure incorporates the Trinity into the model.

---

[100] Wilson, *Pipeline*, 91.

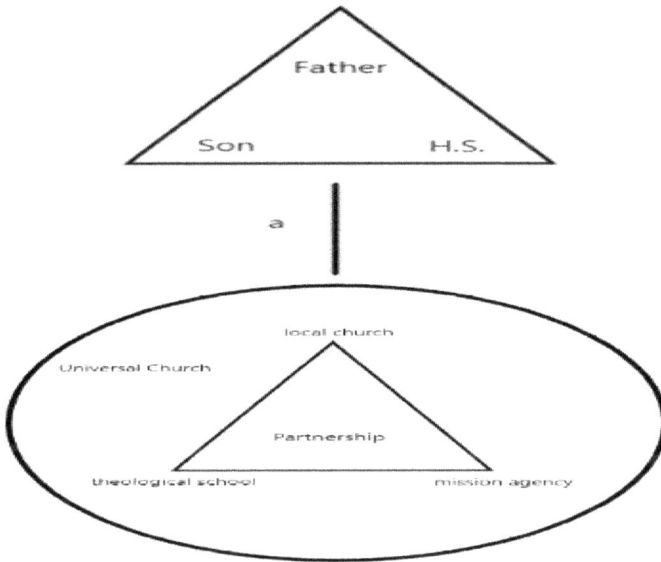

Father

Son   H.S.

a

local church

Universal Church

Partnership

theological school   mission agency

a.   Relational involvement of the Trinity with the Universal Church

Figure 8. Relational Paradigm with the Universal Church

Through this we can see that the model is well grounded in the sound
biblical theology of the Trinity and the Universal Church. Relational Realism
then provides the theoretical framework to undergird the importance of God's
involvement in the process of relational partnership. As believers in Christ, we
are both in relationship with God and with one another (Eph. 4:4-6). It is in
the context of these relationships that we individually fulfill our roles as
members of the one Body (1 Cor. 12:12-31). The local church, university, and
mission agency all fulfill different roles in the Universal Church as
organizations of believers and members of the Body of Christ. The model
meets its full understanding in the following diagram.

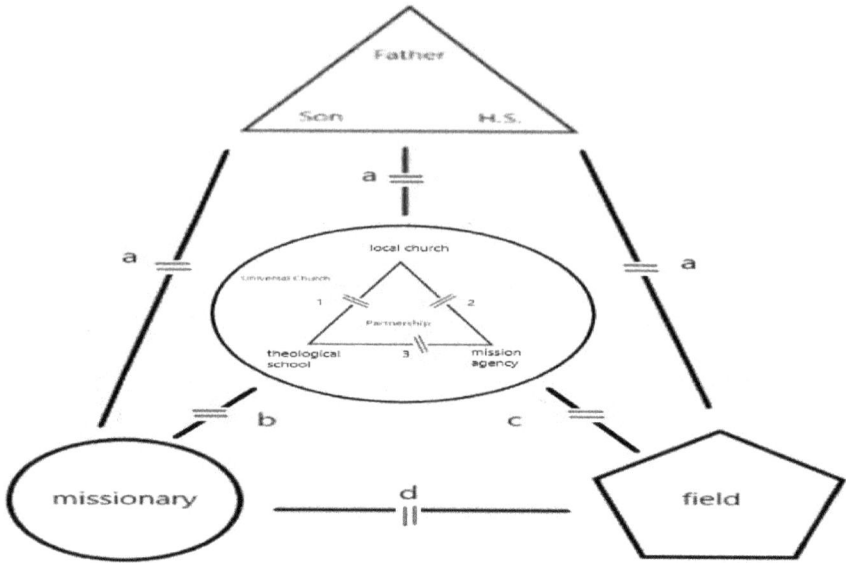

At the Macro level Relational Realism demonstrates the various relationships involved in Christian Missions.

a. Relational involvement of the Trinity with entire process.
b. Missionary's relationship with church, school, agency.
c. Universal Church relationship with mission field (primarily through agency).
d. Missionary's relationship with mission field (lost people).
1. Relationship between local church and theological school.
2. Relationship between local church and mission agency.
3. Relationship between theological school and mission agency
= Transgressional dynamics of spiritual reality, i.e. Satan, worldly system, and the flesh.[101]

Figure 9. Integrated Relational Paradigm for Missionary Mobilization[102]

The diagram in Figure 9 demonstrates the full scope of the relationships involved in missions. Missions is an inherently relational activity and missionary mobilization is primarily relational as well, as each member of the Universal Church cooperates in partnerships to mobilize and equip the next generation. These relationships then continue throughout the years of the missionary's ministry on the field. The focus of this work is the internal relationships seen on the diagram as 1, 2, and 3. I have already examined a

---

[101] "Transgressional dynamics" is the oppositional forces against the "transformational dynamics" of the Triune God. See Harold Lindsell. *The World, the Flesh, and the Devil*. Canon Press. 1973.
[102] Joshua Paxton, "Integrated Relational Partnerships..." IN *Transformational Change in Christian Ministry*. Enoch Wan and Jon Raibley, *Transformational Change in Christian Ministry*, (Portland: Western Academic Publishers, 2022:129).

couple of examples of growing relationships between local churches and mission agencies in the literature review. While the black lines demonstrate the relational connection between each other, it is also important to acknowledge the reality of forces both practical (contracts, agreements, finances, etc.) and spiritual (sin, Satan, the world's system, etc.) which threaten to undermine good relationships.[103]

Local Church, Mission Agency, University Roles

Local churches, mission agencies and universities all represent unique organizational expressions of the Universal Church. They are biblically appropriate and culturally driven forms to achieve the biblical function placed upon every believer of witnessing to the gospel. While the local body of believers as organized into a local church with biblical leadership has great precedence in Scripture for raising up and sending out missionaries (Acts 13:1-4), there is also great leeway given for the agency and university to come alongside and assist the church, as noted earlier. Each one has a unique role to fill in the mobilizing and equipping of cross-cultural servants of Christ for today's unique missions reality. This section will examine the roles that each play as a prerequisite to understanding how cooperative partnerships can be formed.

Local Church

Local churches have been described as, "An assembly of professing believers in Christ in a specific location who are organized under biblical leadership to do God's will."[104] The local church is the visible manifestation of the Universal Church on Earth. A discussion of all the roles of local churches would fill many books, the purpose of this section is to outline the role of the local church in missionary mobilization and equipping.

The main example that we see in Scripture is through Saul's calling and accountability to the church in Antioch in Acts 13:1-4. Several principles can be gained by looking at this verse. First, Saul and Barnabus were called out from among those who were already doing ministry (Acts 13:1, 2). Several individuals are named in verse 1 as being prophets and teachers, those who were involved in the ministry of the church at Antioch and Saul and Barnabus are among them.

From this, we can glean that it should be those who are already actively involved in a local church who are good candidates for the mission field. Ministry in their home context where they know the language and the culture

---

103 See the Appendices for more background on the importance of relationship in partnership, including a review of related literature on the subject.

104 Morgan, *Missions in the Local Church*, 10.

is not only good training but demonstrates the potential missionary's ability to do the work of ministry. A good litmus test for any potential missionary candidate is if they can do ministry in their own culture, because if they struggle here, how much more so when they are in a different context. A second principle is the involvement of the Holy Spirit in the process (13:2). While the church is involved, it is the Holy Spirit who initiates the sending out of Saul and Barnabus. Finally, to be noted is the dual involvement of both the church and the Holy Spirit in the actual sending of Saul and Barnabus. The church at Antioch commissions them through the laying on of hands and praying, sending them off (13:3). However, it is the Holy Spirit who is their ultimate sender (13:4).[105] Further, we can see from Acts 14:27 and 18:22, 23 that Paul repeatedly returned to Antioch to report to the believers there on his ministry.

It should be noted that while the occasion of Saul and Barnabus being sent from Antioch provides us with good principles for the local church's involvement in missions a caution is necessary. The book of Acts is largely recognized as being a historical account of the development of the early church as recorded by Luke. As a historical book it is largely descriptive not prescriptive. The purpose of the book of Acts is to record the historical development of the church and not to explain doctrine.[106] While Acts provides a precedence and explanation for the local church's involvement in missions it does not set hard and fast standards for how things should always happen. It is, however, a good model for the church to follow still today.

A contemporary understanding of the role of the local church in missions can be found in the discussion surrounding the term 'Sending Church.'[107] In the book *Pipeline*, David Wilson goes into detail on what it means to be a sending church as well as the role of the sending church. He outlines the roles for local churches, mission agencies and missionaries. Notably absent is the role of the university in preparing the next generation for the mission field.[108]

The role of the local church is described as this:
a. Sending – primary partner, stakeholder, and participant of the Great Commission
b. Selecting – affirming the character and competence of a missionary

---

[105] Marvin J. Newell, "Who Sent the First Missionaries? A Critical Examination of Acts 13:1-4," (MA Thesis. Grace Theological Seminary, Winona Lake, May 1977), 51, 52.

[106] Mal Couch, ed. *A Bible Handbook to the Acts of the Apostles*, (Grand Rapids: Kregel, 1999), 18.

[107] Wilson, *Pipeline*, 90.

[108] I have spoken at length with David about this very thing and he assures me that the oversight was not in fact his own. While he tried to contact several professors at several schools, he was repeatedly turned down for including their thoughts in the first edition of the book, he hopes to include them in the next.

c. Praying – before field, on the field, ministry contacts, family at home, reentry
d. Mobilizing – short-term trips, mid-term opportunities, and long-term support.
e. Nurturing – providing a spiritual community as a base of primary support
f. Resourcing – ensuring the missionary is well equipped (What are their ministry needs?)
g. Caring – holistic support contributing to effective ministry through missionary care
h. Communicating – ensures a clear and transparent understanding between partners[109]

The local church has a very important role to play in raising up and supporting missionaries. Local churches provide an intimate framework for relationship development in community and discipleship and growth. It can be argued that the local church knows the prospective missionaries the best and can evaluate their calling and readiness for cross-cultural ministry, especially in the realm of personal traits that might be hidden from an agency or school. The local church is also the primary place for raising up financial and prayer support as well as providing personal care for the missionary and his/her family.[110] These relationships are important for not only mobilizing and equipping the missionary but keeping the missionary on the field for the long haul. However, there are also many aspects of cross-cultural ministry that are unique when compared to ministry in any other format. Thus, God has raised up the mission agency to fill many important roles that many local churches, especially smaller ones, would struggle to fulfill.

Mission Agency

As mentioned earlier mission agencies are largely a product of the Great Century of Western mission advance. From the founding of William Carey's *Particular Baptist Society for the Propagation of the Gospel to the Heathen* in 1792[111] to more recent organizations being founded today, missions agencies have served to mobilize and equip Christians around the world for cross-cultural ministry. From their initial beginnings they were founded by gospel-minded Christians to help send and support missionaries to the foreign field. With the biblical precedence for mission agencies established earlier, how

[109] Wilson, *Pipeline*, 91.
[110] David J. Wilson, ed. *Mind the Gaps: Engaging the Church in Missionary Care*, (Redlands, CA: Mind the Gaps, 2015), 6.
[111] Olson, *What in The World is God Doing?* 120.

then do they fit into the overall picture of mobilizing and equipping missionaries in today's world?

As it does with the local church *Pipeline* spells out some of the roles of the modern mission agency.

a. Supervising – overall on-field oversight, leadership, and accountability
b. Facilitating – recognizes the centrality of the church as sender while preserving the mutually deferential roles of each participant
c. Organizing – provides the administrative services that free the missionary to focus on ministry
d. Consulting – offers timely consultation to the church on major decisions regarding personal, family, and ministry difficulties and decisions
e. Caring – holistic support contributing to effective ministry through member care
f. Communicating – ensures a clear and transparent understanding between partners[112]

There is a good degree of overlap between the role of the local church and that of the agency, especially in the areas of 'caring' and 'communicating'. I would also add the role of mobilization to what Wilson has presented here. Mission agencies do a great deal of mobilizing workers for the harvest through advertising, knowledge, awareness and especially having full-time members who visit churches and schools.

Paul Beals further delineates the role of the agency into responsibilities for the local church and the missionaries. Responsibilities towards the church include recruiting personnel, public relations, and financial oversight. Responsibilities towards the missionaries involve financial services, travel/shipping arrangements, and counsel or evaluation.[113] Another important insight to add to the discussion is the importance of the agency's role in forming a bridge between sending churches and national churches on the field.[114]

Mission agencies are biblically based and historically supported. While the argument has been made that the sole responsibility of an agency is to support the local church, both scripture and history attest to the important role they have played in expanding the reach of the gospel. Within the framework of the Universal Church, they have a vital role to play in the mobilization and equipping of the next generation. Perhaps Beals gave the

---

[112] Wilson, *Pipeline*, 91-92.
[113] Paul A. Beals, *A People for His Name: A Church-based Missions Strategy*, Revised ed. (Pasadena: William Carey, 1995), 145.
[114] Beals, *A People for His Name*, 141.

best answer to where the authority lies when he wrote, "If parachurch organizations such as mission agencies have assumed the initiating authority of the local church, they have done so by default. Local churches must prove themselves to be the sending authority."[115] Next, we will examine the role of the university and then establish a comparison for the roles of all three.

Christian University/Theological School

The university, any university, is in the position of trying to recruit individuals to decide to be educated at its particular institution. However, the decision process is largely up to the individual with some input from friends, family, and personal background factors. For this reason, the current model is not greatly developed based on relational partnerships or community but rather the school's ability to market its educational programs. The university is seen largely to be on its own island. Students make an individual decision to come based on factors such as program, size, cost, and distance from home, etc... and then following graduation make an individual decision where they will work/serve in either ministry or the marketplace. While recognizing the rights of individuals to make their own decisions on the one hand, this book is challenging this model by advocating for a greater degree of relational partnership. What then is the role of a university, specifically a Christian one, or a theological school in mobilizing and equipping the next generation of missionaries? Before getting into that question an important distinction is necessary.

Biblical Ministries Worldwide (BMW) reports that the average age of their missionary appointees over the past decade has been 36 years old.[116] The reality of this statistic has forced them to reevaluate their recruiting practices with a shift to more emphasis on the local church. Statistics are interesting things and often can be interpreted multiple ways. While BMW has, rightly so, concluded that churches are the new place to find people, there is another way of viewing this. That is, why are they waiting so long? If the average age of a college graduate is 22-23 then that represents 14 years of ministry lost. While arguments can be made about the need for people to grow and mature after college, or even pay off student loans, a system is needed to mobilize the next generation much sooner. The reality of global evangelism today is such that the birth rate in unreached areas of the world is outpacing our ability to reach people with the gospel.[117] To that end, understanding the role of the university and what it contributes to produce relational partnerships

---

[115] Beals, *A People for His Name*, 138.
[116] Biblical Ministries Worldwide, "Senders Think Tank." unpublished handout.
[117] Justin Long, "Global Diagram 3: Growth in Population and Christianity, AD 1910-2010," Accessed November 7, 2019, http://justinlong.org/resources/gd3.pdf.

becomes extremely important. That said, the model being presented should not be seen as merely proposing a faster process to field deployment. While that situation does exist, it is far more important that missionary candidates be fully prepared and equipped for what lies ahead in their ministry. Matt Rhodes has recently highlighted the dangers of quick solutions to missions problems in his work, *No Shortcut to Success: A Manifesto for Modern Missions*.[118] In this work Matt correctly highlights the importance of accurate training and preparation of missionary candidates. This serves more to highlight the important role that universities play in the preparation of missionaries.

Paul Beals spent significant time on the role of the theological school or university. He outlines several important roles that universities play in the preparation of missionary candidates. "The wheel of missions is not complete, however, without the contribution of the schools that prepare Christian leaders to serve at home and worldwide."[119] Perhaps most importantly, Christian universities serve as the primary training ground for not only missionaries but pastors. This connection back to the local church will have far reaching implications for how the church promotes a theology of missions to its people.[120] Other roles that the theological school plays can be outlined as follows, I will include how Calvary University (CU) provides this in parenthesis:

a. Biblical/Theological Education – theological schools include a lot of time in intensive study of the Bible and theology (students at CU have a minimum of 21-30 semester hours in Bible and Theology, depending on their program)

b. Character Development – theological schools provide an atmosphere for spiritual growth (CU students experience this not only in classes but through chapel, campus life, relationships with faculty/staff/one another)

c. Ministry – theological schools provide opportunities for service in ministry (the Christian Ministry requirement at CU means every student, regardless of degree must participate in ministry for 7 of the 8 semesters of enrollment as an undergraduate student, this is separate from program related internships)[121]

Beals summarizes his chapter on theological schools with this statement,

---

[118] Matt Rhodes, *No Shortcut to Success: A Manifesto for Modern Missions*, (Wheaton: Crossway, 2022).
[119] Beals, *A People for His Name*, 191.
[120] Beals, *A People for His Name*, 192.
[121] Beals, *A People for His Name*, 192-214.

"The school, church, and mission agency must seek specific ways to reinforce each other in the total preparation of those entering international ministries."[122] Beals made this statement in 1995. It is even truer today and is exactly the mutual reinforcement that Synergy seeks to provide.

One other key piece to the role of the theological school is worth mentioning and that is the opportunity that schools have for networking. Local churches and mission agencies have not always had a fantastic relationship. Churches often have the perception that agencies want their money and people but not their input. Agencies, as professionals in their field, can often feel that churches just don't understand the reality of missions, a reality the agency lives with every day. Several agencies have been trying to address this issue and two will be named in the next section. However, the university or theological school presents a good middle ground for local churches and agencies to meet in a non-threatening way. Also, it is at least the case at Calvary, and I suspect elsewhere that the connections Calvary or another university has to both its church constituency (representing the wider student body, faculty and staff) and its connections to multiple missions organizations (well over forty that I could name) serve as a greater opportunity for networking and solutions than the connections of any one church.

Current Models in Church/Agency Partnership

Over the past few years, a change has been developing and more agencies are making concerted efforts to engage the local church in fulfilling its role in missions. Two examples are presented here in Avant's Joint Venture program and Biblical Ministries Worldwide's Think Tanks.

Avant: Joint Venture

David Wilson, author of *Pipeline*, is the Director of Church Relations for Avant. Avant, (formerly Gospel Missionary Union) has been an international church planting mission agency since 1892.[123] As a mobilizer with this mission agency, I am very familiar with them. In 2004, when my wife and I first joined the organization, they launched a program called Joint Venture. As they say on their website, "Joint Venture was created as an opportunity for the church and agency to combine their strengths to plant the church among the unreached."[124] Joint Venture is a cooperative effort between Avant and the

---

122 Beals, *A People for His Name*, 214.
123 "Churches," *Avant Ministries*, accessed October 28, 2019, https://avantministries.org/churches.
124 "Churches," *Avant Ministries*, accessed October 28, 2019, https://avantministries.org/churches.

local church where the local church takes a position of ownership of the mission team. The team of six to ten adults is formed from members of the local church and the church works together with Avant for field location, timeline for deployment, and other administrative details.[125]

Joint Venture presents one example of an agency taking the initiative to involve the local church in the entire process. Avant began to recognize that many mega churches[126] were beginning to take the responsibility for missions solely into their hands. While on the one hand a welcome trend, it also presented complications that are beyond the scope of this paper. Joint Venture was created to be the answer. To allow the local church to have more involvement in the process of sending their people to the mission field. Many of the specifics may vary from church to church but as they say, "the goal is always the same: missionaries are sent, the gospel is preached, and churches are planted!"[127]

Biblical Ministries Worldwide

In July 2019, I had the privilege of traveling to the headquarters of Biblical Ministries Worldwide in Atlanta Georgia and participating in their first "Recruiting Think Tank." BMW leadership took the initiative to bring together missions reps and leaders in their organization along with representatives from schools to lay out their new direction in mobilization. I later asked former BMW President, Paul Seger to give me more details on their "Senders Think Tanks." BMW began hosting these think tanks where they gather a group of pastors from area churches and talk with them about how their church can mobilize its own people for the mission field. Paul reports that it is too early to judge the long-term results of these meetings. However, there has been positive movement in several areas. One positive result was that many of these churches who gathered for the think tank had previously not done much together so this served as an opportunity for networking. Another positive outcome was that the pastors felt this was a wakeup call to something they really hadn't considered before.[128]

At this point, there is not a lot of formal interaction between churches and the agency for Biblical Ministries Worldwide, rather it is based largely on establishing relationships with pastors. One step that they have undertaken is to send the pastor of a sending church to visit their missionary during the

---

[125] "Churches," *Avant Ministries*, accessed October 28, 2019, https://avantministries.org/churches.

[126] They define this as churches of 1000 or more.

[127] "Churches," *Avant Ministries*, accessed October 28, 2019, https://avantministries.org/churches.

[128] "Churches," *Avant Ministries*, accessed October 28, 2019, https://avantministries.org/churches.

missionary's first term. This is an attempt to connect them more with the missionary as opposed to the agency.[129]

Others

There are other organizations currently involved in helping engage local churches to be more involved in the mobilization process. Two others are "Sixteen:Fifteen: Church Missions Coaching" and "The Sending Project". "Sixteen:Fifteen" exists to provide resources and coaching to churches to help them build and establish their missions program.[130] "The Sending Project" is a church networking organization that exists to bring churches together. They report on their website, "The Sending Project is facilitating a city-wide alliance of pastors and church mission leaders from Kansas City area churches so they can; come together, learn from each other, and serve alongside each other."[131]

Multiple organizations and agencies are beginning to come together and join forces for the cause of Christ. Now more than ever a model of relational partnership is needed to foster cooperation among the various parts of the body, the Universal Church.

The Synergy Model

The Synergy model of relational partnerships seeks to take the components of the local church, agency, and university and integrate them into a relational educational design that brings together the best that each has to offer. The main unifying factors in everything are God, (in relationship with all three organizations, the student and the lost), the Universal Church (uniting the local church, university, and agency), and the student. The model exists principally to prepare the student for cross-cultural missionary service. However, its application has implications for other programs and other partnerships within the Church.[132]

The local church, university, and agency all have key roles to play in preparing the students. While all of them contribute to the student's development holistically, they each have a clear area where they fill a role in a greater capacity due to their unique focus and nature. Local churches thrive in providing for the affective (being) of the student, universities are best suited for cognitive development (knowing), and the agency has the practical skills and behavioral (doing) components. The Synergy process of learning is

---

[129] "Churches," *Avant Ministries*, accessed October 28, 2019, https://avantministries.org/churches.

[130] "What We Do for Your Church," *16:15 Homepage*, accessed November 7, 2019, https://1615.org/.

[131] "Vision," *About*, accessed November 7, 2019, http://www.thesendingproject.org/about.

[132] I explore these implications in Chapter 4.

complex enough that no one diagram can truly capture the full reality of the student's experience. Figure 10 helps to illustrate the contributions of each partner to the development of the student.

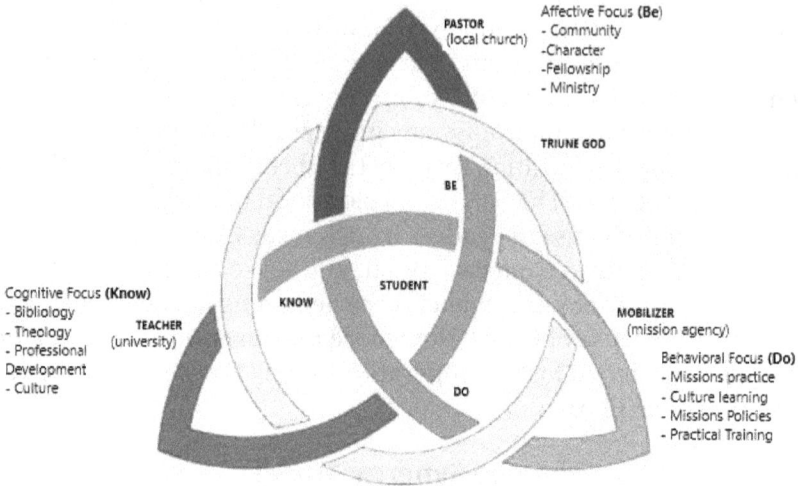

Figure 10. Synergy Cycle of Partnership Learning[133]

In Figure 10 we can see how the student develops in the cognitive, affective, and behavioral areas through the unique contributions of each Synergy partner. Each partner has a main contact who is involved with the student, be that the teacher, pastor, or mentor. And the student is involved in all three communities. In the four stages of experiential learning we have seen that each partner contributes to the experiential learning process in a specific area.[134] The church is the student's primary place for concrete experiences as well as testing new concepts. The agency is the primary place for observation and reflection as the student evaluates how their experiences would work in a cross-cultural context. The university is the key place for forming abstract concepts and generalizations to evaluate those experiences. These processes lead to the student's growth,

As the student progresses through the Synergy process, they will also progress towards spiritual and professional maturity. Working in relationship with all three organizations the partnerships allow the student to not only grow through the cyclical education process but to also progress towards the goal of being a missionary. Synergy culminates in the student's graduation

---

[133] Wan & Raibley, *Transformational Change in Christian Ministry*. 2022:130.
[134] See the literature review in Appendix II.

46

and deployment to the field with the agency they trained with. Not only does the student receive exceptional training in the context of relationships but they are also able to accelerate their deployment to the field by building essential relationships and raising support along the way, rather than waiting until after graduation.

The Synergy Educational Process

The goal of this next section is to take the previous discussion further into the education realm by laying forth an educational framework for the Synergy process and demonstrating how it contributes to student learning. The contributions of the church, university, and agency will be noted, ending with an overall picture of the Synergy Cycle of Learning. The cycle will be further illustrated using curriculum mapping to demonstrate how each course contributes to the student's overall growth and development as a missions-minded Christian and potential missionary. The key idea is to examine the process of moving the Christian student from being a student to be a mobilized member of the Church. Finally, this section will conclude with how Synergy contributes to the transformational growth and change of the student.

First, the figure below offers a deeper glimpse into what Synergy is trying to accomplish through integrated relational partnerships and the relationships involved in the process.

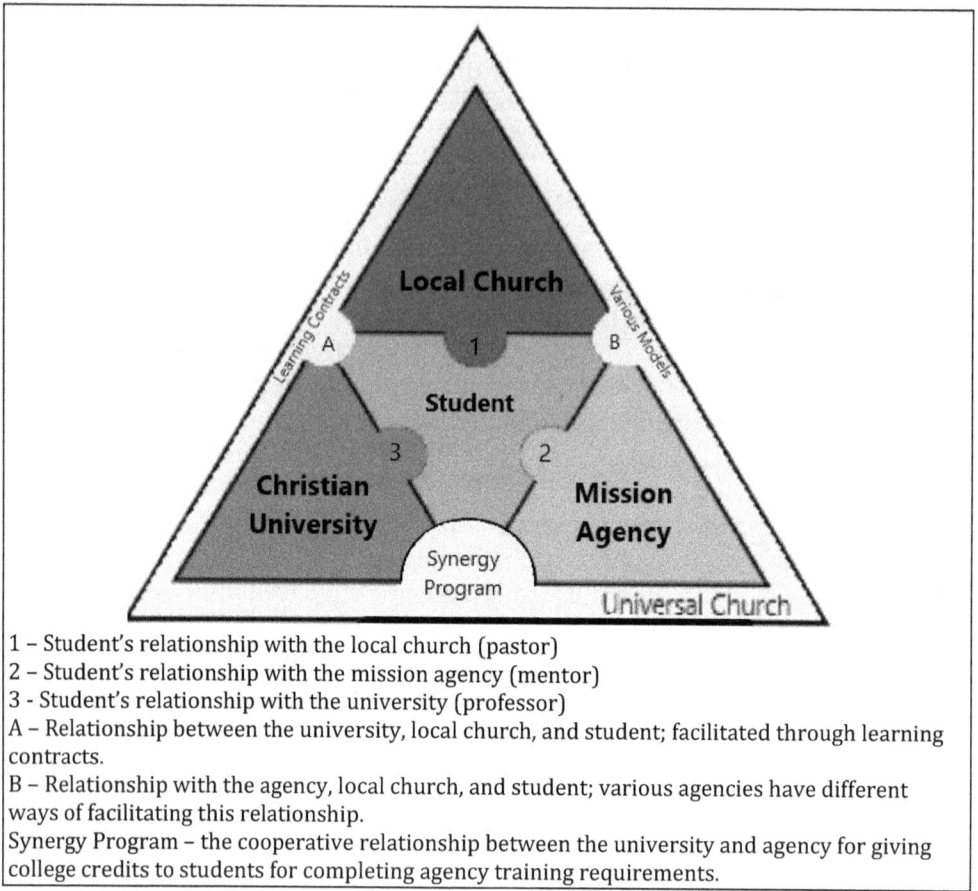

1 – Student's relationship with the local church (pastor)
2 – Student's relationship with the mission agency (mentor)
3 - Student's relationship with the university (professor)
A – Relationship between the university, local church, and student; facilitated through learning contracts.
B – Relationship with the agency, local church, and student; various agencies have different ways of facilitating this relationship.
Synergy Program – the cooperative relationship between the university and agency for giving college credits to students for completing agency training requirements.

Figure 11. Relationships within the Synergy Program

The above diagram demonstrates the relationships present within the Synergy Process and provides insight into where the details of the process need to be worked out. Integrating the Synergy Process into the diagram of the process and progress of relational transformation as adapted from Wan and Hedinger gives us the following overview. [135]

---

[135] Wan and Hedinger, "Transformative Ministry for the Majority World Context," 7. See the literature review in the appendices for more information on Wan and Hedinger's work.

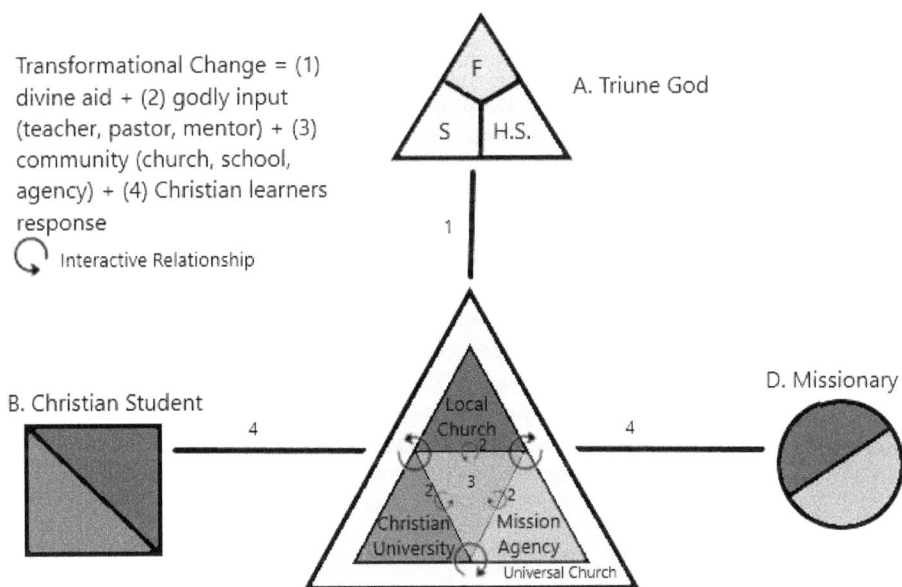

Transformational Change = (1) divine aid + (2) godly input (teacher, pastor, mentor) + (3) community (church, school, agency) + (4) Christian learners response

Interactive Relationship

A. Triune God

F
S   H.S.

1

D. Missionary

B. Christian Student

4

4

Local Church

2

3

2   2

Christian University   Mission Agency

Universal Church

Figure 12. Relational Transformation through Synergy

In this process of relational transformative change, the student begins primarily in relationship with their local church and the Christian University when they arrive on campus. The student then progresses through their academic career in the Synergy program through relational interaction with the three key organizations (local church, university, agency); primarily through the input and relationships with three key individuals (pastor, mentor, teacher). This process represented by the orange area contributes to the student's transformative change from a student to a missionary. While not all students will become vocational missionaries, that remains the goal of the program.

The Synergy model of outcomes-based, experiential learning creates a rich environment for the holistic development of the student. It integrates together sound theology and educational theory into a model that engages the student at multiple levels and through multiple relationships with a singular focus contributes to the student's development into a potential missionary candidate. As these three arms of the Universal Church collaborate with one another, each can contribute its best to the student. Only through real relationships developed under the guidance of the Holy Spirit can we recognize that all three have a distinct role to play in helping prepare the next generation of missionaries. Then, working together, we can mobilize the body of Christ for the completion of the Lord's harvest.

The coursework that student's complete in conjunction with the agency training allows them to receive credit for their work with the agency. Four courses were developed (Intercultural Methods 1-4) that the student enrolls in concurrently or immediately following the training with the agency. Students complete assignments, papers, and a journal and are also evaluated by their agency mentor and sending church pastor. Students are then assigned a grade consistent with the work. Each course builds on the last as the training and the overall development of the student builds as well. This development is tracked using a curriculum map as seen in table 19, as students progress from one level to the next.

Table 2. Synergy Curriculum Map

Ministry Studies PLO's	Courses			
	IC361	IC362	IC363	IC364
The student has demonstrated the Christian Character qualities essential for Christian ministry.	K	A	A	S
The student has demonstrated an understanding of the theology, theories, methodologies, and skills essential for effective Christian	K	A	A	S
The student has developed effective communication skills essential for Christian ministry.	K	A	A	S
The student has developed basic interpersonal skills necessary for addressing the spiritual needs of people.	K	A	A	S
The student has acquired basic ministry skills under the guidance of a mature, seasoned professional supervisor in the kind of ministry setting anticipated	K	A	A	S

K= Knowledge/Comprehension

A=Application/Analysis

S=Synthesis/Evaluation

Utilizing a curriculum map such as that seen above provides the University with the necessary framework for assessing the student's academic and professional growth. The program learning outcomes are traced directly to the student objectives for each course and then individual assignments in courses. Through this Synergy not only prepares the student for missions but also meets the necessary academic rigor of a college education. The Appendices contain more information on the educational basis and research into Synergy's educational design including a discussion of Generation Z and their learning styles. Ultimately, the goal of Synergy is to produce an environment for transformational change in the character and maturity of the student in order to equip them for missionary service.

Relational Interactionism

In the recent book *Transformational Change in Christian Ministry*, Enoch Wan and John Raibley took the concepts within the relational paradigm another step forward to produce the relational interaction model seen below. Wan and Raibley define relational interactionism as, "An interdisciplinary narrative framework that develops from practical considerations of dynamic interaction of personal Beings/beings, forming realistic relational networks to multiply contexts (i.e., theo-culture, angel-culture, and human-culture) and with various consequences.[136]

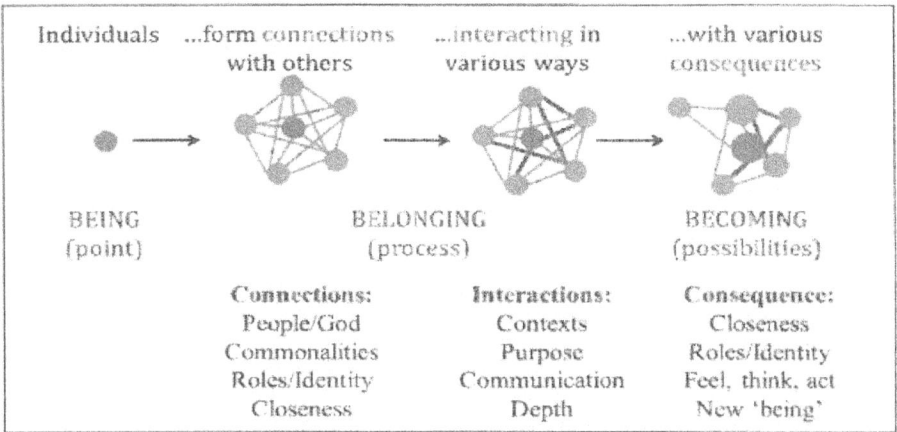

Individuals	...form connections with others	...interacting in various ways	...with various consequences
BEING (point)	BELONGING (process)		BECOMING (possibilities)
	Connections: People/God Commonalities Roles/Identity Closeness	Interactions: Contexts Purpose Communication Depth	Consequence: Closeness Roles/Identity Feel, think, act New 'being'

Figure 13. Relational Interaction Model[137]

Wan and Raibley go into detail in their book on explaining the foundation and outworking of the framework. For our purposes here and relating the framework to Synergy it would be helpful to understand the three phases of transformational change; 'Being, Belonging, and Becoming.'

"'Being' has the individual in view, at a specific point in time. 'Belonging' focuses on the process of relating by forming connections and interacting within those connections. These connections may be vertical, between the person and God, or horizontal with other people. 'Becoming' anticipates the possible outcomes of the interactions."[138]

This framework provides the perfect backdrop for exploring how the Synergy process utilizes relational partnerships to transform the student from

---

136 Enoch Wan and John Raibley, *Transformational Change in Christian Ministry*, (Portland: Western Academic Publishers, 2022), 11.

137 Wan and Raibley, *Transformational Change*, 11.

138 Wan and Raibley, *Transformational Change*, 11.

initially being a student to becoming a mature believer ready to step into the role of a missionary.

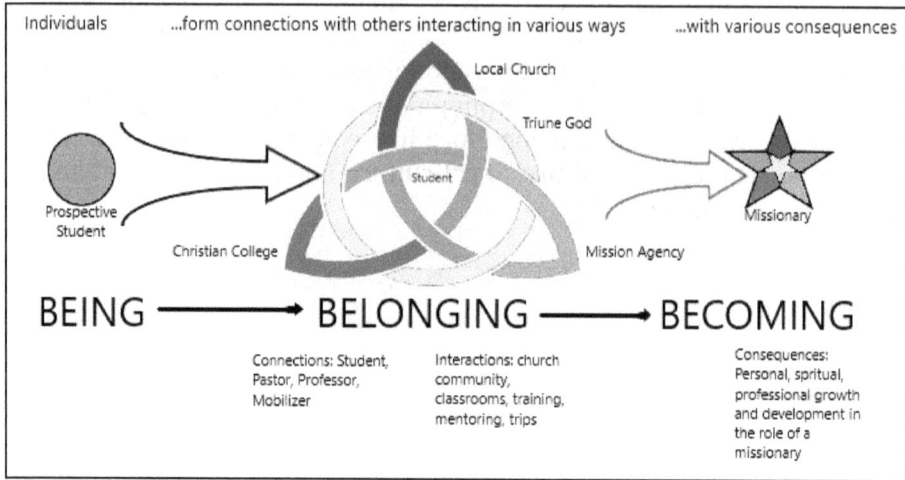

Figure 14. Relational Interaction through Synergy[139]

The Synergy process can easily be demonstrated as the relational interaction of the student, local church, university, agency, and God. In this process 'being' is primarily focused on the student and the student's growth and development. However, the student does not stand alone. Per Wan and Raibley's description above, 'being' can apply equally to those personally involved in the process including the pastor of the local church, the professor at the university, and mobilizers and trainers involved with the agency. The necessary outcome is that everyone involved is growing through the dynamic interaction of the partnership. Relationships between each person and each organization are strengthened and improved. While yes, the goal of the student's ongoing growth and maturity is being accomplished, so too is the side result of social interaction between each one and the growth of each individual member in relationship with God.

Each of these partners operating in their various relationships and interactions with one another throughout the process leads to a sense of belonging. The Church is by nature a community of believers in which we are encouraged not to forsake gathering together (Hebrews 10:25). These personal and organizational connections provide a community in which to foster growth and development. The student learns not only in academic (cognitive) ways but also affective and behavioral through the combined efforts of the relational partnership. Each piece contributes to the total

---

[139] Wan and Raibley, *Transformational Change*, 131.

development of the student. The result then is not a missionary candidate who only knows great theological terms, but one who can also apply those concepts to their own life and others. The result is a candidate who can identify and empathize with people who have lived their whole lives in darkness, not knowing there is a better way through the power of the gospel. Perhaps one of the most common accusations leveled against college graduates is that while they have excellent training and knowledge, they lack the experience to practically apply it in ministry. Through the involvement of the local church and the mission agency the student is able to develop those practical ministry skills, while learning the academic foundation for them. We belong in community, we were made for community, and if COVID-19 has demonstrated anything it is the importance of community when community was taken away for 2 years. Life on life community provides the context for transformation. Transformation in this case results in becoming a missionary.

Summary

Christians grow in community. Perhaps it is an obvious statement and maybe it goes without being said. However, it was vital to the early church. It is so vital that the author of Hebrews told his readers not to forsake it. Scripture presents a clear testimony to the importance of community. Paul goes into great detail to the Corinthians on how they each have a role to play in the local church.[140] The local church is a microcosm of what the Universal church is in macrocosm.[141] This chapter has presented the Synergy process as an educational model to promote transformational growth in the student. We have described growth that progresses from the student's freshman year at college until graduation as an equipped and ready missionary. The next chapter will explain the practical details of what Synergy looks like for each of Calvary's agency partners.

---

[140] 1 Corinthians 12
[141] David E. Stevens, *God's New Humanity: A Biblical Theology of Multiethnicity for the Church*, (Eugene, OR: Wipf and Stock Publishers, 2012), 138.

Chapter 2 Questions for Discussion

1. As you consider the Trinity as a theological basis for partnership, what relationships are essential for your organization?

2. What are the essential roles and responsibilities for each of the partners?

3. What factors outside of your organization need to be considered? For Calvary accreditation is a key issue that drives program design.

4. How does the model of relational interactionism fit your situation?
    Consider the three areas...
        BEING - individual
        BELONGING – community interaction
        BECOMING – consequences, goal, outcomes

CHAPTER 3
THE OPERATION OF THE SYNERGY MODEL

Introduction

An educational process like Synergy which involves many moving parts and requires the cooperation of multiple organizations also requires a high degree of flexibility. While the basic principles of students receiving training from the agency and credit for the university under the supervision of their local church are consistent, yet details, timelines for completion, and eventual deployment to the field can vary greatly with each partner. The process first began as described in chapter one with Crossworld. While the timeline with Crossworld has changed slightly it remains consistent with the initial vision. In this chapter I will go into more detail on how the process works with Calvary's other four partners. The goal is to demonstrate its practical flexibility for the unique context in which the relational partnership takes place. This section will close with a discussion of some common elements as well as ongoing adjustments to the process that came out of the dissertation research.

Ethnos 360

Ethnos 360 was founded in 1942 as New Tribes Mission with a clear vision to reach the most unreached and isolated people groups around the world.[142] Calvary has enjoyed a vibrant relationship with them for many years. Among some of our notable alumni to serve with Ethnos 360 include Martin and Gracia Burnham. Martin and Gracia, both graduates of Calvary Bible College, are well known names because of their kidnapping in 2001. They were held for over a year before being rescued by the Philippine military; sadly, Martin did not survive the rescue attempt.[143] In 2018 Calvary launched the Burnham Center for Global Engagement, which serves as the hub for all our missions related and intercultural studies offerings at the school, including Synergy.

Ethnos 360's training of their missionaries is the most expansive of the three Synergy partners. Involvement in Synergy with Ethnos 360 automatically adds a year to the student's program as they will be spending two years at Ethnos 360's Missionary Training Center in Roach, Missouri

---

[142] "About," *Ethnos 360*, accessed March 26, 2021, https://ethnos360.org/about.
[143] "About Gracia," *Gracia Burnham*, https://graciaburnham.org/gracia/, (Accessed June 8, 2023).

while also finishing their Calvary coursework.[144] An outline of their extensive training is readily available on their website.[145]

This training runs over four, 18-week semesters beginning in August each year. If married, both husband and wife are expected to complete the training, and if a single marries someone who has not gone through the training, they are expected to return so their spouse can complete it. The general training includes Christian life principles, culture and language acquisition, and church planting methods. Additional courses are available for those who are specializing in linguistics. In addition, Ethnos 360 has an aviation wing that requires specialized training at the aviation center in Arizona.[146] The emphasis in the academic courses offered as part of Ethnos 360's training includes:

Church Planting: Worldview, New Testament Church principles, practical ministry skills, folk religions, curriculum development, evangelism, the mature church model.

Christian Living: Foundational Bible teaching, teamwork, stewardship of life and resources, discipleship, effective parenting, conflict resolution.

Culture and Language Acquisition: Phonetics, culture and language methodology, animism, grammar, semantics and translation, literacy, phonemics.

Complementary Courses: Missionary health and wellness, missionary technology, safety, learning styles, communication skills.[147]

In addition to the academic coursework, students also regularly attend chapel, pray for missionaries on the field, and are involved in a relational mentoring program with each other and experienced missionary trainers.[148] Perhaps one of the greatest aspects of Ethnos 360's training is that every trainer is a seasoned missionary who has been through the same training and then utilized it on the mission field to plant an indigenous church among a tribal people group. Students are also expected to contribute to the overall training environment through work detail while they are living on the training center's campus in southern Missouri.

The importance of training to Ethnos 360 can also be seen in the core

---

[144] "Synergy with Calvary University," *Ethnos 360*, accessed March 26, 2021, https://ethnos360.org/training/ethnos360-training/synergy-with-calvary-university.

[145] "Ethnos 360 Training," *Ethnos 360*, accessed March 26, 2021, https://ethnos360.org/training/ethnos360-training/academics.

[146] "Overview of Ethnos 360 Training," (Ethnos 360, Roach, MO, unpublished document), used by permission, 1.

[147] "Overview of Ethnos 360 Training," 1.

[148] "Overview of Ethnos 360 Training," 1.

values of their missionary candidates, summarized below.

Table 3. Ethnos 360 Spiritual Qualities and Ministry Capabilities of Candidates[149]

Core Values	Description (Therefore we commit ourselves to:)
A Spirit Controlled Life	Glorify Christ in our attitudes and actions. Exercise our spiritual gifts so we can be more effective in ministry where God has palced us. Enjoy freedom from striving and self-effort in our daily life and ministry.
Godly Relationships and Interdependence in Ministry	Obey God by maintaining the unity His Spirit has provided for us. Glorify Christ by demonstrating our need for one another as members of His Body. Use teamwork and plurality of leadership effectively to accomplish God's work.
Effective Communication in Evangelism and Church Planting	Understand the culture and learn the language of the people group. Communicate the Gospel clearly to the unsaved. Teach believers the Word of God.
The Word of God as Our Final Authority	Submit to God by gladly yielding to the authority of His Word in all we believe and do. Actively seek direction from God's Word in our decision making, never choosing contrary to it. Remain true to the teaching of the Word of God, including that expressed in our doctrinal statement.
The Certainty that God Desires to Use Any Life	Ecourage believers that God gives each of His children the privilege of serving and glorifying Him. Provide opportunity for service in (Ethnos 360) based on the grace of God in glorifying Himself through the lives of believers. Assign ministries in a way that reflects the diversity of gifts represented by the indviduals who make up (Ethnos 360).
Willingness to Sacrifice for Christ	Carry His Gospel to parts of the world where living and working conditions are often difficult. Persevere in completing His task with joy, even in the absence of ease or comfort. Demonstrate that the Lord is worthy of any sacrifice we may be called upon to make for Him.
Excellence in What We Do	Undertake each task with resolve, giving our best effort for His glory. Reflect the faithful character of God by completing our tasks thoroughly and efficiently. Increase our effectiveness in serving God at our individual and collective tasks by being lifelong learners.
Dependence on God Evidenced by Prayer and Living by Faith	Trust God to supply the personnel, direction, and resources we need to do His will. Glorify God and demonstrate our dependence upon Him by making our needs known to Him through prayer. Depend on God individually and corporately, and not rely on (Ethnos 360) in place of God.
A Sense of Urgency in Ministry	Redeem the time as demonstrated by Christ andA8:B13 His apostles in taking the Gospel to people who have yet to hear it. Stay focused on the eternal value and destiny of souls. Remain mindful of the immensity of the task before us.

Completing Synergy with Ethnos 360 is a longer process than with any of

---

[149] "Spiritual Qualities and Ministry Capabilities," 1-14.

the other partners. Their extensive training program requires the student to spend two years at the Missionary Training Center (MTC) in Roach, MO. Owing to the longer and more specialized training that a prospective missionary receives with Ethnos 360 a student who wishes to participate in the program must understand that completing it will automatically extend their college program to five years as opposed to the traditional four. However, with many of Calvary's students arriving on campus with early college and transfer credit this is less of a concern. Calvary also has options for students to take a lot of classes in the summer, which could further shorten this time frame.

Application and Finances

While the application process has slight variances for each organization the basics are the same as that already given above for Crossworld. Students express interest in the Synergy program, fill out an application for Calvary which includes a pastoral reference and are then directed to complete the agency's application process. Once approved by the agency they enroll at the MTC and in the accompanying coursework. Students enrolled in Synergy will also complete a learning contract which includes input from the pastor of their home or sending church, the professor, and an agency mentor. The learning contract serves as a formal way of binding the relationships between each partner.

Financial arrangements are made separately with Calvary and the agency. The student pays or uses scholarships or other aid for the coursework at Calvary and makes separate arrangements with the agency itself. Calvary has instituted a scholarship program for the coursework to help offset the cost of the training with the agency.

Timeline of Completion

Listed below is the recommended timeline for completion of Synergy-Ethnos 360. While there can be some variation, this timeline helps the student to complete both the university education and missionary training in the best timeframe. Specific dates depend on the year of completion. Students are highly encouraged to take courses over the summer early on to complete the process in five years or even sooner based on their early college or transfer credit.

Table 4. Ethnos 360 Timeline of Completion

Year	Calvary Course	Ethnos 360 Training
Sophomore		
Fall	Complete Synergy Application	
Spring	IC351	Wayumi
Junior		
Fall	Ongoing follow-up	
Spring	Complete Ethnos 360 Application	
Summer	Raise Support and Move to MTC	
Senior 1		
Fall	IC361	MTC 1
Spring	IC362	MTC 2
Summer	IC459	Internship
Senior 2		
Fall	IC363	MTC 3
Spring	IC364	MTC 4
Graduate and Go!		

Upon completion of the process, the student would receive both their degree as well as be appointed as a missionary with Ethnos 360. With continued support raising the potential (depending on field) would be for them to be on the mission field engaged in ministry immediately, or at least within a year. At this point the relational ties with the school would lessen although they are never severed as the student becomes an alumnus and would be prayed for on a regular basis at "The Haystack," Calvary's weekly prayer time devoted to prayer for alumni missionaries.[150] The relationship with the local church and mission agency would continue throughout the missionary's years of fruitful service to the Lord.

Biblical Ministries Worldwide

Biblical Ministries Worldwide (BMW) was formed in 1988 from two post-WWII mission agencies, one focused on the Pacific and South America and the other one Europe. It now has more than 500 missionaries focused primarily on church planting in forty-seven countries, having maintained steady growth over the past two decades. All administrators are former missionaries and see

---

[150] The Haystack is a group of Calvary students who meet regularly on Thursdays throughout the school year to read alumni newsletters and pray for them.

themselves as mentors and guides, viewing missions as a family, rather than an organization. BMW is involved with pioneering mission work among unreached people groups in Africa, Asia, Indonesia, and the Pacific islands.[151] A large portion of the mission family ministers alongside of partner missions in previously reached but needy countries (like Western Europe), strengthening national churches, helping plant churches, and training national leaders formally and non-formally. BMW also has a growing network of tentmakers around the world. The partnership between Calvary and BMW has similar application and financial processes as those of Ethnos 360.

BMW is a longtime friend of Calvary University, and the list of alumni who have gone on from Calvary to serve with them is very long. In addition to having many graduates serve with this organization both at home and abroad, a staff member who works in Calvary's Library is a campus mobilizer with BMW. She has personally been involved in many missions activities on campus and is a mentor to many female students who are contemplating missions service. It is these kinds of relationships that truly form the backbone of our partnership with organizations like BMW.

BMW's purpose statement is to "serve the Lord and local churches by establishing reproducing churches through evangelism, discipleship and leadership development."[152] Each of Calvary's Synergy partners has a unique niche to their ministry; BMW is the only one that has ministries located in both the US and around the world, while others are exclusively international or national in their focus.

The Synergy relationship with BMW began through the efforts of the staff member above to connect David Brown, then BMW's head of training, to the school. Brown has since gone on to head up a ministry on the field in South Africa, and their training program has recently been passed on to David McCrum, who currently serves as the Vice-President of Education.

BMW is mindful of the role of the local church and their own place in missions, stating that they are, "dedicated to helping North American churches fulfill their mission of spreading the gospel and planting churches in gospel-deprived locations around the world."[153] Their pre-field process is outlined on their website[154] as well as their partnership with Calvary through

---

[151] "About BMW," *Biblical Ministries Worldwide*, https://biblicalministries.org/about, (Accessed 5/19/2022).

[152] "Purpose," *Biblical Ministries Worldwide*," accessed March 26, 2021, https://www.biblicalministries.org/about/purpose/.

[153] "BMW's Prefield Process," (Biblical Ministries Worldwide: Atlanta, unpublished document), used by permission, 1.

[154] "training," *Biblical Ministries Worldwide*," accessed March 26, 2021, biblicalministries.org/serve/training/.

the Synergy process.[155]

BMW is strongly committed to local church involvement. Most recently, they have begun making a concerted effort to come alongside local churches more in partnership relationships; this includes hosting Sender's Think Tanks and posting many resources for local churches on their website.[156] Their training currently involves a four-step process. While Synergy with Ethnos 360 automatically results in an extension of the student's program, BMW's training, like Crossworld's, can be worked right into the student's four-year degree and include an on-field experience.

Table 5. BMW Synergy Timeline

Year	Calvary Course	BMW Training
Sophomore		
Fall	Complete Synergy Application	
Spring	Complete BMW Application	
Summer	IC361	Explore
Summer	IC362	Onboard
Junior		
Fall	Ongoing follow-up	
Spring	Ongoing follow-up	
Summer	IC363	Equip
Summer	IC364	Deploy
Summer	IC459	Internship
Senior		
Fall	Finish Calvary coursework	
Spring	Finish Calvary coursework	
	Graduate and Go!	

---

[155] "synergy," *Biblical Ministries Worldwide*," accessed March 26, 2021, biblicalministries.org/serve/training/synergy/.

[156] "Senders videos," *Biblical Ministries Worldwide*," accessed March 26, 2021, https://www.biblicalministries.org/send/senders-videos/.

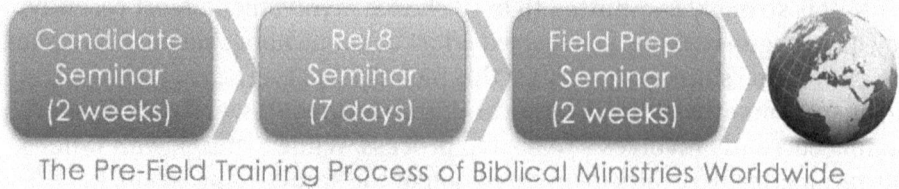

The Pre-Field Training Process of Biblical Ministries Worldwide

Figure 15. BMW's Pre-Field Training Process[157]

BMW's training process begins with the application phase (not pictured above) which includes the establishment of a relational connection between the candidate, agency, and local church. If the candidate is approved and the local church is on board, then their training proceeds through four modules; Explore, Onboard, Equip, and Deploy.[158]

All four training modules are offered over two subsequent weeks in July. This enables the student to travel to Atlanta for these two weeks and accomplish two of the modules in one trip. During their sophomore year, students will complete both Explore and Onboard, enrolling in the accompanying Calvary courses either concurrently or for the following Fall semester. Enrolling for the courses (IC361 & IC362) in the Fall allows the student to focus on the training time while they are at BMW and complete the accompanying coursework for Calvary once they return. The student would then return to BMW for the final two Modules (Equip and Deploy) the following summer between their Junior and Senior years. Like Crossworld and Ethnos 360 this enables the student to complete their training, earning credit towards their degree while also building the necessary relationships along the way.

Village Missions

Village Missions' primary ministries involve church planting and church revitalization in small town and rural churches of North America.[159] They are one of two US focused ministries involved in Cavalry's Synergy process. The other, Midwest Church Extension (MCE) is discussed below. Village Missions focuses on placing "Missionary Pastors" in struggling churches which are on the verge of closing or can't afford to pay a pastor's salary. Founded in 1948, they place a lot of emphasis on the pastor's role and relationships within the community where he ministers. They state on their website that this could

---

[157] "Synergy Handbook," unpublished document, Calvary University, 2020.
[158] "Training," *Biblical Ministries Worldwide*, accessed June 1, 2023, https://learn.biblicalministries.org/library/.
[159] "Home," *Village Missions*, https://villagemissions.org/, (Accessed 5/18/2022).

involve anything from preaching the Word to helping with regular farm chores. Rural America represents a unique cultural environment and the training required to minister there needs to prepare students for that ministry.

The different focus of Village Missions and MCE, from national to international, involves a slightly different course track than that seen above with Crossworld, BMW, and Ethnos 360. While the courses involved with international ministry place a high degree of emphasis on cultural learning and cross-cultural understanding, those for ministry in the US take a more pastoral focus. To this end, we have nicknamed the national focus of Synergy, OnRamp.[160] The name reflects that the goal of this process is to help the student merge into ministry, much like a highway on-ramp helps a car get up to speed and merge into traffic. It should also be mentioned that because of the focus of both organizations this process is limited to men. It is Calvary's position and the position of these organizations, that only men can serve as pastors. Students who are completing OnRamp will take a similar set of coursework to those completing Synergy, however since the focus is slightly different the course descriptions and objectives are slightly different as well. This results in four separate courses MS361-MS364 or Ministry Methods as opposed to Intercultural Methods.

OnRamp Process and Timeline

The process of helping students merge into a national focused ministry allows for a great deal more practical ministry involvement. Village Missions and Calvary have enjoyed a long relationship which includes many alumni serving in rural churches across the United States as Village Missionary Pastors. One of those pastors serves in Blue Mound, KS, slightly more than one hour's drive from Calvary's campus. This close relationship and connection allows for a highly practical residency program for these students, that would be far more difficult at the international level.

The initial steps for a student desiring to complete the Synergy process with Village Missions (VM) involves a series of mentorship weekends and a residency with one of their missionary pastors. The process begins in October of either a student's Freshman or Sophomore year when representatives from VM visit Calvary's campus for a weekend event where they introduce students to the ministry of VM. These events are also opened to others in the area who would like to attend and learn more about the ministry.[161] Following this

---

[160] "On-Ramp Program: Synergy Calvary University," *Village Missions*, https://villagemissions.org/on-ramp-to-ministry/calvary-university/, (Accessed 5/18/2022).

[161] We have already seen the Lord use them to mobilize not only students but other couples and visitors as well. Following the October 2021 event, 3 couples previously unaffiliated with either Calvary or VM ended up joining the ministry

initial event students are invited to complete a pre-application which begins their involvement in Synergy and their relationship with VM. The timeline for a student to complete the process is summarized below.

Table 6. Synergy-Village Missions Timeline

Year	Calvary Course	VM Training
Sophomore		
Fall	Introduced to Synergy/OnRamp	
Spring	MS361	Mentorship Weekend 1
Summer	3 Month Internship	
Junior		
Fall	MS362	Mentorship Weekend 2
Spring	MS363	Mentorship Weekend 3
Summer	MS459	9 Month Residency
Senior		
Fall	Continue Residency	
Spring	MS364	Candidate School
Graduate and Go!		

As seen in the table above, the process of completing Synergy with Village Missions involves incorporating the student's coursework into a series of mentorship weekends and an extended residency program. The student begins with an initial mentorship weekend in the Spring of their Sophomore year. These mentorship weekends involve pre-work and readings, around 16 hours of lecture and then post-work and follow-up by the student to complete both VM and Calvary course requirements. After this time an account is created for the student with VM that allows them to raise support for the internship. During the summer between their Sophomore and Junior years, the student will spend three months interning with a VM Missionary Pastor. This internship early on in the process allows them to get their "feet wet" with rural ministry and see if it really is for them. It is a great benefit for them to have this initial exposure because if they change their mind at this point then they really haven't wasted any time.

In their Junior year the student will participate in two more mentorship weekends and continue their Calvary coursework. Following the completion of their Junior year they will have a nine month residency with a VM Missionary Pastor. Ideally, the student will be able to return to the same pastor and church community that they served in the previous summer. This would allow them to capitalize on an existing relationship and jump right into the ministry. Students who are involved in the Ministry Studies program at Calvary could use this residency to fulfill their academic internship requirement as well. Because the residency is nine months long it will extend into the Fall semester of the student's Senior year. [162] However, all of Calvary's classes are offered in a blended online format, which allows the student to continue their Calvary education from their field of service. The added benefit of this arrangement is that the student can immediately apply what they are learning in class to their ministry context.

The process completes in the student's Senior year with attending VM's candidate school in March. The student will then be able to complete any support raising.[163] All along the way the student has also been maintaining a relationship with their sending church through references, and pastoral mentoring which is built into the Synergy process for national focused organizations like Village Missions just as is done for internationally focused agencies. Village Missions so enjoys this relationship with Calvary that the On-Ramp process which began with Calvary is being worked into the educational programs of other schools as well. They are currently in conversation with both Frontier School of the Bible and Montana Bible College to begin similar programs.[164]

Midwest Church Extension

Calvary University has a long-standing relationship with IFCA International. Many of our faculty and staff attend IFCA churches. Many of our alumni serve with IFCA churches and ministries and they are among our top places for recruiting students. While Calvary is not an IFCA exclusive school, we have very similar doctrinal positions and have been involved in ministry together in many ways. Midwest Church Extension (MCE) as an organizational member of the IFCA International has a close relationship with Calvary as a result.[165] Calvary is also a member organization of the IFCA.

Midwest Church Extension states their mission as "fulfilling the Great Commission by strategically extending the ministry of IFCA International

---

[162] The 3-month internship and 9-month residency are designed to fulfill a 12 month residency requirement for Village Missions Missionary Pastors prior to them receiving their first ministry appointment.

[163] An added benefit of this process is that Village Missions guarantees a salary amount to its missionary pastors reducing the amount they have to raise. The combination of internship and residency allow the student to raise support early and often in the process. This easily creates a situation where a student will already be fully supported upon graduation for their first ministry.

[164] "On-Ramp Program," *Village* Missions, https://villagemissions.org/on-ramp-to-ministry/, (Accessed 5/18/2022).

[165] "Our Identity," *Midwest Church Extension,* https://www.ifcamce.org/, (Accessed 5/18/2022).

churches to Midwestern communities and equipping believers for church planting ministry in whatever community God may call them to."[166] Their focus is on the states of Ohio, Indiana, Illinois, Iowa, Wisconsin, and Missouri. IFCA International has other church extension organizations which focus on other areas of the country. One of these, Rockies Southwest Bible Church Extension, also has a close relationship with Calvary. In many ways the Synergy partnership with MCE also opens the door for the other church planting arms of the IFCA.

MCE Process and Timeline

While both Village Missions and Midwest Church Extension have similar processes MCE's involves a much long residency program that extends throughout the student's Junior and Senior years. This extended residency option allows the student to "learn-on-the-job" by being involved in MCE church planting work as it happens and also continuing their education. Again, Calvary's blended in-class and online course model allows students to continue their education online while in ministry at their residency location. The process carries with it the added benefit of being able to directly apply what the student is learning in his classes to the ministry they are involved in.

Table 7. Midwest Church Extension Timeline

Year	Calvary Course	MCE Training
Sophomore		
Fall	Complete Synergy Application	
Spring	Complete MCE Application	
Summer	MS361	Begin Residency
Junior		
Fall	MS362	Continue Residency
Spring	MS363	Continue Residency
Summer	MS459	Continue Residency
Senior		
Fall	MS364	Complete Residency
Spring	Return to Calvary for final semester	
Graduate and Go!		

Once the student is accepted into the residency they begin immediately

---

[166] "Our Mission," *Midwest Church Extension*, https://www.ifcamce.org/home-page#IdentMission, (Accessed 5/18/2022).

during the summer between their Sophomore and Junior years. Because of MCE's expansive ministry throughout the Midwest a lot of residency locations are available, including right in Kansas City. The student has a variety of church planting options to choose from, everywhere from small town and rural ministry to urban and inner-city church planting. Once the student is paired up with a mentor at the residency location, he will begin to involve himself in that ministry, learning on the job. The content of Calvary's Synergy coursework as well as any other courses can be completed online through Calvary's learning management system. Through the process the student continues to be in contact with their home/sending church, the pastor of which also serves as a mentor for the ministry the student is involved in. After two years at the residency location the student then returns to Calvary for their final semester before becoming a full member of MCE. Following graduation, the student can be immediately sent to an existing field to join a ministry in progress or even launch a new church plant.

Summary

Each one of these organizations emphasizes similar concepts in their training. Missionaries need personal development, a strong relationship with the Lord and others, cross-cultural and ministry skills, and a wide variety of other abilities depending on their field of service. There are many similarities in what they teach as well as how they go about teaching it. Clear parallels can be drawn from their content, methods, and philosophy. It is not surprising that although they have different focus areas (tribal church planting, church planting, business as missions, pastoral ministry, etc.) most of the training remains very similar and can easily be interwoven into the courses involved in the Synergy process at Calvary. Synergy must incorporate biblical/theological principles of missionary training as seen in the examples of Jesus and Paul, a sound missionary training philosophy and the deliberate training of the whole person from a relational framework. These elements reflect key areas of missionary practice in keeping with the realities of what the missionary will face on the field.

The blending of college coursework and missionary training takes some logistical expertise but as demonstrated in the examples above it is doable. In each of these cases the student maintains relationships with the local church, university, and mission agency throughout the training process. This means they are surrounded by a team of supporters who are there to help them succeed, mentor them along the way, and see them reach a place of transformational growth into the ministry God has called them to accomplish.

Throughout this chapter the importance of the relational connections that exist between each of these organizations have been emphasized over and again. We are all bound by our common faith in Christ. The relationships between alumni, students, pastors, supporters, and just historic ties of people who have served together in ministry form a tighter bond than mere contractual agreements. Those same relationships allow for mutual trust and understanding when we all know that everyone has each other's best interest in mind, wants everyone to succeed and is ultimately united in our desire to fulfill the mission of God in proclaiming the gospel.

Chapter 3 Questions for Discussion

As you develop your partnership further it will be necessary to work out the practical details of how it will operate.

1. With the end goal of all partners in mind, what time considerations are
      necessary?
2. How will you work out the financial arrangements, if any?
3. If your partnership involves a change of location (such as a student moving to
      an area of ministry) will this individual still be able to fulfill the
      obligations to both?
4. What technological needs might you have in order to facilitate the operation
      of the program? Synergy would not have been possible for Calvary even
      just a year before it was launched because the online program was not
      in place.

CHAPTER 4

MISSIOLOGICAL, ECCLESIOLOGICAL, AND EDUCATIONAL IMPLICATIONS

Introduction

The dissertation research that resulted in this book was conducted with four research questions in mind.

1. What is the ethnographic profile of Generation Z relevant for mobilizing them for Christian mission?
2. What are the roles/responsibilities of the stakeholders in the mobilization of Generation Z for Christian missions?
3. How does Synergy allow the stakeholders to utilize integrated relational partnerships for mobilizing Generation Z for Christian mission?
4. What are the educational implications from the research findings?

This chapter examines the outcome of the research that was conducted and the implications for local churches, universities, and mission agencies.

Missiological Implications

Research question three highlights two missiological implications for this research. The first is in relational partnerships and the second mobilizing the next and future generations.

Relational Partnerships for Missions

As demonstrated in the literature review, partnership and working together have a long-standing history in missions.[167] That said, those partnerships are often created based on contracts, memorandums of understanding, or in the case of schools, articulation agreements. While these documents are important and they serve a purpose in formalizing many of the arrangements of the partnership, they are not the basis of partnership within a Christian context. Solid partnerships between local churches, schools and mission agencies are the outworking of the relational paradigm.

Partnerships begin with the understanding that the Triune God works in partnership Himself. The Father, the Son and the Holy Spirit are each equally

---

[167] See Appendix 2.

God and yet carry out distinct roles within the Godhead and cooperate fully in creation, redemption, and sanctification. As seen in Table 19 each member of the Trinity cooperates in missions and fills specific roles. This unity in diversity is further demonstrated in the Universal Church. God, writing through Paul, reminds us that though the Body is one it has many members (1 Corinthians 12:12-31). Whether applied individually within one local church or corporately to the Universal Church as a whole, this principle demonstrates the simple fact that we need each other. Local churches, Christian colleges, and mission agencies are each part of the Universal Church through the membership of its people, and each has a distinct role to play in the mobilizing of missionaries. This study demonstrates that the current trend towards local churches "going their own," and forgoing utilizing the resources they have in both Christian colleges and mission agencies is not only practically misguided but biblically unfounded as well. While absolutely there is great precedence for the biblical responsibility of the local church for missions, that precedence does not preclude the involvement of mission agencies and universities bringing their unique resources to the table for the furthering of the Great Commission. Concurrently, it was recognized by the participants of this study that while there is great precedence for the local church's engagement in missions, its current involvement is lackluster at best. Now, more than ever a partnership approach that engages the roles, responsibilities, and gifting of each organization is needed. Much as Hebrews 10:24 calls individual believers to "spur one another on to love and good deeds," local churches, universities, and missions agencies need relational partnerships that will continually motivate and remind them of the relationship they share with the Triune God and the ministry He has called each to accomplish (2 Corinthians 5:18-21). Synergy is one practical example of the relational paradigm at work in partnerships. The reader is encouraged to examine the Literature Review in Appendix II for more helpful information regarding forming relational partnerships.

Mobilizing the Next and Future Generations

Numerous other works have been released recently that demonstrate that mobilizing Generation Z is a frequently discussed topic. Missio Nexus in collaboration with Sixteen:Fifteen hosted a webinar covering the results of the Barna study that was referenced in this research.[168] A book is also to be published soon by Jolene Erlanger and Kay White.[169] There is great interest in how to reach this generation for Christ and also how to mobilize the believers among them for reaching the lost.

At the same time, Generation Z has been called the final generation.[170] While the long-term effects of the Covid-19 pandemic and social distancing remain to be seen on this generation. The simple reality is that the world changes so quickly that change is the new normal and generational distinctions are becoming increasingly blurred. However, one very clear theme has emerged from every study done on Gen Z and that is the overwhelming importance of relationships. Once again, the relational paradigm is noteworthy in contributing to our understanding of the work of mobilization. The relational interaction of the Trinity with the (pastor/teacher/mobilizer) and the student is key to our understanding of the process. In 1 Corinthians 3 Paul reminds the divided Corinthian church that while they have had multiple teachers and workers among them God was the one who did the work. "I planted, Apollos watered, but God gave the growth."[171] The relational paradigm integrated into Synergy as seen in Figure 12 demonstrates clearly the same principle that while the local church may plant and the Christian university and missions agency may water, it is God working through all of them who provides the growth that leads to maturity and ultimately missionary service. All three can be essential ingredients to the process.

For the Mission Agency

It is a simple and yet profound statement, missions agencies need missionaries. While agencies willingly accept workers from all walks of life and ages and professional backgrounds there must be intentionality in raising up the current generation. This study has highlighted the importance of relationships in the mobilization process. Much like the local church and the university must be intentional in relationship building so should the missions agency. From a mobilization perspective, specifically applied to Generation Z,

---

[168] Peer to Peer Virtual Gathering, *Mobilizing Generation Z: Observations, Obstacles and Opportunities*, Online Zoom Meeting, October 6, 2021.

[169] The title is not yet available.

[170] Sparks & Honey Culture Forecast, "Gen Z 2025: The Final Generation."

[171] 1 Corinthians 3:6.

that means building relationships with them, where they are. While the days of the missions conference and the lone mobilizer visiting the college campus once a semester are far from over, their effectiveness in engaging the current generation is rapidly waning. While previous generations actively looked for opportunities, Generation Z looks for relationships. Their identified distrust of organizations makes them wary of the organizational display table and the missions mobilizer looking to recruit them. However, they will respond well to a good conversation, a cup of coffee and an invitation to connect on Facebook, Twitter, or Instagram. While it is more time consuming, the mobilizer who commits the time to building relationships with students, mentoring them, and seeing mobilization as a ministry will meet with much greater success. Mission agencies would do well to invest in dedicated campus mobilizers who can build sustained relationships with particular schools that they have partnerships with. These long-term relationships will serve great dividends than a once or twice a school year campus visit.

Ecclesiological Implications

The implications for the local church as seen through both the literature review and the research is the importance of early discipleship and establishing a strong missions culture. Youth who are involved in a local church that engages them in relational discipleship, not just programs or separate worship services, but life-on-life relational involvement will see great fruit in the spiritual maturity of the younger generation. The local church that equally has a strong emphasis on missions, talking about it from the pulpit, giving time for visiting missionary speakers, offering short-term trips in partnership with like-minded agencies, and challenging its youth to consider missionary service will reap the fruit of young people yearning to reach the lost.

The next step is providing them a pathway to that field. Local churches which intentionally build relationships with like-minded, and like-theology Christian universities can provide their youth with a direct link to Bible training, ongoing discipleship, professional training, and preparation for missions. Then, in partnership with mission agencies this generation can be sent well prepared both spiritually and professionally for the task ahead, with a strong local church behind them.

Finally, and perhaps most important of all, personal involvement with the *missio Dei*, begins in the local church. Local churches must begin to ask themselves how they are intentionally discipling their people, especially the next generation to have a missional vision for what God is doing in the world as revealed in His Word. A "culture of mission" is essential to bringing up a generation that is focused on following the Lord into the harvest field.

Educational Implications

This study has served to highlight several things about education in response to research question four. It has demonstrated the importance of the relational paradigm to the educational process. Education is much more than just the dissemination of facts to the learner. It is the wholistic preparation of the student cognitively, affectively, and behaviorally. Incorporating each partner into the education process allows for the student to learn from the best that each one has to offer. Synergy creates a rich environment for learning that allows the student to develop not just professionally but spiritually as well. Referencing back to Figure 10 it was demonstrated how each partner contributes to the student's education. This process, in the context of the relational paradigm, as seen in Figure 14 results in not just education but transformational change in the student as the student learns, grows, and matures towards the goal of becoming a prospective missionary. Finally, relational interactionism provides a good framework for how transformation happens within the specific Synergy context.[172]

This process, along with the incorporation of professional organizations like missions agencies opens a new avenue for education in the context of professional development that leads immediately to a career. Synergy creates the opportunity for students to immediately progress to the mission field after graduation. This happens through the process of building relationships as well as incorporating organizational membership into the student's education. The student takes all the practical steps of applying, being approved, trained, and beginning their support raising while still a student. This opens a wealth of potential implications for how students are both educated and linked to potential employers. The university, through its exiting relational connections has laid the foundation for the student, creating a pathway to an immediate career following graduation.

Theological schools, universities, and Christian colleges would do well to remember that they are not an island to themselves. The school exists to build on the foundation laid by the local church, to add to the student's professional training, and to bridge the gap between preparation and deployment. The university that is well immersed in a solid biblical foundation offers the student essential and intensive Biblical and theological training, professional development, and cross-cultural preparation. However, none of this happens in a vacuum. The student is still attending their local church, still working a job, and perhaps immersed in other ministries. College professors would do well to take intentional steps toward developing relationships with those same local churches, ministries, and even jobs to wholistically prepare the student for what lies ahead.

---

[172] Wan & Raibley, *Transformational Change in Christian Ministry*. 2022:127-131.

In that preparation, the school must always remember that ministry preparation is much more than just an information brain dump. This generation has the information, but they lack the ability and maturity to properly filter it out.[173] What the current generation needs is professors who will walk with them relationally as mentors and guides. Teachers who will go with them into areas of ministry and educate along the way, rather than remove the process of education from the environment in which it is useful. The college must be intentional to take its educational gifts to the student, in their environment or creating environments where the student can learn through experience and not in isolation.

The implications of this could best be illustrated by a potential next step for Calvary. As the creator and director of the Synergy process, I have begun having a conversation with our business department about a similar project, currently titled "Synergy-Business." The relational philosophy behind Synergy-Business is much the same as the existing Synergy process for missions mobilization and could even feed into the greater picture of ministry, as Business as Missions becomes an increasingly popular method. In much the same way that Calvary has done the groundwork for the student in establishing relationships with like-minded missions agencies, Calvary (specifically the Business Department) would seek to establish relationships with like-minded Christian owned businesses. College level courses (12 hours) could then be created to incorporate on-the-job learning and training in cooperation with those businesses. Following their sophomore year students would apply with the business for a two-year learning internship in which they would work part-time for the business while still in school and earning those 12 credit hours. This would allow the students to take classroom principles and apply them in a real business environment much like Kolb's experiential learning process.[174] Provided the experience is beneficial for both the student and the business, students could potentially be offered temporary or even long-term career opportunities with that business following graduation, creating an immediate pathway for them to use their degree and the experience they learned along the way. With the cost of college increasing and the political debate of student loan forgiveness, colleges will increasingly find that they need to innovate to stay relevant. In 2020, Google announced plans to start accepting "Google Learning Certificates" as replacements for college degrees.[175] Mega-corporations like Google are taking

---

[173] See the Literature Review in Appendix II for a discussion on the characteristics of Generation Z.

[174] Kolb, *Experiential Learning*, 38.

[175] "Google Plans to Replace College Degree with 6-Month Certificates to Help People Develop Skills and Get High-Paying Jobs in Various Fields!" August 30, 2020, *THEMONEYTIME*,

the lead in offering innovative educational and career pathways that bypass the traditional college route. Christian colleges like Calvary which already face increasing challenges in a changing cultural environment would do well to seek out innovative educational opportunities in the realm of relational partnerships.

Conclusion

The purpose of the research study was to further develop the Synergy process at Calvary University for creating a relational partnership model for mobilizing Generation Z for Christian missions. The research was brought about by the recognition that local churches, Christian universities, and mission agencies frequently operate in their own silos with no singular and intentional process for mobilizing believers for the mission field. This frequently results in mobilization being a hap-hazard affair at best and at worst those who are interested in being missionaries not knowing how to proceed toward that goal.

Partnerships are needed. However, partnerships built on a traditional contractual basis that are limited to pragmatic results are insufficient. True partnership is relational and begins with an understanding that relationship is an inherent characteristic of our Triune God. That relationship then extends to his redeemed Church and further as we seek to redeem others. Paul speaks to this necessity in 1 Corinthians 12, as he illustrates the roles and responsibilities of the different parts of the body. While addressing one local church, his encouragement is equally applicable to the Universal Church found all over the world in different cultures and forms. Relational partnerships are built first on the unity that exists within the body of Christ and are primarily relational rather than pragmatic or programmatic.

Ephesians 4 is worthy of more examination related to the importance of relational partnerships in individual growth and discipleship. Moving backwards the end goal is seen in verse 13, "until we all attain to the unity of the faith and of the knowledge of the Son of God, to mature manhood, to the measure of the stature of the fullness of Christ." Given elsewhere in Romans 8:29, God's end goal is that we would be "conformed to the image of His Son." However, this end goal according to Ephesians 4:11 requires various roles fulfilling their parts in equipping the saints for the work of ministry. Yet, the fulfillment of those roles is dependent on the relational unity to be found in the body of Christ in Ephesians 4:3-6. From this perspective we can clearly see that the maturity and growth of the body are dependent on each one working

---

https://themoneytime.com/google-plans-to-replace-college-degree-with-6-month-certificates-to-help-people-develop-skills-and-get-high-paying-jobs-in-various-fields, (Accessed October 19, 2021).

out his/her gifting/role in the body as given by the Lord. This does not come from contracts or memorandums of understanding but rather the "calling to which you have been called." Growth and maturity in the body of Christ originate in relationship.

Synergy was presented and evaluated as an educational model that incorporates the roles and unique contributions of all three partners to the process. It is well grounded in the theology of relational partnership to be found in the Trinity and the universal Church. The relational paradigm presents an understanding of the importance of recognizing the involvement of the Triune God in the entire process and with each individual partner. Relational interactionism demonstrates the unique "being," "belonging," and "becoming" of creating a community of transformational change through the Synergy process.

While Synergy is still new interviews and focus groups with students, pastors, agency representatives, and graduates currently serving on the mission field demonstrated that it is a well-grounded process. Most of the areas for improvement focus on elements that are external to the program itself, such as marketing.[176] Along the way the data collection process contributed to the very relational partnerships being studied by providing interaction among the partners, resulting in some previously unplanned events and ideas to strengthen those relationships and move the Synergy process forward. The research also identified several action steps for this research cycle: marketing specifically to IFCA churches, cooperative events for local churches, conferences, mission rep presence on campus, and including more agencies. The research has also opened new possibilities in educational models that incorporate the Synergy-model in other degree programs, such as business. Calvary's existing institutional effectiveness evaluation process will allow for the continual evaluation and refinement of this important program.

Recommendations for Future Research

This book is the result a participatory action research study of the Synergy process at Calvary University. The study itself represents one cycle of action research into the Synergy process. Future periods of action research will be necessary to continue to develop Synergy and improve the program. The long-term effectiveness of the process is dependent on enough graduates serving as missionaries to evaluate it. In addition, a couple other areas for future research have been brought to light.

The dissertation study was an application of the relational paradigm to education. The relational paradigm could be applied to education in other ways and in other contexts. The study was limited to the United States and

---

[176] See Appendix III for a discussion of the research and findings.

Western cultural background. Application of the Synergy model or similar models in other cultures would require more research into the contextual nature of the local church and partnerships in that area. The relational paradigm could be applied to other educational areas as well as a means of considering the holistic development of the student in relationship with the Triune God, the educational community, and their broader career field.

The Synergy model of partnership-based education also presents other interesting opportunities for research. Besides just business, which was mentioned in the implications, what other career fields could benefit from students who are trained in a cooperative model that combines the college education with real world career training? This brings to mind "apprenticeship" type programs as a way of merging university level education with real world career skills. Could this type of education be a potential solution to the lingering issue of crippling student debt, enabling students to pay for their education while working in their chosen career field and learning on the job? I frequently recall a conversation I once had with a ministry leader who told me that given two candidates for a position, one with 2 years' experience and no degree and one with a degree but no experience, he would choose the individual with experience every time. This issue, faced by more and more college graduates, spurred me to investigate a possible solution. Only more research will be able to determine if partnership-based education models like Synergy are that solution.

Partnerships have been a mainstay of missions activity since the beginning of the Modern Missions Movement. However, they are frequently focused on contracts and pragmatic results rather than being primarily relational. This research highlighted the importance of relationships in partnership development for mobilizing the next generation of missionaries. Further research could be conducted on relational partnerships in other frameworks. A key research question for consideration is: does the strength of the relationship allow the partnership to weather challenges where a contractual partnership would simply end? Further, what relational qualities are necessary (trust, honesty, faithfulness, etc.) to allow for stronger partnerships in other areas. The appendices contain a lot of helpful research information that went into this study and the development of the Synergy model.

Questions for Discussion

1. If you are a pastor of a local church, how will partnerships with a university or mission agency help you church to further its mission to reach all people? Consider also how you are training and discipling the next generation. See the literature review in Appendix II for helpful information concerning Generation Z.

2. If you are a mission agency president, mobilization director, or other leader. how will forming partnerships with universities help you to better fulfill your mission. Is your training structured in such a way that you can partner with universities? What field opportunities do you offer to further the education and training of the next generation? Finally, are you seeking partnerships with local churches?

3. Finally, for other university professors who are investigating partnership or apprenticeship type programs. Who do you need to partner with? Consider first, those organizations that your school has a historic relationship with. They probably already have shared vision and values. How will a partnership-based approach help you to set up your students for success after they graduate? Consider that in today's job market we can no longer be business as usual and leave the job hunting up to them. If you want to build value into your program, how can you help them see direct links to their future career or ministry?

APPENDIX 1
Methodological Matter of the Research Conducted

Introduction

The Synergy process is conducted at Calvary in conjunction with five partners: Crossworld, Ethnos 360, Biblical Ministries Worldwide, Midwest Church Extension and Village Missions. Of these partners three are in a track specifically designed for cross-cultural missionaries and two are in a separate track designed for more local pastoral ministry. Given this distinction, the study focused on the three agencies involved in cross-cultural ministry, Crossworld, Ethnos 360, and Biblical Ministries Worldwide. This appendix focuses on the research methodology behind the study.

Methodological Background: Participatory Action Research

Participatory action research (PAR) was used in this study to involve all stakeholders in the process of revising Synergy. Action research is a qualitative research method that centers around solving a recognized or potential problem in a specific context. Kurt Lewin is widely considered as having coined the term, "action research."[177] As a social psychologist Lewin felt that research and theory should be connected and lead to social action.[178] Lewin's model includes five steps; "fact-finding, planning, taking action, evaluating, and amending the plan."[179] Various models have been proposed by action researchers for how the methodology is to function. The model proposed by Ernest T. Stringer was used for this study. Stringer's model involves three repeatable steps, "look, think, and act."[180]

---

[177] Mark K. Smith, "Kurt Lewin: groups, experiential learning and action research," *infed.org: education, community-building and change*, 2001, accessed October 27, 2020, https://infed.org/mobi/kurt-lewin-groups-experiential-learning-and-action-research/.

[178] R. Burke Johnson and Larry Christensen, *Educational Research: Quantitative, Qualitative, and Mixed Approaches*, 6th ed. (Los Angeles: Sage, 2017), 59.

[179] Craig A. Mertler, *Action Research: Improving School and Empowering Educators* 3rd ed., (Thousand Oaks, CA: SAGE, 2012), 15.

[180] Stringer, *Action Research*, 9.

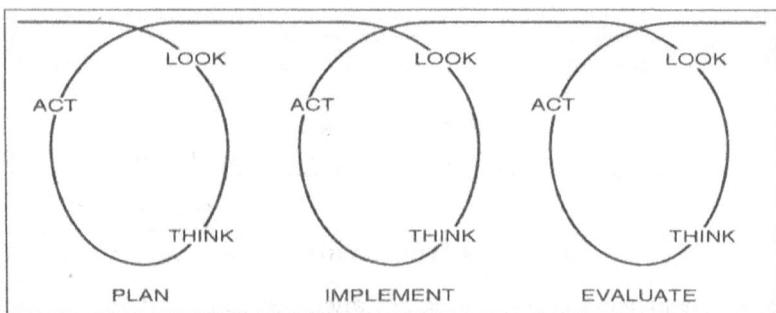

Figure 16. Action Research Interacting Spiral[181]

The power of PAR comes in bringing diverse voices to bear on the issue being studied.[182] It allows all the stakeholders in a given issue to speak into that issue's improvement. In view of this the researcher becomes just one voice among equals as each research participant contributes to the final product.[183]

Action research (AR) is often used in the context of educational research. Educational research involves studying "educational topics, phenomena, or questions."[184] Craig A. Mertler defines action research in an educational context as "any systematic inquiry conducted by teachers, administrators, counselors, or others with a vested interest in the teaching and learning process or environment for the purpose of gathering information about how their particular schools operate, how they teach, and how their students learn."[185] Gilbert, Johnson, and Lewis highlight action research in *Missiological Research* as an appropriate method for conducting research in missiological contexts..[186] They identify four strengths of this research approach for missiological issues.

1. The AR focus on local issues and challenges in cultural context is consistent with desired outcomes in many missiological research projects. Researchers move from larger theological and missiological concepts to their implications for the church and missions in local settings.

---

[181] Stringer, *Action Research*, 9.

[182] E. Alana James, Tracesea Slater, and Alan Bucknam, *Action Research for Business, Nonprofit, and Public Administration: A Tool for Complex Times.* (Los Angelos: Sage Publications, 2012), 7.

[183] James, Slater, and Bucknam, *Action Research*, 8.

[184] Mertler, *Action Research*, 6.

[185] Mertler, *Action Research*, 4.

[186] Marvin Gilbert, Alan R. Johnson, and Paul W. Lewsi, ed. *Missiological Research: Interdisciplinary Foundations, Methods, and Integration,* (Pasadena: William Carey Library, 2018), 239.

2. Engaging local participants in an organizational setting as co-inquirers in the research process provides a vehicle for missiologists to engage national churches, ministers, and other stakeholders in their project. Such broad engagement ensures greater interest and ownership of outcomes of the project and recommended next steps for action.
3. An AR-type missiological research project may ultimately lead to problem-solving action in a local setting while simultaneously drawing tentative conclusions about the generalizability of findings beyond the immediate context. Such conclusions could be evaluated in more conventional research designs.
4. The action-centered-practitioner approach to AR is compatible with the approach of missiologists who tend to be engaged in local contexts as "doers" rather than armchair "reflectors." However, this approach must intentionally be integrated with the academic research rigor of traditional missiological/theological research to maintain the integrity of results and contribute to the larger academy.[187]

Participatory action research, being well rooted in both educational and missiological contexts was well suited for this study. The emphasis on involving all stakeholders in the research process and program design contributes to the overall purpose of the research into integrated relational partnerships. In this way the research design not only provides the methods for action that promotes better process design for Synergy but also contributes to the eventual outcome. Incorporating all stakeholders into the research process helps foster those same relational partnerships.

Creating and revising a process like Synergy which aims to mobilize next Gen missionaries through relational partnerships between churches, agencies, and schools integrates many areas of research. Relational realism, ecclesiology, and missiology provide the theological and theoretical undergirding for the study. Thematic elements of missionary training, relational partnerships, and an ethnographic profile of Gen Z and their learning preferences provide practical insights to incorporate. Participatory action research will enable all stakeholders to give insight to the final Synergy process.

At the end of *Relational Missionary Training,* Hedinger states that the authors' prayer is that the work would spark a conversation for relational issues in ministry and especially in the training of cross-cultural gospel messengers.[188] This dissertation seeks to continue that very conversation as it applies to the training of missionaries through creating integrated relational partnerships for mobilizing Generation Z Christians.

---

[187] Gilbert, Johnson, and Lewis, *Missiological Research*, 241-242.
[188] Wan and Hedinger, *Relational Missionary Training*, 295-296.

Research Process and Procedures

Integrative Research Approach

This research was informed and guided by Enoch Wan's "STARS" approach to integrative research.[189] As this research incorporates both educational and missiological research the "STARS" approach provides a five-step process for conducting research that is, "characteristically evangelical, doctrinally sound and theologically grounded."[190] The table below outlines the steps in this research approach.

Table 8. Wan's Way of Integrative Research ("STARS") [191]

CRITERIA	*	EXPLANATION
1. Scripturally sound	S	Not proof-text; but the "whole counsel of God" (Acts 20:26-27
2. Theologically Supported	T	Not just pragmatism/expedience; but sound theology
3. Analytically Coherent	A	Not to be self-contradictory, but to be coherent
4. Relevantly contextual	R	Not to be out of place; but fitting for the context.
5. Strategically practical	S	Not only good in theory, but can be strategically put into practice.

Conducting this study in this manner allowed for the results to not only be specifically applicable in the context of Synergy at Calvary but also for drawing both educational and missiological implications for the evangelical community at large.

Participatory Action Research Design

There is great variety in the steps and design of an action research study. Drawing from the literature review and comparing various models, I arrived at the following model for this study based largely on Stringer's model as noted above.

---

[189] Enoch Wan, "Inter-Disciplinary and Integrative Missiological Research: The 'What,' 'Why,' and 'How,'" www.GlobalMissiology.org, July 2017.
[190] Wan, "Inter-Disciplinary and Integrative Missiological Research," 5.
[191] Wan, "Inter-Disciplinary and Integrative Missiological Research," 5.

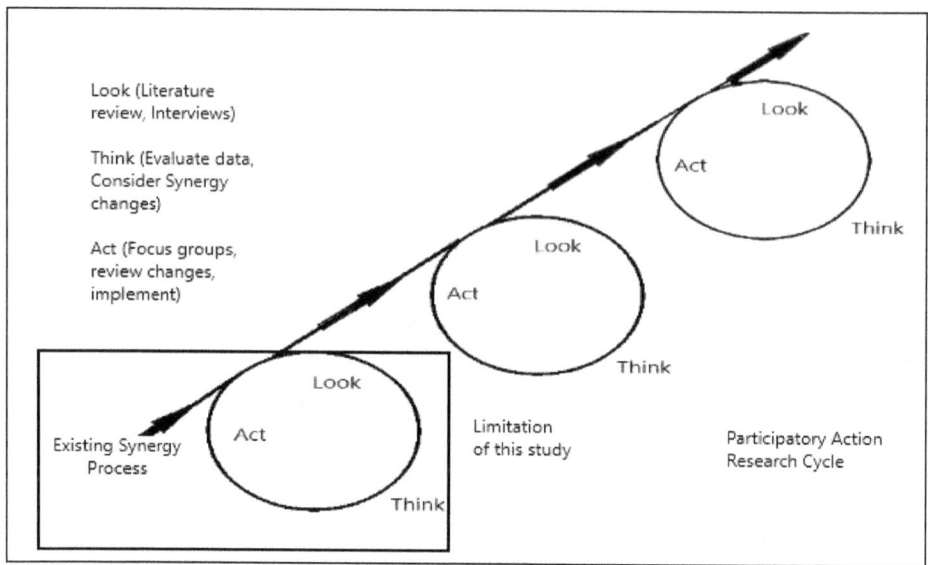

Figure 17. Participatory Action Research Cycle

The square indicates the realm that this study occupies within the cycles of action research. The limitations of the study only allowed for one cycle to be conducted, arriving at improvements to the process that can be implemented and then evaluated through further cycles. Calvary's existing organizational review process conducted by the office of institutional effectiveness will allow for further review of Synergy beyond this study.

Beginning with the existing Synergy process and partners, this study progressed through the action research cycle following the stages of look, think, and act.[192] The look stage incorporated the identification of the problem, research questions, literature review and interviews. The think stage included the evaluation of the data gathered from the look stage and consideration of possible revisions of Synergy based on that data. Information gathered from the interviews was collated and presented to Focus Groups of interview participants to find key areas of improvement. Finally, the act stage involved implementing those change areas as discovered during the focus groups. At this point, Synergy needs to be allowed time to run with the considered improvements before further cycles of action research can be accomplished.

---

[192] Stringer, *Action Research*, 9.

Technique and Data Collection

Three primary techniques were utilized in this study. The literature review along with scriptural analysis provided the theological and theoretical background for the study as well as collecting data necessary to the process development. Interviews with Synergy partners and participants allowed for their involvement and gathering data for considering improvements. After a review of the data and changes to the process, focus groups of interview participants were used for evaluation of the final process and validity assessment.

Participant Interviews with Key Stakeholders (Look)

Pursuant to the nature of participatory action research, participant interviews with primary stakeholders were a key element of the look stage of research. Purposive sampling was used to interview those individuals who are key to the development of the Synergy process. This resulted in a total of 12 interview participants. Three of these from the mission agencies themselves (Crossworld, Ethnos 360, Biblical Ministries Worldwide) who have chosen individuals to oversee this partnership process already. Three were pastors of local churches within Calvary's constituency, specifically, pastors of churches with a history of sending and supporting Calvary graduates. Three interviewees were current (2) or recently graduated (1) students from the Synergy process itself. Finally, three interviewees were former graduates who are now serving in missions that did not have the opportunity of the Synergy process.

Prior to interviewing the agency partners, pastors, and missionaries they were given the opportunity to read the literature review for the study. Foundational to participatory action research is that the participants are fully involved in the research.[193] Giving the Synergy partner organizations the opportunity to read this material will help them make informed decisions about the nature of the process. The students to be interviewed did not read the literature review. The purpose of their interviews was to gauge their experience of either the process or what they may have benefited from in having gone through it. Allowing them to read the literature review could have had a negative impact on their responses.

---

[193] Stephen Kemmis and Robin McTaggart, "Participatory Action Research," *The Handbook of Qualitative Research*, 2nd ed. (Thousand Oaks, CA: Sage Publications, 2000), 597.

Data Analysis and Evaluation (Think)

Interviews were conducted via Zoom for recording and transcription. Transcripts were then sent to interview participants for verification. Following the interviews, data collected was analyzed and evaluated for themes and items relevant to improving the process. This incorporates the 'think' stage of action research. Once themes from the interviews were identified three separate focus groups were created with one representative from each of the key stakeholders (1 agency leader, 1 pastor, 1 Synergy student, 1 missionary). These focus groups were conducted via Zoom for recording purposes and to due to the COVID-19 pandemic. Participants received an outline of the Synergy revisions prior to the group meeting so that the time could be utilized for evaluation of the new process. One benefit of focus groups for this purpose was that it helped with the triangulation of the data as each stakeholder was able to interact with suggested changes from other sources. Creswell and Poth point out that focus groups are advantageous when the interaction of group members will yield the best information.[194] Once more, the research methodology contributed to the overall goal of integrative relational partnerships.

Implementation of the Revised Synergy Process (Act)

After the focus groups identified key areas of improvement for this research cycle those changes were incorporated into the Synergy Handbook as well as a new marketing and partnership plan. These changes will need to be implemented and allowed to run for a period of time before another cycle of action research can be done pursuant to Calvary's institutional effectiveness process.

Summary

Participatory action research methodology was used through interviews and focus groups to gather data on proposed changes and improvements to the Synergy process. Interviews and focus groups with key stakeholders in all areas of the process (agency, church, student, missionary) allowed for thorough data collection and evaluation of the existing process while also contributing to the desired goal of integrated relational partnerships.

---

[194] John W. Creswell and Cheryl N. Poth, *Qualitative Inquiry & Research Design: Choosing Among Five Approaches*, 4th ed. (Los Angeles: SAGE, 2018), 164.

APPENDIX II
Review of Relevant Literature

Introduction

The literature review for the dissertation is presented here in part to establish the theological and thematic background for relational partnerships. Synergy is grounded in a theological/theoretical paradigm of relational realism (based on the Trinity), and robust missiology. The first section focuses on these areas. Some parts of the literature were moved to earlier in the book in order to lay the framework for Synergy's design.

The second section of the review focuses on the thematic areas; research related to missionary training, focusing on works employed by partner organizations and those developed from the relational paradigm. It also includes research on Generation Z, focusing on their learning preferences and motivations for missions. Research related to relational partnerships is also to be considered. Synergy is also an educational process so a solid grounding in educational theory is necessary.

Theological/Theoretical Background

Theology of Mission(s)

What is Missions?

What Is the Mission of the Church? is not just the title of a contemporary book by Kevin DeYoung and Greg Gilbert, but also a primary question being asked by the current generation.[195] Having a scriptural understanding of what the church is to do, as missions, is integral to mobilizing the next generation for that work. A recent Barna study reports that "for many engaged Christian young adults, humanitarian work is and must be an essential aspect of 21st-century missions – at least as and sometimes more important than sharing the gospel of Christ."[196]

Most missiological research and practice centers upon the concept of the Great Commission as revealed in Scripture with a strong emphasis upon the functional and pragmatic aspects of making disciples. Below is a list of definitions of mission/missions which demonstrate this functional emphasis.

---

195 Kevin DeYoung and Greg Gilbert, *What Is the Mission of the Church? Making Sense of Social Justice, Shalom, and the Great Commission*, (Wheaton: Crossway, 2011).
196 Barna, *The Future of Missions*, (Ventura, CA: The Barna Group, 2020), 44.

C. Gordon Olson (former Professor of Theology and Missions at Northeastern Bible College) and Don Fanning (former Director of Global Ministries and Chair of Intercultural Studies at Liberty University) define missions as,

> Missions is the whole task, endeavor, and program of the Church of Christ to reach out across geographical and/or cultural boundaries by sending missionaries to evangelize people who have never heard or who have little opportunity to hear the saving gospel.[197]

Kevin DeYoung (senior pastor at University Reformed Church) and Greg Gilbert (senior pastor of Third Avenue Baptist Church), mentioned above, spend the greater part of their book, *What Is the Mission of the Church?* Developing a definition by asking, "What is the specific task or purpose that the church is sent into the world to accomplish?"[198] They spend a significant amount of the book on verses related to the Great Commission (Matt 28:16-20; Mark 13:10; 14:9; Luke 24:44-49; Acts 1:8) before arriving at,

> The mission of the church is to go into the world and make disciples by declaring the gospel of Jesus Christ in the power of the Spirit and gathering these disciples into churches, that they might worship the Lord and obey his commands now and in eternity to the glory of God the Father.[199]

George Peters (professor of world missions at Dallas Theological Seminary for many years) wrote a seminal work in *A Biblical Theology of Missions*.[200] In it he provides a more holistic definition of mission than DeYoung and Gilbert and a definition of missions as,

> Mission, in my usage, refers to the total biblical assignment of the church of Jesus Christ. It is a comprehensive term including the upward, inward, and outward ministries of the church. It is the church as "sent" (a pilgrim, stranger, witness, prophet, servant, as salt, as light, etc.) in this world.[201]

> Missions is a specialized term. By it, I mean the sending forth of authorized persons beyond the borders of the New Testament church and her immediate gospel influence to proclaim the gospel of Jesus Christ in gospel-destitute areas, to win converts from other faiths or non-faiths to Jesus Christ, and to establish functioning, multiplying local congregations

---

[197] Olson and Fanning, *What in the World is God Doing?*, 11.
[198] DeYoung and Gilbert, *What is the Missions of the Church?*, 20.
[199] DeYoung and Gilbert, *What is the Missions of the Church?*, 62.
[200] George W. Peters, *A Biblical Theology of Missions*, (Chicago: Moody 1972).
[201] Peters, *A Biblical Theology of Missions*, 11.

who will bear the fruit of Christianity in that community and to that country.[202]

Enoch Wan takes issue with the functional approach to defining mission(s). This overly pragmatic emphasis on the Great Commission de-emphasizes the relational component with the Triune God.[203] The key issue with this emphasis is to place the Great Commission (Doing) before the Great Commandment (Being).[204] In the process, the task becomes more important than the relationship. The following table illustrates Wan's comparison between the popular approach and a relational missiology.

Table 9. Relational Paradigm & Popular Missiological Paradigm[205]

#	(A) Relational Paradigm		(B) Popular Missiological Paradigm
	Great Commandment + Great Commission		Great Commission
1	BEING: vertically God works in **us**	->	DOING: horizontally God works **through us**
2	PERSONHOOD: Christians being **in Christ**	->	PERFORMANCE: Christians doing **for Christ**
3	MESSENGER: saved/shepherd/sent **by Him**	->	METHOD: making disciples **for Him**
4	WITNESS: by life and by living (**to serve**)	->	WINNING: strategize to win the lost (**to save**)
5	VERTICAL: Triune God and His own	->	HORIZONTAL: enterprising and managerial
6	RELATIONAL: vertical + horizontal	->	FUNCTIONAL/PROGRAMATIC: (vertical) horizontal
7	PROCESS: open ended and unpredictable, convergence or tri-systems (i.e. theo-/angelic/human) without "excluded-middle"	->	PROGRAM: structured plan and procedure, lip service to vertical, secularized with "excluded middle"

An understanding of the theology of missions from the paradigm of relational realism is a vital component of this study. The study seeks to integrate relational realism into the mobilizing process of Synergy.

Who is a Missionary?

The term "missionary," is widely used and widely thrown around the church today. Statements such as Charles Spurgeon's well known and oft quoted, "Every Christian is either a missionary or an imposter,"[206] while making for a good sermon do little to provide clarity. Complicating the issue is the oft heard statement that the word "missionary" is not in the Bible. Of course, the Bible was not written in English either.

Tracing the terms "missions" and "missionary" backwards we arrive at the Latin terms, *missionem* and *mittere*, "act of sending" and "to send"

---

202 Peters, *A Biblical Theology of Missions*, 11.
203 Wan, *Diaspora Missions to International Students*, 12.
204 Wan, *Diaspora Missions to International Students*, 15.
205 Wan, *Diaspora Missions to International Students*, 19.
206 C. H. Spurgeon, *The Metropolitan Tabernacle Pulpit Sermons*, vol. 54, (London: Passmore & Alabaster, 1908), 476.

respectively.[207] In his Latin Vulgate translation Jerome used the word *mittere* to translate the verb form of the Greek *apostello*. However, the translation is a curious one as Jerome translated the verb form into a comparable Latin term but left untranslated the Greek noun, *apostolos*.[208] The Latin Vulgate is not an inspired text compared with the original Greek manuscripts upon which it is based. It appears that Jerome wished to make a distinction between the verb form of the activity of sending and the noun which designated the office of Apostleship. There is also a connection from 'missionary' back to the Roman Catholic origins of missions among the Jesuits. The Jesuits first used the term to refer to their members who were sent overseas; as such, foreign travel was an important component of the word's initial religious usage.[209] From mission to *mittere* to *apostelos*, tracing the origins and etymology of the term we arrive at the biblical concept of apostles.[210] The apostles, therefore, are the chief example for us of missionaries in the Bible.

Example of the Apostles

Apostles are found in two distinct ways in the New Testament. The first is those who were uniquely called by Christ and set apart to be his Apostles[211]. They are named in Matthew 10:1-5; Mark 3:13-29; and Luke 6:12-16. John's gospel, while recording the specific callings of some, does not include the special reference to the twelve as a set apart group. Luke 6:14-16 records them as,

> Simon, whom he named Peter, and Andrew his brother, and James and John, Philip, and Bartholomew, and Matthew, and Thomas, and James the son of Alphaeus and Simon who was called the Zealot, and Judas the son of James, and Judas Iscariot who became a traitor.

These twelve are clearly indicated in Scripture as having a unique ministry, what has come to be called the 'office of Apostleship.' Indeed, Jesus at one point tells them that they will have the honor of sitting on twelve thrones in His kingdom and will be judges over the twelve tribes of Israel (Matt. 19:28). Theirs was a unique role and ministry, and as such the twelve form an exclusive group.

---

[207] "mission," *Online Etymology Dictionary,* accessed February 10, 2021, https://www.etymonline.com/word/mission?ref=etymonline_crossreference.

[208] Willie Rodriquez, "Missionaries, Prophets Or Apostles?" *Bearurcross,* accessed February 16, 2021https://bearurcross.com/biblestudies/missionaries-prophets-or-apostles/.

[209] "mission," *Vocabulary.com,* accessed February 16, 2021https://www.vocabulary.com/dictionary/mission#:~:text=Mission%20comes%20from%20a%20Latin,to%20those%20trips%20as%20missions.

[210] George W. Peters, *A Biblical Theology of Missions,* 249.

[211] Throughout this paper "Apostles" is used to designate the office, while "apostles" refers to the more general usage of the term.

Following Jesus' ascension, the remaining 11 decide to choose a replacement for Judas. In doing so, Peter names two very specific qualifications for this office of Apostleship. Acts 1:21, 22 records these two qualifications for replacing Jesus as being first, someone who had been a part of their ministry since the beginning. It is incredibly specific, from the baptism of John to Jesus's ascension. The second is that they would be a witness of his resurrection. At this point they choose two people and cast lots; Matthias is added to the eleven apostles, bringing their number back up to 12. These two qualifications are incredibly significant because they lay out for us today that there are no Apostles in the sense of the office of Apostle. It was a unique ministry for the very beginning of the Church. However, we find another individual who does inhabit a special office of apostleship.

That individual is Paul. Several times throughout Scripture, Paul is called an Apostle. Acts 14:14 sees the term applied to both Paul and Barnabus, Paul uses it himself in the greetings of many of his letters (Rom. 1:1, 1 Cor. 1:1, 2 Cor. 1:1, Gal. 1:1, Eph. 1:1). What is more, Paul understands his apostleship to fill a unique roll compared to that of the twelve. Acts 13 records the first missionary journey of Paul and Barnabus. They first travel to Cyprus; Barnabus, it appears, is merely visiting home (Acts 4:36). Then, they continue to Antioch in Pisidia, where Paul begins what will become his regular routine of first going to a synagogue to share about Jesus (Acts 13:14). This would become a regular habit of Paul's to the point that when he arrives at a new location and does not first go to a Synagogue, such as Philippi (Acts 16:13), we can reasonably assume there was no synagogue there, and indeed that was the case. As often happened wherever Paul went, a riot broke out in Antioch; at this point Paul reveals in Acts 14:47, for the first time, his understanding of the unique character of his Apostleship. "For so the Lord has commanded us, saying, 'I have made you a light for the Gentiles, that you may bring salvation to the ends of the earth.'" Paul recounts the very words of Jesus instructing him to go to the Gentiles in Acts 22:21 and 26:15-18. Further evidence is given in Galatians 1:15-16 as Paul recounts his meeting with the Apostles in Jerusalem. Paul's ministry stands apart from the twelve as being unique in taking the gospel to the Gentiles. I will return to Paul later; however, this is not the last time we see the term apostle applied to someone outside of the office.

So far, the term apostle has been used in a unique way of individuals who held a special ministry during the early church period.[212] However, there are several other occasions in which we encounter this term applied to other individuals who just do not fit the mold of the office. We already saw earlier how it was used of Barnabus in Acts 14:4, 14. Paul later uses the term on three

---

[212] Peters, *A Biblical Theology of Missions*, 254.

occasions, applying it to Epaphroditus (Phil. 2:25) and several unnamed individuals (2 Cor 8:23). In writing to the Thessalonians, Paul includes Timothy and Silvanus (Silas) in his greeting and later refers to all of them as "apostles of Christ" (1 Thess. 2:1, 6).

Examining Scripture, we discover that the term apostle is used in two very distinct ways. The first, being the office of the twelve and Paul, while the second usage is a more general sense of others who had an expansive traveling ministry. Finding this in Scripture forces us to ask how these individuals can bear the label of apostle and yet not be of the office? In every case it is applied to individuals who appear to have a ministry that includes traveling and reaching new areas with the gospel message. This then forms the essential character of all these individuals' ministry, that they were sent out to take the gospel where it had not yet gone.[213]

Throughout the book of Acts and his numerous letters, Paul stands as the chief example for us of this type of pioneering apostolic ministry. His aim was always to take the gospel where it had not yet been (Rom. 15:20); and wherever he goes we find him engaging in three primary activities, given for us in Acts 14:21-23, preaching the gospel, making disciples, and establishing churches.

Paul's ministry, along with his companions', is also primarily cross-cultural. As a Hellenistic Jew, he was raised in and familiar with Greco/Roman culture, and it is to the gentiles that he primarily takes the gospel. A fascinating and somewhat hilarious story is recounted in Acts 14 of a cross-cultural misunderstanding in Paul's ministry. Arriving in Lystra, Paul heals a man who was crippled from birth and could not walk. Upon seeing this, the crowds immediately attribute the miracle to Paul and Barnabas being Hermes and Zeus respectively, come down to them in human form. Greco/Roman mythology was replete with stories of the gods visiting human beings, so the crowd immediately interprets this event through their own worldview and wrongly began to worship and offer sacrifices to Paul and Barnabas. Interestingly, although the crowd is praising them, it is not until the priest comes to offer sacrifices that they realize what is happening and cry out to the crowd to stop. A hint why is given in 14:11, the people were speaking their native language, Lyconian, a language which Paul and Barnabus likely did not understand. All these accounts taken together allow us to arrive at a definition for a missionary as seen in Scripture. *A missionary is a believer in Jesus Christ sent by God and the Church across geographical and/or cultural boundaries to preach the gospel, make disciples, and plant churches.* It is this definition that is in mind while considering how missionaries should be trained.

---

[213] Peters, *A Biblical Theology of Missions*, 249.

Thematic Background

The Thematic literature review is broken into three parts, 1) related research on missionary training, 2) research related to an ethnographic profile of Generation Z, and their motivations for missions and 3) relational partnerships.

Missionary Training

Introduction

A great deal of information exists on the topic of missionary training. Here the literature review presents a summary of some of the most common themes for inclusion in missionary training theology, philosophy, and practice. To keep the review relevant to the study, it is those works employed by the partner agencies (Crossworld, Biblical Ministries Worldwide, Ethnos 360) which will be primarily focused on.

A foundational book for this study is Wan and Hedinger's *Relational Missionary Training*.[214] This work incorporates Wan's relational paradigm into the training and equipping of new missionary candidates. The conclusion of Wan and Hedinger's work lists several implications for what it means to train missionaries from the relational paradigm. They include:

- The program will understand that mission work is a series of relationships, with God first and secondarily with people.
- The program will understand that the purpose of mission is relational: to facilitate a relationship between Triune God and the people who are being reached.
- The program will strive to use good teaching and outreach methods, yet always see those methods as serving relationship, not the other way around.
- It means that mission skills, attitudes, knowledge are designed for and evaluated on the basis of relational outcomes.
- It means that desired training outcomes are relational.
- It means that training is dependent on more than one person/Person to be effective.
- It means that we assume relationships to be dynamic, not static.
- It means that training will not be seen as the mechanical following of a prepared curriculum, but as the flexible interaction of content, training methods, and training relationships within a flexible philosophy of education.

---

[214] Wan and Hedinger. *Relational Missionary Training.*

- It means that the trainee is prepared to be transformed even as he/she takes a message of Gospel transformation to the unreached.
- Training based on the Paradigm of Relational Realism is accepted, appreciated, and consistent with lifestyle patterns of most of the non-Western world as well as a growing number of Western civilization's younger generations.
- It means that we are equipping a generation of leaders from Jesus's church who have developed relational skills and insights in vertical and horizontal directions, both within and across cultures.[215]

These elements will be included in conversation with interviewees and integrated into the final Synergy process.

Theology of Missionary Training

There are several things to consider when attempting to establish a theological basis for missionary training: First, as Jesus uniquely called and set apart the twelve in scripture to fulfill the role of being his Apostles, how did he go about preparing them for that role? Second, if Paul is our primary New Testament example of a missionary, then what should we observe about who he was and how he was uniquely suited for that ministry? Third, do we find in Scripture any examples of how Paul prepared those who worked alongside him in this ministry? Finally, what does Paul's example tell us about the nature of the missionary's task and what a missionary should be prepared to encounter? There are many other questions that could be asked for considering the nature of modern missions. However, these will provide a biblically solid theological basis. So, we start where we should always start, with Christ and his preparation of the Apostles.

Jesus' Training of the Apostles

While over the course of His earthly ministry Jesus had thousands of followers, He did exclusively reserve certain lessons for the twelve Apostles. "Though many were focused on Him, He focused on a small group whom the Father had given Him to equip for ministry (John 17:6)."[216]

Clark Macaulay, while highlighting the intense relational nature of Jesus' training of the twelve "a personal trainer, tutor and teacher," mentions three specific ways that He prepared them.[217] The first was "practical learning,"

---

[215] Wan and Hedinger, *Relational Missionary* Training, 289-295.

[216] Clark Macaulay, "The Training Methods of Jesus," *Biblical Ministries Worldwide*, accessed February 19, 2021, https://www.biblicalministries.org/see/blog/2014/03/31/the-training-methods-of-jesus/.

[217] Macaulay, "The Training Methods of Jesus."

Jesus had the apostles participate in His ministry throughout their time with Him. This was real "hands-on ministry training."[218] There are several occasions in Scripture where we see the apostles practically engaged in ministry, including baptizing (John 3:22, 4:1-2), preaching (Mark 3:14, Matt. 10:7), casting out demons (Mark 3:15, Matt. 10:1), and healing (Matt. 10:1, 8). The second is "private learning."[219] Jesus often spoke to his disciples alone and taught them things that He did not share with the crowds. Macaulay points out that often this was to deal with their heart issues, such as "selfish ambitions (Mark 9:33-35), testing their affections (John 21:15-17), and affirming what they had learned (Matt. 16:13-17)."[220]

While Jesus clearly taught truth, doctrine, and knowledge, it was always in the context of His special relationship with these twelve men. Finally, the Apostles were present for Jesus' "public learning".[221] They were with Him when He taught the crowds (Matt. 5:1, Luke 12:1). They not only heard the same teaching but observed His teaching methods and practice and often received private instruction following this (Mark 4:1, 10).

Additionally, Jim Putnam has pointed to six things that Jesus did to prepare his disciples. These include bringing them into situations where they would encounter others who had needs, giving them real teaching, connecting them relationally to God and one another, equipping them and releasing them for ministry, sharing new truth with them, and modeling discipleship while they were together.[222]

Gene Wilkes gives five steps from Jesus' ministry on equipping others to serve: encourage them, qualify them, understand their needs, instruct them, and pray for them.[223] Encouraging those who are being prepared once again speaks to the relational component and can most clearly be seen in John 14 where Jesus is encouraging them upon the eve of His death. Qualifying them is to ensure that they are spiritually a good fit for the ministry that will be asked of them.[224] Understanding their needs means listening to them and knowing what they are lacking in skills and resources. Instructing them involves teaching in theology and doctrine, while praying for them is clearly illustrated by Jesus in John 17.[225] Perhaps the most outstanding characteristic of how

---

[218] Macaulay, "The Training Methods of Jesus."
[219] Macaulay, "The Training Methods of Jesus."
[220] Macaulay, "The Training Methods of Jesus."
[221] Macaulay, "The Training Methods of Jesus."
[222] Jim Putnam, "Here Are 6 Things Jesus Did to Equip His Disciples For Ministry," accessed February 19, 2021, *jimputman.com*, http://jimputman.com/2018/07/08/6-things-jesus-did-to-equip-his-disciples-for-ministry/.
[223] C. Gene Wilkes, *Jesus on Leadership: Discovering the Secrets of Servant Leadership from the life of Christ*, (Wheaton: Tyndale, 1998), 189
[224] Wilkes, *Jesus on Leadership*, 191.
[225] Wilkes, *Jesus on Leadership*, 198.

Jesus trained His Apostles was simply the daily experience of life and relationship, taking them along as He performed His earthly ministry. A. B. Bruce indicates,

> From the time of their being chosen, indeed, the twelve entered on a regular apprenticeship for the great office of apostleship, in the course of which they were to learn, in the privacy of an intimate daily fellowship with their Master, what they should be, do, believe and teach, as His witnesses and ambassadors to the world.[226]

Jesus' training of the Apostles presents several key components. He trained them in the three areas of cognitive, affective, and behavior (know, be, do); he trained them in a highly relational way; and he demonstrated a genuine care for them as His followers. There were clear things that they needed to know, doctrine and truth regarding the Father and the Son. He focused on developing in them the right character traits and the necessary skills for ministry. He was also very hands-on and practical, inviting them into the work to learn ministry by doing ministry.

One important element remains to be mentioned. As much as Jesus trained and equipped His Apostles for the work to come, apart from the Holy Spirit's indwelling they were not ready. This can be clearly seen in His instruction for them to wait in Jerusalem before carrying out the mission entrusted to them (Luke 24:46-49, Acts 1:8). It was only following the coming of the Spirit in Acts 2 that we see them begin to minister; and once the Spirit falls, they do so immediately.

We next turn our attention back to Paul as the chief example of New Testament missions. We will first consider how he was uniquely equipped to be the Apostle to the Gentiles and then how he equipped others.

Paul's Personal Training

"Paul was not only a missionary; he also deliberately went about training others to be missionaries."[227] Paul is perhaps Scripture's most unlikely hero. We first see him in Acts 7:58 and 8:1 giving approval of Stephen's death. We next find him in Acts 8:3 heavily persecuting the church, and then in 9:1 seeking to root out followers of Jesus outside of Jerusalem. By his own testimony he tried to destroy the church (Gal. 1:13). All this, however, was before he met Jesus on the road to Damascus (Acts 9). However, it would be wrong to consider Paul as having only begun training for his ministry after his conversion. Indeed, Paul indicates in Galatians 1:15 that God, "set me apart

---

[226] A, B, Bruce, *The Training of the Twelve: How Jesus Christ Found and Taught the 12 Apostles: A Book of New Testament Biography*, (Pantianos Classics, first published 1871), ebook ed. Kindle Version, location 611.

[227] Wan and Hedinger, *Relational Missionary Training*, 79.

before I was born."

What then is there about Paul that uniquely equipped him for his ministry to the Gentiles that we might consider in the training of missionaries? Scripture indicates several things about Paul that we could point to as well as a training period he went through following his conversion. First, Paul was a Jew. As a Jew, he was also a Pharisee (Acts 23:6; Phil. 3:5), who trained under Gamaliel (Acts 22:3), the same teacher who encouraged the Sanhedrin to show leniency to the Apostles (Acts 5:34). He boasts often of his zealous following of the Law and adherence to the codes of the Pharisees. As such, Paul was well versed in the Old Testament. We encounter him soon after his conversion engaging with the Hellenistic Jews in Jerusalem and giving evidence from Scripture that Jesus was the Christ (Acts 9:29). So good is his testimony and defense that they plot to kill him! As Paul is giving his defense before Agrippa and Festus (Acts 26), Festus comments, "Paul you are out of your mind; your great learning is driving you out of your mind (Acts 26:24)." It is evident from Scripture that Paul was well educated.

Second, Paul was naturally suited to debating with the Hellenistic Jews (those who were ethnically Jewish but culturally Greek) because he was himself familiar with Greco/Roman culture. Paul was a native of Tarsus (Acts 22:3), a city in Asia Minor located well outside of Judea in the province of Cilicia. Growing up in Tarsus, Paul would have become very familiar with the culture.[228] It is not surprising that we see him specifically debating with Jews who have strong Greco/Roman cultural influences because he was well suited for the task. This background serves him well again when he arrives in Athens in Acts 17. Delivering his message to the Areopagus he is familiar with their manner of worship and even quotes two of their own poets (Acts 17:28).

Both characteristics of being a Pharisee, well acquainted with Jewish scriptures and a Hellenistic Jew familiar with Greco/Roman culture, made Paul an ideal missionary to Gentiles. Also, while not directly related to training, his Roman citizenship (Acts 16:37, 22:25) afforded him some advantages in his ministry as well.

Scripture also gives some testimony regarding a special equipping that Paul received from the Lord. In recounting his testimony to the Galatians, he indicates a time of going away to Arabia and then returning to Damascus for three years (Gal. 1:17). How long he spent in Arabia we are not told. There is also some indication of special revelation he received from the Lord in being caught up to the third heaven (2 Cor. 12:2). What this means and what he was told is not clear.

Paul's own life presents us with at least three key principles in developing a theology of missionary training. The first, just as Paul was well versed in the

---

[228] "Tarsus," *Ancient History Encyclopedia*, accessed February 19, 2021, https://www.ancient.eu/Tarsus/.

Old Testament, so too must today's missionaries be well-versed in the Bible. Second, cross-cultural ministry requires cross-cultural understanding. Paul's unique knowledge of Greco/Roman culture combined with his knowledge of scripture allowed him to speak directly to the heart of the Greco/Roman worldview, something that afforded Paul great success as time and again in the book of Acts we encounter gentiles receiving the gospel with gladness. Finally, Paul had a personal encounter with Christ. His deep and abiding relationship with the Lord cannot be overlooked as a key component in his ministry.[229] "Knowledge of Scripture, his world, and of the crucified and risen Christ formed Paul into the great missionary apostle to the Gentiles. Likewise, these elements deserve priority in shaping future missionaries for Christ."[230] Paul was well suited for this role. How then do we see him training and preparing others?

Paul's Training of Others

Paul trained/mentored both Timothy and Titus and was himself mentored for a time by Barnabus (Acts 9:27; 11:25). Paul's relationship with Timothy is especially noteworthy. Paul first encounters Timothy in Lystra and circumcises him as a testimony to the believing Jews (Acts 16:1-3) because he wants Timothy to join their party. He is left with Silas in Berea when Paul must flee the city (Acts 17:14), only to join him later in Athens. In Acts 19:22 we see that Paul has sent him to Macedonia, along with Erastus. Throughout Scripture there are multiple references to Paul sending Timothy on various errands. Stacy E. Hoehl (Professor of Communications, Wisconsin Lutheran College) has highlighted several lessons from Paul's mentoring relationship with Timothy. Paul recognizes Timothy as the right person to be his own successor (Acts 16:3).[231] Paul equips Timothy for the task of ministry; while Paul recognizes that circumcision is of no value (Galatians 2:3-4), doing so demonstrates his recognition of Timothy's need to relate to his Jewish audience (1 Cor. 9:19).[232] Paul empowers Timothy throughout their relationship in how he describes him to others (1 Thess. 3:2), by being an example (Acts 18:1-5) and by keeping him focused on the goal (1 Timothy

---

[229] H.H. Drake Williams, III, "Three Influences in the Training of Paul, the Missionary Apostle," accessed February 19, 2021, *Training Leaders International*, https://trainingleadersinternational.org/jgc/13/three-influences-in-the-training-of-paul-the-missionary-apostle.

[230] Williams, III, "Three Influences in the Training of Paul, the Missionary Apostle."

[231] Stacey E. Hoehl, "The Mentor Relationship: An Exploration of Paul as Loving Mentor to Timothy and the Application of This Relationship to Contemporary Leadership Challenges," *Journal of Biblical Perspectives in Leadership*, accessed November 13, 2020, https://www.regent.edu/acad/global/publications/jbpl/vol3no2/JBPL_Vol3No2_Hoehl_pp32-47.pdf, 35.

[232] Hoehl, "The Mentor Relationship," 36.

6:12).[233] Paul gives Timothy opportunities to grow in ministry experience by giving him multiple assignments, most notably the task of leading the church in Ephesus (1 Timothy 1:3).

Finally, the depth of Paul's personal relationship with Timothy can be seen in how he refers to him as a son (Php. 2:19-24). Clearly, Paul and Timothy had a deep and abiding relationship with one another. Paul's training of others is, much like Jesus', done in the context of relationship. Paul taught Timothy (1, 2 Timothy), encouraged the development of his character (1 Timothy 3:11-16), and gave him practical ministry experience (Phil. 2:19-24). Regarding others that were part of Paul's team and who he invested special interest in we also see Titus and Epaphroditus. Both men, along with Silas, were traveling and ministry companions of Paul. Epaphroditus, also called an apostle (Phil. 2:25), is seen being sent by Paul to encourage the Philippians. Titus receives instruction (just like Timothy) in doctrine and character development as well as the practical assignment of his ministry in Crete (Titus). Enoch Wan and Mark Hedinger specifically highlight the relational component of Paul's missionary training, "The training that Paul offered was through the highly relational form of inviting them to learn ministry by doing ministry together with Paul."[234]

Mark Hedinger, in writing his dissertation, conducted an inductive study of 1 and 2 Timothy and Titus to arrive at seven themes that Paul included in his missionary training.

1. Theme Number One: The Missionary's Focus on Scriptural Truth
   Teaching on Sound Doctrine (1 Tim. 4:6 – 16)
   The Gospel Itself (1 Tim. 1:12 – 17; 2 Tim. 1:8-10; Titus 3:5)
   Teachings on False Doctrine (Titus 1:10 – 16)
2. Theme Number Two: The Missionary As a Person
   The Activities of a Missionary (1 Tim. 1:3; 2 Tim. 2:2; Titus 1:5)
   The Attitudes of a Missionary (1 Tim. 4:11 – 12; 2 Tim. 2:15; 3:10-11)
3. Theme Number Three: The Missionary As Teacher
   Content that the Missionary Should Teach (1 Tim. 2:8; 6:17 – 18; Titus 3:1)
   Content to Avoid Teaching (1 Tim. 6:20; 2 Tim. 2:23; Titus 3:9)
   Relationship Patterns of the Missionary as a Teacher
   In Relationship to All People (1 Tim. 2:24)
   In Relationship to Certain People (1 Tim. 2:25; 5:1 – 2; Titus 1:12 – 13)
   Who Should Teach (1 Tim. 5:17; 2 Tim. 2:2)
   False Teachers (1 Tim. 6:3 – 10; 2 Tim. 2:16 – 18)

---

[233] Hoehl, "The Mentor Relationship," 38.
[234] Wan and Hedinger, *Relational Missionary Training*, 80-81.

4. Theme Number Four: The Missionary As Developer of Church Leadership
   Choosing Leaders for the Church (1 Tim. 2:12; Titus 1:5)
   Character of Leaders (1 Tim. 3; Titus 1)
   False Leaders (related to false teachers) (1 Tim. 4:1 – 5)
5. Theme Number Five: The Missionary As Defender against Opposition
   From False Teachers (1 Tim. 1:3; 6:20; 2 Tim. 1:8)
   From Persecution (2 Tim. 2:9-10; 2:14; Titus 1:11)
   From Desertion (2 Tim. 4:16)
   From Divisive Persons (Titus 3:10)
6. Theme Number Six: The Missionary and Specific Relationships
   God/missionary (1 Tim. 1:12-17)
   God/unredeemed (1 Tim. 2:4)
   Missionary/old man (1 Tim. 5:1)
   Missionary/young man (1 Tim. 5:1)
   Missionary/old woman (1 Tim. 5:2)
   Missionary/young woman (1 Tim. 5:2)
   Man/woman (1 Tim. 2:11 – 15)
   Church leader/his family (1 Tim. 3:4; Titus 1:6)
   Missionary trainer/trainee (1 Tim. 1:2; 2 Tim. 1:5; Titus 1:4)
   Slave/master (1 Tim. 6:1)
   Believers/government (Titus 3:1)
   Believers/their families (1 Tim. 5:8) [235]

Working with Enoch Wan, Hedinger added a seventh theme in *Relational Missionary Training*.

7. Theme Number Seven: The Missionary and Spiritual Warfare
   Satan – the enemy (1 Tim 1:20; 5:15)
   Profane babblings and oppositions of the knowledge (1 Tim 6:20-21)
   The snare of the devil (2 Tim 2:26)
   Godly in Christ Jesus shall suffer persecution (2 Tim 3:12)
   Evil men and imposters shall grow worse and worse
   Deceiving and being deceived (2 Tim 3:13)
   Enemy (2 Tim 4:10; cf. 1 Jn 2:15; 4:13)
   Ungodliness and worldly lusts (Titus 2:12) [236]

Wan and Hedinger conduct an extensive study on the training methods of Paul, considering what he taught new missionaries as well as how. They

---

[235] Mark Hedinger, "Towards A Paradigm of Integrated Missionary Training." (D. Miss. Dissertation, Western Seminary, Portland, 2006), 82-83.

[236] Wan and Hedinger, *Relational Missionary Training*, 87-88.

primarily demonstrate the relational component of Paul's training as based on trinitarian theology and the relational realism paradigm. The following are specific items that Paul taught Timothy.

1. Cultural Sensitivity (Acts 16:1)
2. Multi-ethnicity in the church as Jews and Gentiles came together (Acts 16:3)
3. Church growth (Acts 16:6)
4. The Spirit's involvement in directing missionary outreach (Acts 16:6)
5. Evangelism and baptism (Acts 16:15)
6. Recognition of and reaction to demonic activity (Acts 16:16)
7. Persecution, jail, beating and suffering for the gospel (Acts 16:22)
8. Strategy of who goes to new towns and who stays to disciple new believers (Acts 17:14, 15)
9. Preaching in difficult circumstances (Acts 18:5)
10. Missionary finances (Acts 18:5)
11. Missionary team formation (Acts 20:4)
12. Doctrines and their application to Christian Life (Rom 16:21; 1 Cor 4:17; 1 Thess 1:1; Philemon 1:1) [237]

Finally, Wan and Tin Nguyen in a study of the relationship between Paul and Timothy arrive at five "timeless guiding theological principles for mission training."

1. Relationship is prominent before, during, and after the training process.
2. The goal of training [is] to build up spiritual Christians who possess and display biblical values.
3. Trainers and trainees create a community of faith in which they fellowship, set examples for one another and for the world.
4. Spiritual maturity, the outcome of the vertical relationship between God and the trainer and trainees, is the primary objective of mission training. Holiness is the most important qualification of God's servants.
5. Only spiritual trainers can produce spiritual trainees. [238]

---

[237] Wan and Hedinger, *Relational Missionary Training*, 90.
[238] Enoch Wan and Tin V. Nguyen, "Toward a Theology of Relational Mission Training – an Application of the Relational Paradigm," *Global Missiology* no. 11, accessed February 26, 2021, http://ojs.globalmissiology.org/index.php/english/article/view/1626/3599, 11.

Summary

Taken together, these studies into God's Word of the training of Jesus' Apostles, Paul's unique equipping, and Paul's subsequent training of his companions, chiefly Timothy, provide a solidly biblical foundation for a theology of missionary training. Next, I will apply this theological framework to a philosophy of missionary training, building on the biblical principles with a view to the relational paradigm[239] and educational models.

Table 10. Summary of Biblical/Theological Principles for Missionary Training

Seven Key Themes[240]	Paul's Teaching of Timothy[241]	Timeless Principles[242]
The missionary's focus on Scriptural truth The missionary as a person The missionary as a teacher The missionary as developer of church leadership The missionary as defender against opposition The missionary and specific relationships The missionary and spiritual warfare	Cultural sensitivity Multi-ethnicity in the church Church growth The Spirit's involvement Evangelism and baptism Recognition and reaction to demonic activity Persecution, jail, beating, and suffering Strategy for deployment Preaching in difficult circumstances Missionary finances Missionary team formation Doctrines and their application to life	Relationship (before, during, after training) The goal of training is to build up spiritual Christians Trainers and trainees create a community of faith and fellowship Spiritual maturity is the primary objective of training Only spiritual trainers can produce spiritual trainees

---

239 Wan, "The Paradigm of 'Relational Realism.'"
240 Wan and Hedinger, *Relational Missionary Training*, 87-88.
241 Wan and Hedinger, *Relational Missionary Training*, 90
242 Enoch Wan and Tin V. Nguyen, "Toward a Theology of Relational Mission Training," 11.

Philosophy of Missionary Training

Several recent research studies have focused on the philosophy and practice of missionary training in different contexts. As the focus of this study is primarily in the United States, I begin with studies conducted in a Western context and then move to others as well. The goal is to find those common essential elements that can be built into a philosophy of missionary training founded on theological principles as noted above and in the context of relationship.

Missionary Training in Western Contexts

Mark E. Sarracino conducted a study of field-based missionary leadership training.[243] His purpose was to assess on field leadership development by North American mission agencies. While not directly equivalent to the study at hand, several of his points are worth noting. The field-based training program (or any training program) should focus not just on academics or skills but also character development, "both the 'being' and the 'doing.'"[244] Another key universal theme is that mission agencies need to define the outcomes of their training, that is, what they want their missionaries to look like.[245] Sarracino ultimately pointed to several important components for missionary training including: relationship, mentoring, character development, contextual relevance, active learning (andragogy), and cross-cultural understanding,[246] After surveying ten North American mission agencies[247] he arrived at several conclusions relevant to this study.

Throughout the study there was a strong emphasis on character development. Five qualities were specifically found: godly character, intimacy with God, relational skills, people development, and gifting.[248] One particularly important highlight was the weight given to cross-cultural training. Ninety percent of the organizations recognized cross-cultural adaptability as important with fifty percent saying they have had people leave the field because of cross-cultural issues.[249]

In another research study Mark H. Swank investigated creating a new

---

[243] Mark E. Sarracino, "A Study of Field-Based Missionary Leadership Training," (D. Min. Dissertation, Colombia Biblical Seminary and Graduate School of Missions, Colombia, 2001).

[244] Sarracino, "A Study of Field-Based Missionary Leadership Training," 4.

[245] Sarracino, "A Study of Field-Based Missionary Leadership Training," 7.

[246] Sarracino, "A Study of Field-Based Missionary Leadership Training," 46-61.

[247] Organizations surveyed were Conservative Baptists International, Foreign Mission Board of the Southern Baptists, Operation Mobilization, Overseas Crusade, Overseas Missionary Fellowship, TEAM, WEC, Wycliffe, Young Life and one anonymous agency.

[248] Sarracino, "A Study of Field-Based Missionary Leadership Training," 109.

[249] Sarracino, "A Study of Field-Based Missionary Leadership Training," 113.

missionary training paradigm for Church of God World Missions.[250] His research is particularly interesting to this study as it focused on the training of young adults (18-25) who feel a call to missions.[251] Swank developed the educational framework of his program around holistic discipleship, focusing on formal, non-formal, and informal education for the trainees. "Training is accomplished then by integrating formal education or "knowing," informal education or "being," and non-formal education or "doing."[252] The table below is a summary of the training elements that were included.

Table 11. Church of God World Missions Training Elements[253]

Knowing/Formal Education	Being/Informal Education	Doing/Non-Formal Education
Biblical Knowledge	Personal Prayer	Local Church Ministry
Church Doctrine	Time	Children's Outreach Services
History of CoG	Accountability	Evangelism Outreaches
World Missions	Groups	Homeless Feeding Programs
Biblical	Mentoring Time	Tutoring Programs
Foundations for	Corporate	Youth
Missions	Worship	Services/Retreats/Conferences
Evaluating Cultural	Journaling	Inner-city Invasions
Dynamics	Steps to Freedom	Overseas Mission Trips
Church Planting	Spiritual Retreats	Drama/Dance/Music Ministry
Movements	Evaluations and	Prayer Walks
Specialized	Conflict	Adopt-a-block
Cultural/Religious	Resolution	Coffee House Outreaches
Studies	Community	
Language Learning	Living	

Swank's training also includes academic credit available to students through Lee University and The Church of God Theological Seminary.[254] One of his most relevant findings in conducting a survey of on field missionaries was that 88% of them saw value in integrating academics into the training program.[255] This was an element of the training that was initially resisted by the project leader Swank served under. Recognizing the importance of practical training combined with academic study is a key component of this

---

[250] Mark H. Swank, "Developing A New Missionary Training Paradigm for Church of God World Missions," (D. Min. Dissertation, Trinity International University, Bannockburn, 2006).

[251] Swank, "Developing A New Missionary Training Paradigm," 2.

[252] Swank, "Developing A New Missionary Training Paradigm," 2.

[253] Swank, "Developing A New Missionary Training Paradigm," 48-54.

[254] Swank, "Developing A New Missionary Training Paradigm," 45.

[255] Swank, "Developing A New Missionary Training Paradigm," 68.

study.

Missionary Training in the Majority World

One of the most comprehensive resources on missionary training is *Internationalizing Missionary Training: A Global Perspective*. While the focus of this work is on the two-thirds world, it contributes several elements to an overall philosophy of missionary training. William Taylor, in the opening chapter of the book, gives a six-fold process for missionary training which includes "personal disciplines, local church, biblical/theological studies (formal and non-formal), cross-cultural studies (formal and non-formal), pre-field equipping by the agency, and on-field career training."[256] He presents the following diagram for a comprehensive perspective of missionary training.

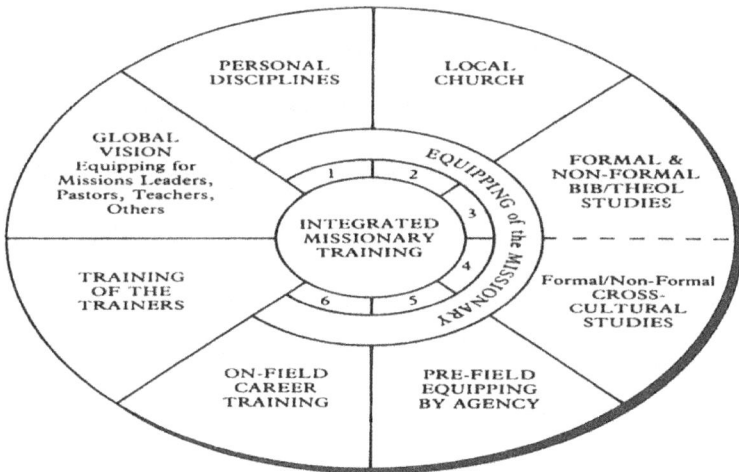

Figure 18. Missionary Training a Comprehensive Perspective[257]

Taylor emphasizes several aspects of this training perspective. Missionaries should have a good handle on personal spiritual disciplines and be growing in their personal lives and character. This is one area that is frequently a struggle for higher education institutions.[258] The missionary needs to be actively engaged in healthy spiritual disciplines and involved in a local church. Taylor specifically highlights the importance of a "mobilizing

---

256 William David Taylor, ed. *Internationalizing Missionary Training: A Global Perspective*, (Grand Rapids: Baker Book House, 1991), 3.

257 Taylor, ed. *Internationalizing Missionary Training*, 4.

258 Taylor, ed. *Internationalizing Missionary Training*, 5.

church", one that is actively sending and supporting missionaries.[259] He also highlights the importance of cooperation in biblical and theological studies noting that many missionary training centers sometimes erroneously assume that students come with the necessary biblical background so that training can be more ministry focused.[260]

Like many others, Taylor also indicates the importance of cross-cultural training. In both biblical and theological studies and cross-cultural training, he echoes others (including Lois McKinney in the same book) who point to the need to integrate formal, non-formal, and informal methods to educate the whole person.[261] Taylor's model is not a step-by-step procedure but rather a philosophy of an overall integrated approach to missionary training. Missionaries are called on to fulfill a variety of roles, and their training must prepare them for whatever they might face. Taylor ends with the necessity of continuing education for missionaries on the field so that they stay fresh in their task.[262]

C. David Harly conducted a survey of six missionary training centers in the two-thirds world.[263] His research focused on historical background, theological principles, educational theory, holistic training, contextualization, evaluation, and development rationale.[264] Harly identified ten common themes among these training centers. First, each one of them had a clear goal, "to train those who will cross cultural barriers in the proclamation of the gospel."[265] Harly's conclusions are summarized below.

---

[259] Taylor, ed. *Internationalizing Missionary Training*, 5.
[260] Taylor, ed. *Internationalizing Missionary Training*, 6.
[261] Taylor, ed. *Internationalizing Missionary Training*, 8.
[262] Taylor, ed. *Internationalizing Missionary Training*, 9-10.
[263] Nigeria Evangelical Missionary Institute, Africa Inland Church Missionary College, Outreach Training Institute India, Asian Cross-Cultural Training Institute, Global Missionary Training Center Korea, The Antioch Mission Training Course Brazil.
[264] C. David Harley, "A Comparative Study of IMTF-Related Missionary Training Centers in the Two-Thirds World," (D. Min. Dissertation, Columbia Biblical Seminary and Graduate School of Missions, Columbia, 1992), 5-9.
[265] Harley, "A Comparative Study," 131.

Table 12. Ten Themes in Two-Third's World Missionary Training Centers[266]

Themes	Explanation
A Clear Goal	Each center focused on the goal of training cross-cultural missionaries.
The Right Location	The location of the center considered cost and student access to ministry.
Cooperation	While each center was founded by one organization being interdenominational allowed for greater cooperation.
Living in Community	Residential programs allowed for both formal and informal relationships.
The Right Staff	Each center had staff with cross-cultural ministry experience.
The Right Students	Students had a clear calling to cross-cultural ministry
The Local Church	The Centers were committed to the primacy and authority of local churches and student involvement in one.
Educational Theory	Culturally contextualized education, interactive, group discussions, andragogical, focused on practical skills
Holistic Training	Educating the whole person, cognitive, affective, and behavioral; cross-cultural sensitivity
Training Families	Married couples are trained together

David Tai Woong Lee conducted research towards establishing a cross-cultural missionary training program for South Korean university students.[267] In his research he discussed several elements related toward building a philosophy of missionary training. He highlights that while theological knowledge is essential so too is knowledge in anthropology, sociology, language, communications, and vocational skills.[268] It bears mentioning that the program was also primarily aimed at the training of tentmakers. He emphasized an integrated approach to training that is grounded in God's Word.[269] Several of his points are noteworthy: candidates must be trained to have a Christian worldview, the integration of ministry skills and cross-cultural principles, emphasis on social sciences and character development, continuous training, servanthood, and balance.[270] He also highlights an

---

[266] Harley, "A Comparative Study," 131-140.

[267] David Tai Woong Lee, "A Missionary Training Program for University Students in South Korea," (D. Miss. Dissertation, Trinity Evangelical Divinity School, Bannockburn, 1983).

[268] Lee, "A Missionary Training Program," 138.

[269] Lee, "A Missionary Training Program," 143.

[270] Lee, "A Missionary Training Program," 144, 156.

andragogical training method.[271]

Returning once more to the biblical/theological principles, we arrive at several key elements that should be present in missionary training. Summarizing the three sections of table 1 we can see that biblically; missionary training should be: relational, emphasize character development, incorporate both knowledge and skills, and incorporate a holistic andragogical approach.

Relational

Whether it was Jesus with the twelve or Paul with Timothy, a deep and abiding personal relationship between trainer and trainees is an essential component of the learning experience. Wan and Hedinger's work in *Relational Missionary Training* stands out here. Theologically, it begins with a solid trinitarian framework for relationship.[272] The relational paradigm then provides a framework for understanding the trainer and trainee relationship in context with the relationship each has with the Trinity.[273] Each of these establishes a basis for missionary training that begins with the relationships between God, trainer, and trainees. Everything else that follows, the educational philosophy, the content of training and even the goal, should be viewed through this relational lens. Multiple other authors, as noted above, have highlighted the importance of relationship in missionary training. Any missionary training program should therefore include ways and means for personal interaction between trainer and trainees. As Wan and Hedinger summarize, "this means that training will take place in the context of interactive connections between the trainer, the trainee, and other beings and Beings who are part of the picture."[274]

Emphasis on Character Development

Closely behind relationship, many researchers indicate the importance of character development in missionary trainees. A key component of Paul's training of Timothy was his character development (2 Tim. 2-4). Character development was repeatedly mentioned as valuable to missionary training in the research. Sarracino indicated five specific qualities: godly character, intimacy with God, relational skills, people development, and gifting.[275] However, for the cross-cultural missionary it is not just the practice of

---

271 Lee, "A Missionary Training Program," 176.
272 Wan and Hedinger, *Relational Missionary Training*, 17.
273 Wan and Hedinger, *Relational Missionary Training*, 20.
274 Wan and Hedinger, *Relational Missionary Training*, 239-240.
275 Sarracino, "A Study of Field-Based Missionary Leadership Training," 109.

personal spiritual disciplines which matter but living them out in the cultural context they find themselves. Missionaries must also develop intercultural character, much like Paul stated in 1 Corinthians 9:19-23; the missionary needs to be an intercultural person, following the example set forth by Hudson Taylor and many others. Missionaries must be culturally sensitive, avoiding behaviors and practices which could hinder their ability to communicate the gospel in the host culture because of thoughtless cultural mistakes.[276]

What the Missionary Needs to Know

What should the content be of a missionary training program? In short, missionaries need to know a lot! At the top of the list is a solid biblical foundation. Missionaries need to be able to practice both solid hermeneutics and exegesis of the text as well as having the ability to contextualize it to the culture of the hearers. To that end they must be able to exegete the culture. Only by accurately understanding the culture of those they are trying to reach can they begin to grasp how best to explain the gospel to them. The training of missionaries needs to include a solid biblical and theological foundation as well as instruction in anthropology and culture. This might also include language acquisition, although the degree of language training will depend greatly on the field and type of ministry. Biblical Ministries Worldwide, for example, includes very little language training; however, a ministry such as Ethnos 360 which expects its missionaries to be able to learn a tribal language, develop an alphabet, teach natives to read their own language, and translate Scripture into that language necessitates a great deal of training in linguistics.

What the Missionary Should be Able to Do

While the Bible and culture could be said to form the core of what a missionary should know, many other elements could be necessary parts of training as well. Ethnos 360, one of Calvary's Synergy partners and participants in this study, has perhaps the most extensive missionary training program of any agency. Their two-year program includes training in organization, time management, communication, teaching, study habits, witnessing, work ethic, motivation, vocational skills (carpentry, plumbing, welding, etc...), discipleship, confrontation, church planting, physical health,

---

[276] Roland Müller, *The Messenger, The Message, The Community: Three Critical Issues for the Cross-Cultural Church Planter*, 3rd ed. (British Colombia: CanBooks, 2013), 4.

and finances.[277] All of these are aspects of training that need to be taken into consideration by any missionary training program. However, the exact nature of the training will depend a great deal on the specific ministry and context being prepared for.

Holistic Training with an Andragogical Education Philosophy

Two other important aspects stand out from the research for developing a philosophy of missionary training. The first, already demonstrated in the last three points, is that training should be holistic; it should involve educating the whole person. Swank, highlighted the roles of formal, informal, and non-formal education, specifically for what the missionary should know, be, and do.[278] Harley listed holistic training as one of his 10 conclusions.[279] Wan and Hedinger provide the following diagram to give a biblical reference for holistic discipleship according to the relational paradigm.[280]

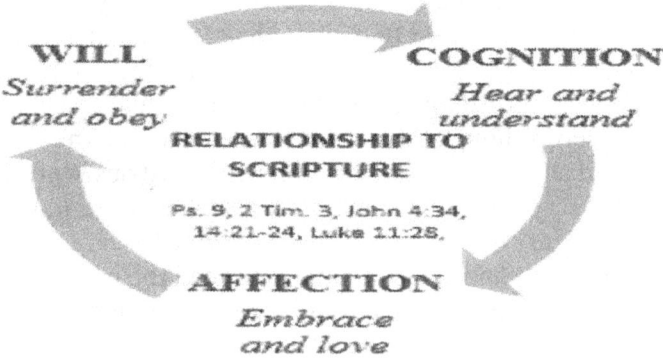

Figure 19. Multi-dynamic Relationship to Scripture

Missionary training should also use adult educational models, andragogy as opposed to pedagogy. "We are training adults and so adult education methods are essential.[281] Harley listed adult education among his ten conclusions.[282] Robert Ferris in outlining standards of excellence for missionary training centers listed "gifts for teaching and mentoring adults"

---

[277] "Spiritual Qualities and Ministry Capabilities," (Ethnos 360: Roach, MO, unpublished training outline), used by permission.
[278] Swank, "Developing A New Missionary Training Paradigm," 48-54.
[279] Harley, "A Comparative Study," 131-140.
[280] Wan and Hedinger, *Relational Missionary Training*, 151.
[281] Wan and Hedinger, *Relational Missionary Training*, 154.
[282] Harley, "A Comparative Study," 131-140.

among the qualifications for missionary trainers.[283]

Summary

A philosophy of missionary training based on a sound theology of Jesus' training of the twelve and Paul's training of Timothy will be relational, holistic (focusing on knowledge, character, and skills), and andragogical. Many models of missionary training exist; George Schultz has summarized them into three broad categories. In his dissertation work he assessed different models for missionary training.[284] Schultz specifically assessed three different models of missionary training within agencies of the Interdenominational Foreign Mission Association (IFMA).[285] He identified three primarily models of training: those he called "providers" (20 agencies) who conducted their own training, "outsourcers" (15 agencies) who utilized third party training organizations, and "partners" (9 agencies) who cooperated in working with others.[286]

The practice of missionary training should incorporate previous research into a model that is practical and relevant for mobilizing and equipping the next generation of missionaries. It should be transformational in the life of the trainee and demonstrate the fullest expression of the Universal Church cooperating to reach the lost.

Practice of Missionary Training

As we delve into the practice of missionary training, this section will focus specifically on the training provided by Calvary University's Synergy partners, Crossworld, Biblical Ministries Worldwide, and Ethnos 360.[287] How does their training methodology reflect the theological and philosophical principles covered so far? This is an important component to the Synergy program. As the director of that program and the one in charge of offering students credit for their experience, I must be assured that my students are getting the vital training that they need to thrive on the mission field.

Furthermore, as an educational institution, Calvary must be able to prove

---

283 Robert Ferris, "Standards of Excellence in Missionary Training Centers," *Training for Cross-Cultural Ministries*, Vol. 2000 No. 1, January 2000.

284 George H. Schultz Jr. "Models of Missionary Training: An Assessment of Alternative Approaches to Training for Cross-Cultural Ministry," (D. Min. Dissertation, Columbia Biblical Seminary and School of Missions, Columbia, 2001).

285 In 2012 the Interdenominational Foreign Mission Association (then CrossGlobal Linke) merged with the Mission Exchange (formerly the Evangelical Fellowship of Mission Agencies) to create MissioNexus.

286 Schultz, Jr. "Models of Missionary Training," xi.

287 This section of the literature review was moved to chapter 3 in discussing the practical aspects of the Synergy partnership.

to its accreditation agencies that we are meeting the educational needs of our students. Does Synergy really accomplish the kind of missionary training that these students need to be successful on the mission field? While success in missions is difficult to measure, it is vital to examine the degree to which our partner's training lines up with what has been discovered so far in this study. This will enable me to tell students that yes, the training they will receive through these organizations will equip them for the task ahead.

Relational Missionary Training

In *Relational Missionary Training* Enoch Wan and Mark Hedinger have taken the paradigm of relational realism and applied it to the task of training missionaries. Their work is foundational to the study at hand because it has the same theological and theoretical starting points in the Trinity and the relational paradigm. Having worked through the theological, theoretical, and practical aspects of missionary training, they conclude with suggestions for moving forward in practice.[288]

First, the "organizing principle for training is relational."[289] As we have seen throughout this study in both the examination of Jesus and Paul as well as the research conducted by others, relationship is a key component of missionary training. Wan and Hedinger carry this into four specific areas related to the program of missionary training. The program will...

1. understand that mission work is a series of relationships, with God first and secondarily with people.
2. understand that the purpose of mission is relational: to facilitate a relationship between Triune God and the people being reached.
3. strive to use good teaching and outreach methods yet will always see those methods as serving relationship not the other way around.
4. be measured in terms of healthy relational patterns; first of all, with Triune God, and then between training staff, training cohorts, and members of a given ministry team.[290]

Second, the content, context, methods, and task of teaching and learning will be relational. "Mission skills, attitudes, knowledge are designed for and evaluated on the basis of relational outcomes." [291]

Third, missionary training according to the relational paradigm will have relational training outcomes. The outcomes and objectives of the training

---

[288] Wan and Hedinger, *Relational Missionary Training*, 289.
[289] Wan and Hedinger, *Relational Missionary Training*, 289.
[290] Wan and Hedinger, *Relational Missionary Training*, 289-290.
[291] Wan and Hedinger, *Relational Missionary Training*, 290.

program will be based not just on cognitive, affective, and skill development but on overall transformation of the person.[292] Missionary training, relational or not, forces the prospective missionary to come face to face with their own preconceived ideas and cultural biases. These issues must be confronted to engage others with the gospel apart from the missionary's own cultural baggage. Missionary training is not just education but transformation.[293]

Fourth, relational missionary training is "dependent on more than one person/Person to be effective."[294] There are a couple of important components to this conclusion. First is the recognition of the role that God plays in the transformative process in both the trainers and trainees' lives. Missionary training is not just all about the man-made curriculum and program but the interactive relationship that occurs between trainer, trainee, and the Triune God. Second, and especially for this study, is the recognition that no one trainer can fully equip the trainees. It takes a team of trainers from a variety of backgrounds and experiences with relational connections to the trainee to truly effect transformative learning. An important concept in bringing together churches, schools, and agencies in the life of the missionary trainee is understanding their unique roles in the process.

Fifth, relational missionary training "assumes relationships to be dynamic, not static."[295] Because human relationships are dynamic, no one training approach can be successful in all circumstances with all individuals. Wan and Hedinger continue that, "a relational paradigm approach to training will not create a single approach, yet will develop multiple approaches, and will vary methods until a good fit between trainer and trainee is found."[296] A better description of the Synergy program would be incredibly hard to find. As the program brings students into relationship with the school through multiple agency partners and connections to their local church, students are provided with a variety of training pathways to follow towards their unique ministry/calling. This is made possible through the relationship already established between the school and agency.

Sixth, "training will not be seen as the mechanical following of a prepared curriculum, but as the flexible interaction of content, training methods, and training relationships within a flexible philosophy of education."[297] Once more the uniqueness of the Synergy program can be seen to fit the principles of relational missionary training. While some components of the curriculum are fixed within certain classes, there is a high degree of flexibility. As each course

---

[292] Wan and Hedinger, *Relational Missionary Training*, 290.
[293] Wan and Hedinger, *Relational Missionary Training*, 291.
[294] Wan and Hedinger, *Relational Missionary Training*, 291.
[295] Wan and Hedinger, *Relational Missionary Training*, 292.
[296] Wan and Hedinger, *Relational Missionary Training*, 292.
[297] Wan and Hedinger, *Relational Missionary Training*, 292.

in the Synergy program is an elective, the full program can be taken by any student in any degree program at Calvary; as such, business majors, education majors, intercultural studies, and even theater have access to missionary training. Students have a choice of three agencies with unique training methods and ministry approaches to choose from.

Seventh, "the trainee is prepared to be transformed even as he/she takes a message of Gospel transformation to the unreached."[298] As students begin to be confronted by their own cultural biases within the context of their vertical and horizontal relationships, they will need ongoing support. The transformative learning process seeks to develop the student's being, not just give them extra knowledge and skills. Through Synergy, the interconnection of mentoring, classes, and missionary training in a relational environment helps them through this transformative process to becoming an intercultural person of God.

Eight, "Training based on the Paradigm of Relational Realism is accepted, appreciated, and consistent with lifestyle patterns of most of the non-Western world as well as a growing number of Western civilization's younger generation."[299] Once again, two key components of relational missionary training can be seen at work in Synergy. The first, demonstrated later in this dissertation is the importance of relationships to Generation Z. The target generation for the Synergy program exhibits the very qualities that are highlighted in relational missionary training. Furthermore, as Calvary continues to expand its online educational offerings and we build a larger base of international students studying in their home countries, relational missionary training provides for educational models that are more acceptable to those students.

Wan and Hedinger conclude with one final observation that training within the relational paradigm is focused on much more than just missionaries.[300] The importance of this one final point could not be overstated with the current generation. We live in a time of unprecedented globalization and cross-cultural conflict. Much of the issues surrounded racism and police brutality, the rise of the Black Lives Matter movement, can be traced to cultural and worldview differences. There has never been a greater need for all people, but Christians especially, to approach the tough issues of life with cultural understanding. Every neighborhood is increasingly diverse, and those who educate Christians must prepare them for that diversity.

The Synergy program at Calvary is actively meeting many of the qualifications that go into relational missionary training. Each of the partners focuses on these areas in the preparation of the missionary candidates. In

---

[298] Wan and Hedinger, *Relational Missionary Training*, 293.
[299] Wan and Hedinger, *Relational Missionary Training*, 294.
[300] Wan and Hedinger, *Relational Missionary Training*, 295.

addition, working in conjunction with the local church and university helps to fill in any potential gaps.

Models

Each of the organizations involved in Synergy conducts their training in-house. By doing so they are better able to control the content of the training as well as work towards establishing good relationships with their missionaries. George Schultz Jr., in conducting his study of agency training models, found most of them to be in-house, models that he described as "providers."[301] He defined "providers" as, "those agencies which provide all or most of the pre-field training to their own candidates."[302] This definition accurately describes the training that is conducted by Crossworld, Ethnos 360, and Biblical Ministries Worldwide. Indeed, for the Synergy partnership model to work, the training needs to be in-house to the missions organization. However, a chief concern that Schultz points out is that in-house or provider training can often be very "company or task-specific," resulting in it not being transferable to other situations or contexts.[303] A key finding of his study was that organizations which provide in-house training, labeled as "corporate universities," can benefit greatly by partnering with academic institutions to provide a greater degree of portability to their students.[304]

Finally, in analyzing what model of training each organization in his study would move towards if they were to change, the greatest difference was in those who would move towards a partnership training model. Providers would go from twenty to fourteen, Outsourcers would go from fourteen to thirteen, and Partners would go from nine to sixteen.[305] Schultz conducted his study in 2001; a similar study would be interesting today to see how much this transition in models has proven correct.

Summary

All of the Synergy partners emphasize similar concepts in their training. Missionaries need personal development, a strong relationship with the Lord and others, cross-cultural and ministry skills, and a wide variety of other abilities depending on their field of service. There are many similarities in what they teach as well as how they go about teaching it. Clear parallels can be drawn from their content, methods, and philosophy. It is not surprising that although they have different focus areas (tribal church planting, church

---

[301] Schultz Jr. "Models of Missionary Training," xi.
[302] Schultz, Jr. "Models of Missionary Training," 5.
[303] Schultz, Jr. "Models of Missionary Training," 16.
[304] Schultz, Jr. "Models of Missionary Training," 28.
[305] Schultz, Jr. "Models of Missionary Training," 73.

planting, business as missions, etc.) most of the training remains very similar and can easily be interwoven into the courses involved in the Synergy program at Calvary. Synergy must incorporate biblical/theological principles of missionary training as seen in the examples of Jesus and Paul, a sound missionary training philosophy and incorporates training the whole person from a relational framework, and key areas of missionary practice in keeping with the realities of what the missionary will face on the field.

Ethnographic Profile of Generation Z

Who is Generation Z?

Current college students are members of Generation Z (Gen Z), those born between 1995 and 2010.[306] They are the first generation to grow up in a world where the internet has always existed and are also referred to as the "Net Generation" and "iGeneration".[307] Marc Prensky makes the statement, "Today's students are no longer the people our educational system was designed to teach."[308] Thiers is a world in which the internet, computers, video games, and cell phones have always existed. They have never known a world without these conveniences of modern life and their lives and learning styles have been completely shaped by them. Their childhoods were shaped by screens. Where my own generation (Generation X) witnessed the development and growth of much of this technology and can remember a childhood without it, Gen Z does not know any different. Life comes at them at blazing speed and all the knowledge of humanity throughout all time is available to them at the touch of a button through a device they carry with them every day.

Andragogy vs. Pedagogy

Prior to entering a discussion of Generation Z's learning preferences, it is important to lay a foundation on the difference between Andragogy and Pedagogy. The educational philosophy of pedagogy is defined by Malcolm Knowles as the "art and science of teaching children."[309] The word itself is derived from two Greek words, παιδ, meaning "child" and αγωγός, meaning

---

[306] Corey Seemiller and Meghan Grace, *Generation Z Goes to College*, (San Francisco: Jossey-Bass, 2010), 6.

[307] Marc Prensky, "Digital Natives, digital immigrants," *On the Horizon*, 9, 5, Accessed March 8, 2019, https://www.marc prensky.com/writing/Prensky%20%20Digital%20Natives,%20Digital%20 Immigrants%20-%20Part1.pdf.

[308] Prensky, "Digital Natives, digital immigrants."

[309] Malcolm S. Knowles, Elwood F. Holton, and Richard A Swanson. *The Adult Learner.* 7th ed. (New York: Routledge, 2012), 60.

"leader of".[310] The Greek word itself, παιδαγωγός, is defined by Strong's Concordance as "a trainer of boys, a tutor" and is summarily used to refer to the tutor or guardian of boys or more generally a slave who was to instruct boys in the morals of the family, it was not strictly used to refer to teachers.[311]

Beginning from a scriptural standpoint, the word itself occurs three times; 1 Corinthians 4:15 and Galatians 3:24, 25. Paul uses it in 1 Cor. 4 to refer to the many tutors or guides that the Corinthian church has in Christ, in contrast to himself as their spiritual father as the one who brought them the gospel. In Galatians 3:24, 25 it is used in reference to the law as a guardian until Christ was to come and they are under this guardian no longer. In the general sense, pedagogy refers to the various theories and methods involved in education. Specifically, it is used in the education of children.

Many pedagogical theories have been developed to describe the way children learn and grow. Well-known names in the development of pedagogical theory include Gagne, Kolb, Gardner, Piaget, Dewey, and Montessori.[312] Some of these theories include cognitivism, constructivism and behaviorism. All of them contribute to a growing understanding of how learning is achieved. However, all of them assume certain things about the nature of learning from the perspective of a child.

Knowles, in his comparison of pedagogy and andragogy, gave six basic assumptions of each. First, children only need to know what they need to know to pass the test, get the promotion, or advance in their field, it is not necessary for them to know how this learning will apply to their lives.[313] In other words, children do not need to know why the learning is important, they just need to learn what is being taught. It is the teacher who, understanding why the learning is important, provides the impetus for them to learn the material. To this end, the second assumption is that the learner is dependent on the teacher.[314] This position of dependency changes throughout time as individuals mature and grow. The more mature a person is the better able they are to self-direct. This rate of change can be seen in the figure below. It is this assumption that really forms
much of the basis of this review as we examine where Gen Z as college students really fit on this continuum.

---

[310] Knowles, Holton, and Swanson, *The Adult Learner*, 59.

[311] "Παιδαγωγός," *Bible Hub*, accessed April 1, 2019, https://biblehub.com/str/greek/3807.htm

[312] Colleen M. Halupa, "Pedagogy, Andragogy and Heutagogy," accessed April 1, 2019, https://www.researchgate.net/publication/297767648_Pedagogy_Andragogy_and_Heutagogy.

[313] Knowles, Holton, and Swanson, *The Adult Learner*, 60.

[314] Knowles, Holton, and Swanson, *The Adult Learner*, 60.

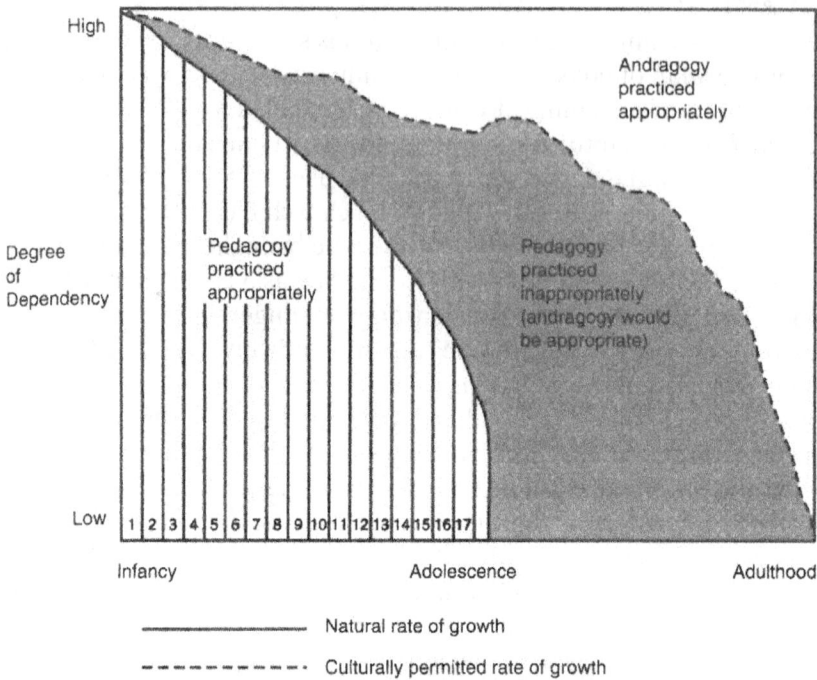

High

Andragogy
practiced
appropriately

Degree
of
Dependency

Pedagogy
practiced
appropriately

Pedagogy
practiced
inappropriately
(andragogy would
be appropriate)

Low | 1 | 2 | 3 | 4 | 5 | 6 | 7 | 8 | 9 |10|11|12|13|14|15|16|17|

Infancy   Adolescence   Adulthood

————————— Natural rate of growth

— — — — — — — —· Culturally permitted rate of growth

Figure 20. The natural maturation toward self-direction as compared with the culturally permitted rate of growth of self-direction[315]

The next assumption in pedagogy is that the learner has little to no experience of value to contribute towards their learning.[316] Instead, it is the experience of the teacher, the textbook writer, or the pedagogical theorist that really matters. Children clearly have limited experiences and even with what experiences they have, they may lack the cognitive ability to interpret experience in a way that will contribute to learning. The fourth assumption is that learners become ready to learn what the teacher tells them to learn.[317] Learning is still fundamentally teacher-directed in that the teacher is deciding what is necessary to know to advance to the next level or move on to the next grade.

The student's orientation to learning in pedagogy is subject centered.[318] Learning revolves around subjects or topics such as, math, history, and science. Furthermore, study of these subjects is based on the logic of the subject itself. For instance, in math, the student needs to learn to add before

---

[315] Knowles, Holton, and Swanson, *The Adult Learner*, 60.
[316] Knowles, Holton, and Swanson, *The Adult Learner*, 60.
[317] Knowles, Holton, and Swanson, *The Adult Learner*, 62.
[318] Knowles, Holton, and Swanson, *The Adult Learner*, 62.

they can subtract, before they can multiply, before they can divide and then move on to higher order equations. The final assumption in pedagogy is that the learner is motivated primarily through external means.[319] Awards, grades, recognition, even punishment; these are all used to provide the learner with the motivation necessary to learn the material and advance to the next grade.

Perhaps the most fundamental principle behind pedagogical theories of education is that the teacher is the one who is driving the learning process. It is largely held that the student needs the teacher to be the driving force behind learning. This fundamental principle is still highly regarded as true for instructors in higher education and especially for theological education. In contrast, perhaps the most fundamental principle for andragogy is its focus on the student as the one in charge of the learning process.

The term Andragogy was first used in 1833 by Alexander Kapp to describe the lifelong necessity of learning.[320] Kapp neither explained the term nor developed a theory around its use. The term was summarily used by different authors and social scientists (Rosenstock, Pagelet) until eventually it came to Malcolm Knowles.[321] Knowles has summarily been described as the "Father of Andragogy" in the United States and is chiefly credited with its development as a theory of adult education.[322] Andragogy was first introduced by Knowles in 1975 as a set of four basic assumptions about adult education. It has since grown to six, these will be examined here in contrast to the six basic assumptions of pedagogy.[323]

The first basic assumption of pedagogy as presented above was that children do not need to know why they need to learn something. In contrast, adults have been found to have a fundamental need to know the value of what they are learning before they will exert the energy to learn it.[324] Adults are self-directed as learners rather than being teacher directed. They need to understand and recognize the value of what they are learning and how it will help them to attain their ultimate goals. While the teacher of children has the benefit of a position of authority to essentially tell the child what they need to know, the adult educator must build a case for why the information is important.

Unlike children, "adults have a self-concept of being responsible for their own decisions, for their own lives".[325] This principle is closely related to the

---

[319] Knowles, Holton, and Swanson, *The Adult Learner*, 62.

[320] Jost Reischmann, "Androgogy: History, Meaning, Context, Function," in Knowles, Holton, and Swanson *The Adult Learner*. 7th ed. (New York: Routledge, 2012), 336.

[321] Reischmann, "Androgogy: History, Meaning, Context, Function," in Knowles, Holton, and Swanson *The Adult Learner*, 338

[322] Knowles, Holton, and Swanson, *The Adult Learner*, v.

[323] Knowles, Holton, and Swanson, *The Adult Learner*, 67.

[324] Knowles, Holton, and Swanson, *The Adult Learner*, 63.

[325] Knowles, Holton, and Swanson, *The Adult Learner*, 63.

first, in that adults take charge of their own education. Adults may even become resentful when teachers hold them in a state of dependence rather than releasing them to be self-directed learners. The adult learner is expected to evaluate their own progress and track whether they are learning the material or not. Responsible adults will then take necessary steps to correct any habits or practices that are impeding the learning process.

The third assumption of andragogy relates to the greater wealth of experience that an adult has over a child. Children, through a lack of experience, can be said to 'not know what they don't know.' In other words, it is hard for them to determine what they need to know to succeed. Adults, however, can draw from their experiences to determine areas of weakness in their knowledge base, areas where they may have lacked information before or at least recognized that they did not have the knowledge or skills they needed for a particular task. Adults are different in that they have both a quantity and quality of experience that is different from children.[326] They have a quantity of experience simply because they have lived longer. Their experiences are also more varied, and different in quality, having done more things with their lives.

Adults are also ready to learn what they need to be successful.[327] As opposed to being told what they need to know to advance, adults recognize the gaps in their knowledge between where they are and where they need to be. Generally, readiness to learn a particular task is assigned to a certain level of experience.

A fifth assumption of andragogy is the individual's orientation to learning. Where a child's learning is subject-centered, the adult's learning is life-centered.[328] As noted above, children learn in a very compartmentalized way. Adults, however, may struggle with learning that does not apply directly to their life situation. Knowles uses the example of university extension courses in which adults were taught in evening courses the exact same way as teenagers were during the day. Success was minimal until the method of teaching was changed from a general focus on composition to specific tasks such as "Writing Better Business Letters" or "Improving Your Professional Communication".[329] Adults who are engaged in learning that is directly applicable to their day-to-day experience learn better.

Finally, while adult learners are responsive to external motivators, their primary motivation to learn comes from internal pressures.[330] While positive and negative reinforcement will still motivate an adult, things such as a

---

[326] Knowles, Holton, and Swanson, *The Adult Learner*, 64.
[327] Knowles, Holton, and Swanson, *The Adult Learner*, 65.
[328] Knowles, Holton, and Swanson, *The Adult Learner*, 66.
[329] Knowles, Holton, and Swanson, *The Adult Learner*, 66.
[330] Knowles, Holton, and Swanson, *The Adult Learner*, 67

personal desire to succeed, increased quality of life, better job satisfaction, or simply a desire for personal growth are more important to the adult learner. On the next page is a comparison table of pedagogy and andragogy. Next, I will examine the qualities of the current generation of college students. Gen Z and those students will later be added to the chart for comparison.

Table 13. Andragogy vs. Pedagogy[331]

Trait \\ Method	Pedagogical	Andragogical
The Learner	- The Learner is dependent upon the instructor for all learning. - The teacher/instructor assumes full responsibility for what is taught and how it is learned. - The teacher/instructor evaluates learning.	- The learner is self-directed - The learner is responsible for his/her own learning. - Self-evaluation is characteristic of this approach.
Role of the Learner's Experience	- The Learner comes to the activity with little experience that could be tapped as a resource for learning. - The experience of the instructor is most influential.	- The Learner brings a greater volume and quality of experience. - Adults are a rich resource for one another. - Different experiences assure diversity in groups of adults. - Experience becomes the source of self-identity.
Readiness to Learn	- Students are told what they have to learn in order to advance to the next level of mastery.	- Any Change is likely to trigger a readiness to learn. - The need to know in order to perform more effectively in some aspect of one's life is important. - Ability to assess gaps between where one is now and where one wants and needs to be.
Orientation to Learning	- Learning is a process of acquiring prescribed subject matter. - Content units are sequenced according to the logic of the subject matter.	- Learners want to perform a task, solve a problem, live in a more satisfying way. - Learning must have relevance to real-life tasks. - Learning is organized around life/work situations rather than subject matter units.
Motivation for Learning	- Primarily motivated by external pressures, competition for grades, and the consequences of failure.	- Internal motivators: self-esteem, recognition, better quality of life, self-confidence, self-actualization.

Generation Z's Learning Preferences

Most of the research on Gen Z and their learning preferences is grounded in three key research studies. Corey Seemiller and Megan Grace conducted a study in 2014 as Gen Z was just beginning to enter college. Their findings are reported in the book *Generation Z Goes to College.* Of the 1223 students they began with 613 both fit the qualifications of their study and completed the entire survey.[332] Pearson reports on research conducted by the Harris Poll of 2,587 respondents between the ages of 14 to 40.[333] Their research was focused primarily on comparing Millennials and Gen Z. Barnes and Noble College also conducted a survey of 1300 middle and high school students in 49 states between the ages of 13-18.[334] Their research focused on those getting ready to enter college.

How They Learn

The Learner

The table above includes two of Knowles main points into the one aspect of the learner. Namely, the learner's need to know and self-concept. According to Seemiller and Grace, Gen Z has a very healthy view of themselves describing themselves as loyal (85%), compassionate (73%), thoughtful (85%), open-minded (70%), responsible (69%), and determined (74%).[335] One interesting fact of note as it relates specifically to preparing them for intercultural ministry, is that "they have already been exposed to many different cultures, identities, and ways of living."[336] This exposure may give them a unique perspective on adapting for cross-cultural ministry and culture-shock since through technology and globalization they have already encountered many different perspectives on life.

Adults are described as being highly self-directed and responsible for their

---

[331] Adapted from floridatechnet.org as reported in *Educators Technology, accessed February 25, 2019,* https://www.educatorstechnology.com/2013/05/awesome-chart-on-pedagogy-vs-andragogy.html.

[332] Seemiller and Grace, *Generation Z Goes to College,* xxv.

[333] Pearson, "Beyond Millennials: The Next Generation of Learners" in *Global Research & Insights,* August 2018, https://www.pearson.com/content/dam/one-dot-com/one-dot-com/global/Files/news/news-annoucements/2018/The-Next-Generation-of-Learners_final.pdf.

[334] Barnes & Noble College, *Getting to Know Gen Z: Exploring Middle and High Schoolers' Expectations for Higher Education,* accessed February 25, 2019, https://next.bncollege.com/wp-content/uploads/2015/10/Gen-Z-Research-Report-Final.pdf, 2.

[335] Seemiller and Grace, *Generation Z Goes to College,* 8-11.

[336] Seemiller and Grace, *Generation Z Goes to College,* 10.

own learning. These same characteristics can be seen in Gen Z. Seemiller and Grace report that Gen Z students are comfortable with learning independently and at their own pace.[337] They prefer hands-on and participatory learning over being lectured to and see their instructors as facilitators of learning. Students from this generation "want to play an active role in creating their learning, not listen silently to their instructors' pontification."[338]

The Barnes & Noble study also supports that this generation of students is self-directed, finding that they are more likely to turn online for researching answers to their questions.[339] They are more likely to seek higher education than previous generations with 89 percent of the respondents rating that a college education is valuable.[340] Sixty-seven percent of the respondents in Pearson's study found the same thing.[341] Interestingly, some of the Pearson study's findings seem to be contradictory. Only 22% of the students they surveyed indicated that they preferred self-directed learning over 78% who indicated that teachers are very important to learning and development.[342] However, 71% of them indicated that when confronted with a problem, they would try to find the answer themselves before consulting a teacher.[343] This seems to indicate that while Gen Z students are self-directed in their learning, they still highly value the involvement of the teacher in the learning process. From this it appears that an andragogical focus would be well placed in educating Gen Z.

One other study offers some insight into the self-directed nature of Gen Z as well, that informs how a college program might be structured. This study, conducted by Stefanie Hassel and Nathan Ridout, sought to "determine what expectations students hold when starting university education, and what expectations university lecturers have of students entering university."[344] One aspect of their research led them to conclude that students and teachers alike expect a more teacher-driven approach among younger students, mainly in the first year. They propose that this expectation is due to these students having just left secondary school.[345] This seems to support the idea that over the course of a student's college career a pedagogical or andragogical

---

[337] Seemiller and Grace, *Generation Z Goes to College*, 178.
[338] Seemiller and Grace, *Generation Z Goes to College*, 179.
[339] Barnes & Noble College, *Getting to Know Gen Z*, 2.
[340] Barnes & Noble College, *Getting to Know Gen Z*, 3
[341] Pearson, "Beyond Millennials," 7.
[342] Pearson, "Beyond Millennials," 19.
[343] Pearson, "Beyond Millennials," 20.
[344] Stefanie Hassel and Nathan Ridout, "An Investigation of Frist-Year Student's and Lecturers' Expectations of University Education," *Frontiers in Psychology*, January 2018, https://www.frontiersin.org/articles/10.3389/fpsyg.2017.02218/full, 1.
[345] Hassel and Ridout, "An Investigation of Frist-Year Student's and Lecturers' Expectations of University Education," 9.

approach may be appropriate depending on the student's level of familiarity with the subject and the teaching style. Students who are coming right out of high school and are used to a pedagogical, teacher-centric, style may require time to adjust and explanation of a more student-driven approach to education. This point can be further emphasized in the next assumption regarding the role of the learner's experience.

Role of the Learner's Experience

Andragogical approaches to teaching place more emphasis on the role of the student's experience in the learning process. Adults, generally have a great degree of life experience to draw from to engage with the material that is being taught. Some valid points could be made both ways for Gen Z. On the one hand, they are still young, entering college around 18-19 years of age. Their age clearly only allows for them to have so much life experience and should be a factor in determining whether a pedagogical or andragogical approach is better.

However, the research suggests that the connectedness that this generation experiences as well as the wealth of information at their fingertips gives them a degree of life experience that was not present in earlier generations as they enter college. Barnes & Noble College reported in their study that 35% of the 13–18-year-olds they surveyed already own their own business or plan to start one in the future.[346] These students are already familiar with the world of the future and with its technology, more so than their professors, who are still trying to catch up. Much of the research resulted in article after article about how to engage these students within the technological world they already live in. In these terms the experiences of the students and their familiarity with the technology may be more important than the teachers experience with the subject.

On the other hand, Gen Z struggles to sift through all the information that is coming at them. They have a wealth of information at their fingertips; however, they frequently find it overwhelming.[347] Another survey of Advanced Placement and National Writing Project teachers found that 83% of these educators believe that the information available online is simply overwhelming to their students.[348] So while, Gen Z has a wealth of information available to them they require guidance to filter it out and determine what is valuable. Most of Gen Z take it for granted that if it is on the internet, it is

---

[346] Barnes & Noble College, *Getting to Know Gen Z*, 5.

[347] Barnes & Noble College, *Getting to Know Gen Z*, 27.

[348] Purcell, K., Raine, l, Heaps, A., Buchanan, J., Friedrich, L., Jacklin, A., ... Zickuhr, K. (2012). *How teens do research in the digital world*, accessed February 26, 2019, http://www.pewinternational.org/2012/11/01/how-teens-do -research-in-the-digital-world/.

true.[349] This presents an educational situation in which teachers in the classroom do not necessarily need to focus on content delivery but rather on content filtration; helping students to develop appropriate ways to determine the validity of the information available to them. It also presents an interesting classroom situation when students can immediately fact-check the professor. Today's college students are accustomed to instant gratification and an immediate return on their efforts.[350]

All of this presents a picture in which the classroom of today requires a great degree of cooperation between teachers and students. The students have experience with the technology and know how to use it, however, they require the wisdom of the teacher to filter it all out. This again lends itself towards a more learner-centric, andragogical approach that focuses more on content filtration and less on content delivery. The flipped classroom is a good example, where students conduct outside research into the content of the class and then spend class time with the teacher, discussing and filtering through it all.

Readiness to Learn

Generation Z is ready to learn. They have a greater optimism about the future with 56% reporting that they have more opportunities to succeed than their parents did.[351] A slight majority of Gen Z is optimistic about their futures (57%) and this optimism lends them to a higher degree of risk taking than Millennials.[352] The correlation between their willingness to take risks and how many are already business owners should not be overlooked.

Having a readiness to learn means that they recognize the reality of where they are and where they need to be. Another way to phrase that would be, that they acknowledge that a college education is important. The Pearson study found that 67% of Gen Z view college as an important step to success while only 1 in 4 expect to have a rewarding career without going to college.[353]

An important factor in this, is that many students in Gen Z are preparing for college long before they arrive there. While previous generations were told that we need to take certain classes in high school to be ready, most Gen Z students are taking college courses while still in high school. Forty-nine percent of older teens (16-18) have already taken a class for college credit and

---

[349] Seemiller and Grace, *Generation Z Goes to College*, 27.
[350] Seemiller and Grace, *Generation Z Goes to College*, 28.
[351] Pearson, "Beyond Millennials," 4.
[352] Pearson, "Beyond Millennials," 5.
[353] Pearson, "Beyond Millennials," 7.

84% of younger teens plan on doing so.[354] A simple Google search on early college programs turns up many options for high school students who are looking to earn college credit while still in high school. This has also become a very popular option among homeschoolers. Calvary University alone, has seen a rise in students taking advantage of this option and some students get so far ahead as to graduate high school with enough credits to already be considered Juniors in college.

Gen Z demonstrates a clear readiness to learn. Their access to technology, interconnectedness with the global economy and options for higher education have presented them with an appreciation for a college degree. For several years now it has been stated that a college degree is the new high school diploma. While having a college degree is not mandatory in the United States, it has become common place for it to be a requirement for many entry-level positions.[355] Generation Z students are already aware of what it will take for them to achieve their goals.

Orientation to Learning

One aspect of the study conducted by Seemiller and Grace pointed out that owing to their increased interconnectedness, Gen Z has a more flexible understanding of time and space constraints.[356] They are not limited to the normal 8-5 class day nor even to sitting in a classroom at all. Their learning methods incorporate a variety of technologies that can be accessed in many different locations, making the whole world their classroom. However, despite this increased interconnectivity with people 83% of Gen Z prefers face-to-face communication.[357]

Generation Z is accustomed to using technology to find their own answers to problems. Several studies have indicated that their favorite learning tool is, in fact, YouTube.[358] Other preferred learning methods are group activities and apps or interactive games.[359] However, Generation Z still demonstrates a desire for relational approaches to learning. While they are accustomed to using technology, they also prefer to study with their friends.[360]

The Barnes & Noble study also found that Gen Z students prefer to learn by doing, namely working through real life examples.[361] Their preference is to

---

354 Barnes & Noble College, *Getting to Know Gen Z*, 5.
355 Vauhini Vara, "Is College the New High School?" *The New Yorker*, January 13, 2015, https://www.newyorker.com/business/currency/college-new-high-school, 1.
356 Seemiller and Grace, *Generation Z Goes to College*, 30.
357 Seemiller and Grace, *Generation Z Goes to College*, 61.
358 Pearson, "Beyond Millennials," 14.
359 Pearson, "Beyond Millennials," 14.
360 Barnes & Noble College, *Getting to Know Gen Z*, 6.
361 Barnes & Noble College, *Getting to Know Gen Z*, 7.

recognize how their learning connects with real-world problems. Once again owing to their access to information and news, Gen Z is more in touch with current affairs in the world around them. They desire to make a difference and want to know that what they are learning will help them.

Motivation for Learning

Perhaps the key difference between the way a child learns and the way an adult learns is the motivation behind why they seek to learn new information. For Generation Z that motivation is largely intrinsic. A large percentage of respondents to Barnes & Noble College's survey indicated that a college education is valuable. They also found that Gen Z has a strong love of learning and that they thrive when challenged.[362] Gen Z's chief concern is whether they will be able to find a job following college and among their top three factors in choosing a college is career preparation.[363] These motivations are more commonly found among adults then children.

Generation Z students are highly independent, they are accustomed to finding their own answers and making their own decisions. "Their preference for self-learning fuels a curiosity and concern about personal fulfillment and social impact."[364] Once again the research indicates that an andragogical approach to education is more consistent with who Gen Z is. They are highly motivated to learn what they need to succeed in life. If anything, a picture begins to emerge that Gen Z needs less to be "taught at" and more to be "guided" and "directed" in the process of learning.

Summary

Bringing it all together, the following table with the characteristics of Gen Z added to the right demonstrates that they have more in common with the andragogical assumptions than they do the pedagogical. Be that as it may, there has still been indication in the research both by Knowles[365] and by Hassal and Ridout[366] that a gradual shift from pedagogical to andragogical teaching methods is in the best interest of the student. First year college students may be better served by 100 level classes that take a primarily pedagogical approach with some andragogical elements incorporated into them. Then moving on to the second and continual years a higher degree of andragogical teaching methods will help them transition appropriately.

---

[362] Barnes & Noble College, *Getting to Know Gen Z*, 3

[363] Barnes & Noble College, *Getting to Know Gen Z*, 4

[364] Barnes & Noble College, *Getting to Know Gen Z*, 2

[365] Knowles, Holton, and Swanson, *The Adult Learner*, 61.

[366] Hassel and Ridout, "An Investigation of Frist-Year Student's and Lecturers' Expectations of University Education," 9.

Beginning with the 2021 school year, Calvary will be implementing a new first year student experience that will place incoming Freshman into cohorts were learning is overlapped

Table 14. Comparison of Generation Z with Pedagogy and Andragogy

Method / Trait	Pedagogical	Andragogical	Generation Z
The Learner	- The Learner is dependent upon the instructor for all learning. - The teacher/ instructor assumes full responsibility for: -what is taught -how it is learned & evaluates learning.	- The learner is self-directed - The learner is responsible for his/her own learning. Self-evaluation is characteristic of this approach.	- Comfortable with learning independently and at their own pace. - Likely to turn to researching their own answers. - Want to be involved in the learning process. - Younger students still expect a more teacher-driven approach.
Role of the Learner's Experience	- The Learner comes to the activity with little experience that could be tapped as a resource for learning. - The experience of the instructor is most influential.	- The Learner brings a greater volume and quality of experience. - Adults are a rich resource for one another. - Different experiences assure diversity in groups of adults. - Experience becomes the source of self-identity.	- Still young, entering college at 18-19 yrs., the quantity of their experience is limited. - Have a much greater degree of interconnectedness and information about contemporary issues. - Have already experienced great diversity & wealth of info but struggle to filter it.
Readiness to Learn	- Students are told what they have to learn in order to advance to the next level of mastery.	- Any Change is likely to trigger a readiness to learn. - The need to know in order to perform more effectively in some aspect of one's life is important. - Ability to assess gaps between where one is now and where one wants and needs to be.	- High degree of optimism about the future and willingness to take risks. - 67% view a college education as necessary for success 49% have taken early college courses with another 84% planning to.
Orienta-tion to Learning	- Learning is a process of acquiring prescribed subject matter. - Content units are sequenced according to the logic of the subject matter.	- Learners want to perform a task, solve a problem, live in a more satisfying way. - Learning must have relevance to real-life tasks, organized around life/work situations rather than subject matter units.	- Prefer to learn by doing, working through real life problems. - High desire to make a difference in the world around them. - Wants their learning to be connected with real world problems.

Method / Trait	Pedagogical	Andragogical	Generation Z
Motiva-tion for Learning	- Primarily motivated by external pressures, competition for grades, and the consequences of failure.	- Internal motivators: self-esteem, recognition, better quality of life, self-confidence, self-actualization.	- Largely internal motivators: love of learning, self-confident, thrive when challenged, career preparation, social impact.

between courses and students are able to receive extra help. This is specifically designed to improve retention rates.

Christian Adult Transformational Learning

One potential way forward can be seen through the work of Enoch Wan. Incorporating a biblical worldview into Meizerow's transformational learning theory, Wan arrives at an educational approach that is both relational and transformational.[367] This approach is summarized below.

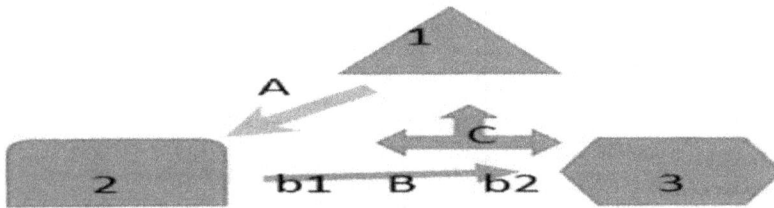

Beings/beings:
1 = Triune God; 2 = transformed teacher; 3 = learner

Interaction:
A = Triune God transforming teacher (vertical)
B = interaction between teacher & learner (horizontal)
    b1: External manifestation in teacher (special grace and appoint-ment as teacher):regeneration, calling, endowment and empowerment (vertical);
    b2: External manifestation in learner (general grace and provi-dential arrangement for learner) (vertical):
C = transformative learning (vertical + horizontal)

HORIZONTAL INTERACTION
— Divine level: within 1—— Father, Son, Holy Spirit horizontally and internally interacting in love with harmony
— Human level: within 2——teacher from Christian community trans-formed by the Triune God horizontally and internally interacting in love and with harmony

PROCESS
A — Christians (2) transformed by the Triune God (vertical)
B — teacher & learner establish relationship (horizontal)
C — then 2 is instrumental in the transformative learning of 3: thus b1 a b2 (vertical + horizontal)

Figure 21. Christian Adult Transformational Learning[368]

Wan's key contribution to transformative education was the inclusion of

---

[367] Enoch Wan and Mark Hedinger, "Transformative Ministry for the Majority World Context: Applying Relational Approaches," *Occasional Bulletin,* Spring 2018, 6.
[368] Wan and Hedinger, "Transformative Ministry," 7

the Relational Realism Paradigm.[369]

> Wan added complexity and accuracy to the concept of transformative education by reminding us that relationship with God is an important part of transformation, and that besides individual teacher/student relationships there is also the important and dynamic involvement of the *"koinonia* and *ecclesia"* – Christian fellowship and church."[370]

We have already seen how andragogical theories of adult learning are appropriate for Generation Z. Now we will see how the process of Christian Adult Transformational Learning is applicable to the Christian University environment using Calvary University as an example. Wan's figure below proposes a representation of the transformational process and progress beyond just the relationships that foster transformative education as seen above.

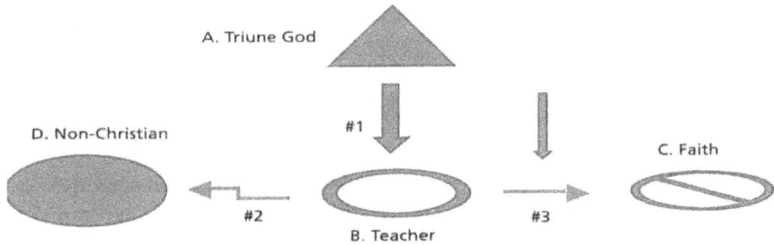

A: Triune God; B: teacher; C: faith community: *ecclesia, koinonia*, etc. (horizontal) D: Non-Christian community

Operational process:
#1 — regeneration, calling, endowment and empowerment (vertical)
#2 — Prior to learning
#3 — transformational change through interaction vertically and horizontally
Ø Interaction between teacher and learner (horizontal) leading to transformational change
Ø transformative change = divine aid + godly teacher's input + Christian learner's response

Figure 22. Relational Transformation: Process & Progress[371]

---

[369] Wan, "The Paradigm of 'Relational Realism,'" 1-6.
[370] Wan and Hedinger, "Transformative Ministry for the Majority World Context," 7.
[371] Wan and Hedinger, "Transformative Ministry for the Majority World Context," 7.

The next figure shows some slight variation in the process and process of relational transformation as applicable for the Christian university setting.

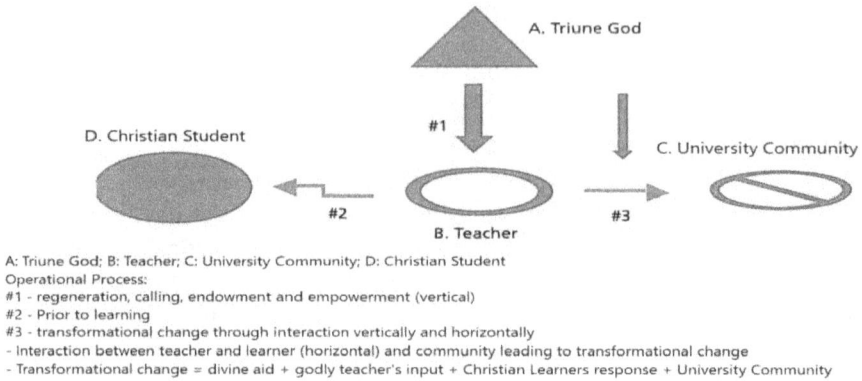

A: Triune God; B: Teacher; C: University Community; D: Christian Student
Operational Process:
#1 - regeneration, calling, endowment and empowerment (vertical)
#2 - Prior to learning
#3 - transformational change through interaction vertically and horizontally
- Interaction between teacher and learner (horizontal) and community leading to transformational change
- Transformational change = divine aid + godly teacher's input + Christian Learners response + University Community

Figure 23. Relational Transformation: Process & Progress in a Christian University

It can be seen how Christian Adult Transformational Education can be carried out in a university setting. The faith community of the student involves both the church and the university. Wan summarizes figures 11 with the following statement, "Transformative Change = divine aid + godly teacher's input + Christian learner's response (i.e. adults who are willing to grow and change can experience transformation by entering a relational community)."[372] In figure 12 I have added (+University Community) to note the role of the community in the process. Students at a Christian university are not only in meaningful relationship with God and their professors but in the wider community of fellow students, staff, faculty, visiting lecturers and more, to say nothing of their home churches.

Outcomes-based Education

Calvary University, like many universities in the U.S., focuses on an outcomes-based education. This is mandated by our two accrediting bodies: the Higher Learning Commission and The Association for Biblical Higher Education.[373] One way in which this is practically demonstrated is using curriculum mapping to trace the institution's objectives through departmental objectives and course objectives all the way down to individual assignments in courses.

Maureen Tam, at the Hong Kong Institute of Education in Hong Kong China,

---

[372] Wan and Hedinger, "Transformative Ministry for the Majority World Context," 8
[373] Calvary University Catalog 2018-2020, (Kansas City: Calvary University, 2018), 19.

has written an excellent and succinct article summarizing outcomes-based education. She states that its development and popularity has risen in large part with a need for quality assessment in higher education.[374] Gosling and Moon state, "The outcome-based approach has been increasingly adopted within credit frameworks and by national quality and qualification authorities."[375] This emphasis on assessment results in outcomes-based education has two starting points. One is for the institution. Outcomes-base education enables the institution to provide evidence to its accrediting agencies that it is in fact accomplishing what it claims and advertises to its constituents. The second, is in the program itself. Outcomes-based education promotes a more andragogical style of teaching that emphasizes student involvement in the learning process. This style has become increasingly popular, as Tam states, "International trends in higher education show a shift away from the teacher-centered model that emphasizes what is presented, towards the learner-based model focusing on what students know and can actually do."[376] While somewhat cliché, the purpose of an outcomes-based approach is to begin with the end in mind. The end goal of all education should not just be the sharing of the professor's pontification but the student's actual learning and growth. It is that transformation will take place, moving the student from a place of immaturity to a place of maturity and usefulness in the Body of Christ.

With the above in mind, there are three levels to outcomes-based education. This explanation will move from the broad to the more specific. The first level is that of the outcomes of the educational institution itself (IO's). These are broadly defined and specific to the assessment of the institution for quality and performance (accreditation).[377] The institution will collect various self-assessments from students as well as academic and non-academic departments to provide evidence that it is upholding what it claims to accomplish through its mission statement and institutional objectives. This evidence is then used as verification for the accreditation process. Since Synergy is a program at Calvary University it is Calvary's IO's that are relevant to this case.

The second level is the program or sometimes department level outcomes (PLO's). These outcomes are broadly defined, although specific to the program, as the desired development of the student as a result of completing

---

374 Maureen Tam, "Outcomes-based approach to quality assessment and curriculum improvement in higher education", *Quality Assurance in Education* 22 No. 2, (2014), 158-168.

375 David Gosling and Jenny Moon, *How to Use Learning Outcomes and Assessment Criteria*, (London: SEEC Office, 2001).

376 Tam, "Outcomes-based approach to quality assessment and curriculum improvement in higher education," 159.

377 Tam, "Outcomes-based approach to quality assessment and curriculum improvement in higher education," 161.

a program of study.[378] Each program within the university has its own PLO's that will be used to determine if the student has accomplished the purposes of the program and become a practitioner in their field. For example, does a program in pastoral ministry produce graduates who can pastor a church? Does a program in education produce graduates who can teach? The PLO's help the program director determine if the program is accomplishing its goals and adjust the program as necessary. Synergy is not technically an 'academic program' in that it does not lead to a degree. It is a collection of elective courses, taken as a whole. As such it is not subject to the same requirements of an academic program. While this allows for greater flexibility in the coursework, it creates the potential for less oversight and evaluation. In order to ensure that outcomes-based learning is taking place consistent with Synergy's partnership model and the goal of graduating students who are ready for the mission field, Synergy's PLO's will be developed based on the partner agency's "ideal candidate checklist" or interviews with agency leaders and mobilization directors. Gleaning insight from the agencies themselves on the qualities that are most needed in their missionary candidates will allow for the program to focus on what is truly necessary. The Synergy courses themselves are part of the Intercultural Studies concentration of the Ministry Studies Program. As such, the courses have the designation "IC" in front of their course number, and from the institution's perspective it is the Ministry Studies PLO's to which the Synergy courses must adhere.

Student Learning Outcomes (SLO's) form the final level of outcomes-based education. These are the learning outcomes that are typically tied directly to a course. They are the specific results of what a student should be able to do because of the learning acquired during that course.[379] SLO's are often framed by the cognitive, affective, and psychomotor categories put forth by Benjamin Bloom.[380] Cognitive outcomes (know) are those that refer to knowledge of the content itself. Definitions of term and understanding of theories and concepts are all aspects of the cognitive area. Affective outcomes (be) go deeper into the student's values and perspectives; the affective outcomes are typically the hardest to achieve as they impact the student's worldview, identity, and subsequent behavior. Finally, psychomotor outcomes (do) are those specific skills that the student has mastered because of the course content. Skills can include performing a task, such as writing a paper, or be more the attainment

---

[378] Tam, "Outcomes-based approach to quality assessment and curriculum improvement in higher education," 161.

[379] Tam, "Outcomes-based approach to quality assessment and curriculum improvement in higher education", 160.

[380] Benjamin Bloom, M.D. Engelhart, E.J. Furst, W. Hill, and D. Krathwohl, *Taxonomy of Educational Objectives, Volume 1: The Cognitive Domain*, (New York: McKay, 1959).

of new abilities, such as problem solving or cross-cultural communication.[381] SLO's are written utilizing specific verbs to convey the learning domain that they fall into.

One final step in the process that doesn't really represent a distinct level is tying the SLO's to student activities and assessments within the course. Having determined what the outcomes are for the student, then it is a natural process to find learning activities that will guide the student towards those outcomes and assessments that will help both the student and the teacher know when the SLO's have been achieved.

Relational Framework of Educational Design

Wan and Hedinger have developed a framework for education design that incorporates the elements mentioned thus far: relational realism, transformative andragogy, and outcomes-based education. Their design process is seen below.[382]

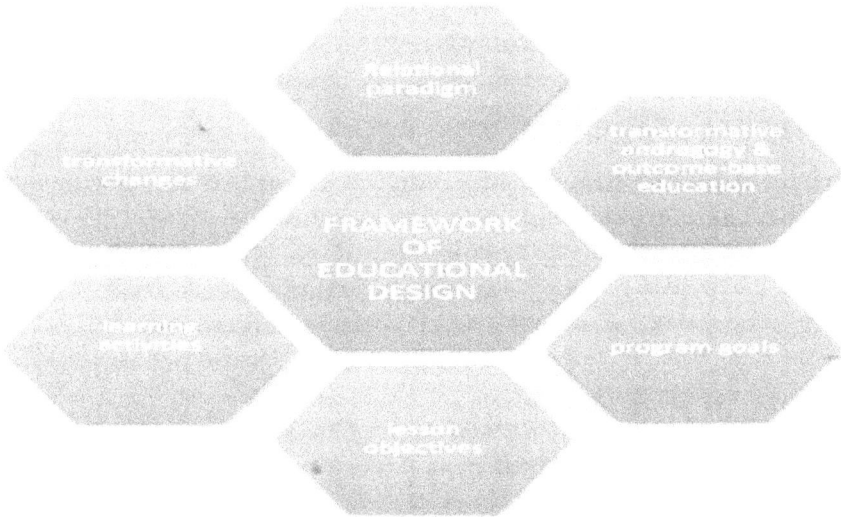

Figure 24. Cyclical Pattern of Transformative Process of Educational Design

1. Theological and theoretical foundation: relational paradigm.
2. Educational philosophy: transformative andragogy and outcome-based education.
3. Program Goals: cross-cultural missionary training.

---

[381] Tam, "Outcomes-based approach to quality assessment and curriculum improvement in higher education", 160.
[382] Wan and Hedinger, "Relational Missionary Training," 124.

4. Lesson Objectives: developmentally specific to particular stage.
5. Learning Activities: multiple dimensions of cognition, volition, affection and action.
6. Program Outcomes: transformative change in belief and behavior.
7. Cyclical: filtered through the theo-theoretical framework of "relational paradigm" and shaped by the educational philosophy of transformative andragogy and outcome-base.[383]

Wan and Hedinger's "Framework of Educational Design" integrates various elements that have thus far been considered. While not specific to a higher education environment with some slight changes, this framework is still relevant in that context. Changes to the above would chiefly be the consideration of the institutional outcomes as well as the program outcomes/goals. One other element that I briefly mentioned earlier in discussing the program learning outcomes is that those would be derived from the agency partners in Synergy. Where number 3, program goals, is listed as cross-cultural ministry training, the agency would be involved in determining these goals.

Experiential Learning

An important theory for consideration with Synergy is that developed by David Kolb and referred to as experiential learning.[384] Kolb's theory was that "learning is the process whereby knowledge is created through the

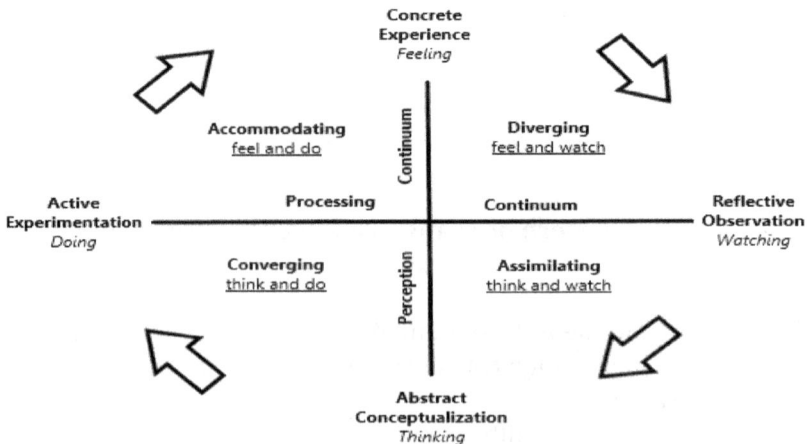

---

[383] Wan and Hedinger, *Relational Missionary Training*, 124-125.
[384] David Kolb, *Experiential Learning: Experience as the source of learning and development, Vol 1*, (Englewood Cliffs, NJ: Prentice-Hall, 1983).

transformation of experience."[385] Kolb's theory consists of two levels, a four-stage learning cycle and four separate learning styles.[386] Figure 12 is a diagram of Kolb's experiential learning and learning styles.[387]

Figure 25. Kolb's Experiential Learning Cycle

Kolb's learning styles are not a significant focus of this paper except to say that learning style theory's main contribution to education is to make the teacher aware that not all students learn the same way. There is no consensus as to who said it and it is frequently misattributed to Albert Einstein, but the quote, "Everybody is a genius, but if you judge a fish by its ability to climb a tree, it will live its whole life believing itself a failure," is appropriate to learning style theories. Some students learn best by lecture and some by experience and some by interacting with technology. Any educational framework should seek to accommodate multiple learning styles.

The key point for including Kolb's experiential learning theory is seen in the four stages of the cycle itself. These four steps (described below) are the key elements in the cycle.

1. Concrete Experience – the learner has a new experience or situation or a reinterpretation of a previous experience.
2. Reflective Observation – the learner notes differences between prior experience and the new experience.
3. Abstract Conceptualization – the learner's reflection allows for the creation of new concepts or modification of old concepts in order to make sense of the new experience and how to respond in the future.
4. Active Experimenting – the learner tries out the new concept in a similar situation in order to validate the concept; if all goes well the learner knows how to better handle the situation in the future, but if not, the cycle continues.[388]

Note that the experiential learning cycle includes Bloom's learning dimensions of cognitive (watching, thinking), affective (feeling), and behavioral (doing). The two theories are congruent with each other. Some debate remains regarding the starting point of the cycle. Muriel and Duane Elmer consider both theories in the creation of their own learning cycle.[389] Their critique of Bloom is that the three domains are not integrated

---

[385] Kolb, *Experiential Learning*, 38.

[386] Saul McLeod, "Kolb's Learning Styles and Experiential Learning Cycle," *Simply Psychology*, accessed July 9, 2020, https://www.simplypsychology.org/simplypsychology.org-Kolb-Learning-Styles.pdf.

[387] Adapted from; Mcleod, "Kolb's Learning Styles and Experiential Learning."

[388] McLeod, "Kolb's Learning Styles and Experiential Learning Cycle."

[389] Muriel J. and Duane H. Elmer, *The Learning Cycle: Insights for Faithful Teaching from Neuroscience and the Social Sciences*, (Downers Grove: IVP, 2020).

sufficiently to represent the reality of life and that the cognitive domain is overly emphasized.[390] Their chief problem with Kolb's theory is that Kolb begins with experience as the "driving force," and they would rather begin with the content and have truth be the driving force for learning.[391] I will next consider the Elmer's model as they attempt to integrate Bloom and Kolb within their own framework.

The Learning Cycle

The Elmers have developed their learning cycle after years of research and experience in education. Its similarities to Bloom, Kolb, and Wan and Hedinger's models are immediately apparent in Figure 12.[392]

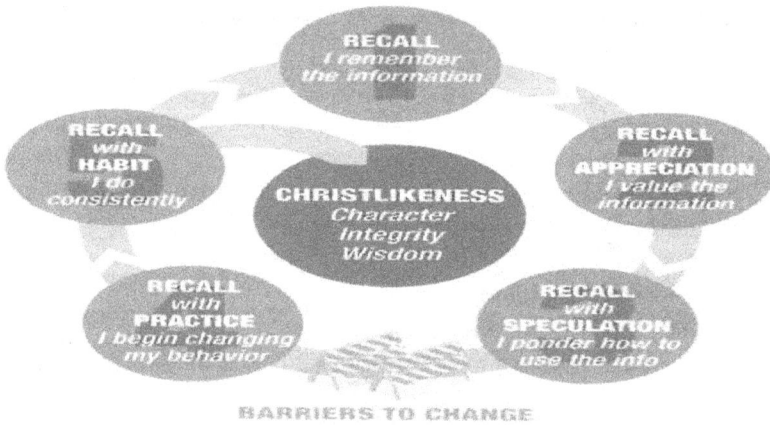

Figure 26. The Learning Cycle (Elmers)

As shown above, the Elmer's learning cycle model includes 5 steps intended to integrate learning with real life. These five steps they can be seen to fit within Bloom's domains. There is also a distinct resemblance to experiential learning as the Elmer's admit they were influenced by both theories. Consistent with their belief that the content takes priority, the first step in the Learning Cycle is recalling the information itself. This is similar with Bloom's emphasis on the cognitive domain. Knowledge of the content becomes the important first step in this process. Calvary University must demonstrate to its accreditors that students are progressing through Bloom's cognitive domains of knowledge, comprehension, application, analysis,

---

390 Elmer and Elmer, *The Learning* Cycle, 9.
391 Elmer and Elmer, *The Learning* Cycle, 10.
392 Elmer and Elmer, *The Learning Cycle*, 7.

synthesis, and evaluation.[393] The main way that this happens at a higher education institute is through course leveling. Courses are applied a 100, 200, 300, or 400 level designation, dependent on the course content being appropriate for students at that level. It is expected that first year students taking 100 level courses will be primarily focused on knowledge development, 200 and 300 level courses have some knowledge content but primarily deal with application of the knowledge from earlier courses. A 400-level course is expected to bring the student to the level of synthesis, evaluating or even creating their own knowledge based on what they have previously studied.

The second and third steps in Elmer's model progress into the affective dimension as students begin to internalize the content and make it their own. This is consistent with Bloom as well as the *feeling* and *watching* aspects of Kolb's experiential learning. The fourth and fifth steps then proceed into the behavioral category of Bloom or the active experimentation stage of Kolb. While each model brings unique aspects and different emphasis to the discussion, three fundamental pieces continually come up again and again. Regardless of the cycle or the starting point in the learning process, knowledge (know), being (be), and doing (do) are the three key elements involved in learning that result in transformation. An overreliance on any one area leads to problems in the development of the student.

Learning Contracts as a Means of Transformational Learning

One way that the literature review has already impacted Synergy is the use of learning contracts as a means of facilitating the transition from pedagogical to andragogical learning. As demonstrated above, Gen Z fits most of the principles for andragogy. However, one area of concern for them, is coming out of a highly pedagogical environment that is teacher-driven and having difficulty transitioning to a student-driven approach. Learning contracts are one way of helping the student take the initiative in the learning process and help them understand that they are an active participant, not just a passive receiver.

Perry Shaw writes an excellent work entitled *Transforming Theological Education* in which he details the journey of Arab Baptist Theological Seminary in developing an integrated approach to learning throughout their curriculum.[394] Several statements that Shaw makes indicate that he is applying similar theories to his work as that represented by Christian Adult Transformational Education. Shaw writes, "An essential element of building

---

[393] Perry Shaw, *Transforming Theological Education: A Practical Handbook for Integrative Learning*, (Carlisle, Cumbria: Langham Global Library, 2014), 162-163.
[394] Shaw, *Transforming Theological Education*, 1.

intentionality into a program of ministerial training is to teach students how to self-educate…"[395] Shaw also points out the importance of relationship, especially relationships with God in a learning paradigm of theological education.[396]

Learning contracts are one of the elements that were implemented at Arab Baptist Theological Seminary (ABTS). For ABTS; learning contracts are implemented in the second year following the completion of foundational learning in the first year.[397] Implementing learning contracts with the student even from the very beginning will help them to recognize the importance of being self-directed and also show them why the foundational material that is covered in the first year of studies is so vital to everything else. Students who understand why they need to learn something will be more motivated to put forth the necessary effort. Shaw writes,

> As with all curricular elements outside the classroom, quality learning contracts entail careful planning in which students' detail what they desire to learn, why they perceive this learning to be significant for their future ministries, in what activities they intend to engage themselves towards accomplishing the learning, and how their learning might be assessed.[398]

Learning contracts provide great potential in allowing the student, even in their first year, to recognize the role that they play in their own education. A contract could also be designed in such a way, as to emphasize the role that mentors, the church community, ministries, and pastors play in the life of the student.

In keeping with the changing nature of education and expanding theories on how learning is achieved, an overall change to andragogical teaching principles at the university level is highly encouraged. This switch also allows for the practical implementation of theories such as Christian Adult Transformational Learning which include an understanding of the importance of the relationship between not only the teacher and the student, but God and the learning community as well.

Mobilizing Generation Z for Christian Missions

Introduction

It is no secret that the Church in the West faces many obstacles in reaching the unreached, not only abroad but in our own postmodern communities.

---

[395] Shaw, *Transforming Theological Education*, 40.
[396] Shaw, *Transforming Theological Education*, 68.
[397] Shaw, *Transforming Theological Education*, 7.
[398] Shaw, *Transforming Theological Education*, 115.

Church membership is drastically down in the United States.[399] More and more members of recent generations are identifying as either Atheist or what has come to be called "nones", in that they have no religious affiliation at all.[400] Even among churched and engaged Christians in the United States involvement in missions activities is shrinking even while it is on the rise in much of the majority world.[401] I have taught in a Christian University for the past nine years and one class I teach that every Calvary University student is required to take is Introduction to Christian Missions. While it is anecdotal to my own experience, I can attest to seeing over the past nine years that more and more students are arriving at Calvary with very little knowledge of missions or why it is an important element in a biblical worldview.

The purpose of this section is to examine some of the contemporary research on Gen Z and what lies behind their motivations. What are the primary motivating factors that this generation is considering in making long term life decisions? How does that compare to some of the traditional ways that the Church has expressed a motivation or calling for missionary service and how might we as the Church need to engage them differently? In the context of partnerships between the local church, mission agency, and theological school, which one of these plays the biggest role in motivating this generation and how might the others come alongside to assist?

Traditional Motivations for Missions

There may well be as many motivations for engaging in missions work as there are believers. To begin, let's examine some of the most common motivating factors and then compare them to current research on Generation Z and their values.

Before discussing motivations for missions, it is important to here define what is meant by missions in the traditional sense. As the research seems to indicate it is possible that one reason for Gen Z's lack of movement towards missions could be the nature in which it has been presented to them. From a Western perspective, missions has traditionally been viewed as a task to be completed. George Peters definition of missions reflects this mentality,

---

[399] Jeffery M. Jones, "U.S. Church Membership Down Sharply in Past Two Decades," *Gallup*, accessed March 17, 2020, https://news.gallup.com/poll/248837/church-membership-down-sharply-past-two-decades.aspx.

[400] James Emery White, *The Rise of the Nones: Understanding and Reaching the Religiously Unaffiliated,* (Grand Rapids: Baker Books, 2014), 16-17.

[401] Center for the Study of Global Christianity, "Christianity in its Global Context, 1970-2020: Society, Religion, and Mission," Gordon Conwell Theological Seminary, accessed March 17, 2020, https://archive.gordonconwell.edu/ockenga/research/documents/ChristianityinitsGlobalContext.pdf.

Missions is a specialized term. By it I mean the sending forth of authorized persons beyond the borders of the New Testament church and her immediate gospel influence to proclaim the gospel of Jesus Christ in gospel-destitute areas, to win converts from other faiths or non-faiths to Jesus Christ, and to establish functioning, multiplying local congregations who will bear the fruit of Christianity in that community and to that country.[402]

Another, shorter definition and one I have used in my own teaching, is that given by C. Gordon Olson, "missions is the whole task, endeavor, and program of the Church of Christ to reach out across geographical and/or cultural boundaries by sending missionaries to evangelize people who have never heard or who have little opportunity to hear the saving gospel."[403]

These definitions have much to commend them and are by no means incorrect in defining the task of missions. However, therein lies a potential problem in conversations with Generation Z and that is the focus on missions as a task. In contextualizing missions for this next generation how do we communicate with them in a way that is simultaneously biblical and meets them in their own context? I will continue to explore this question later, for now let us turn to the traditional motivations for missions, I will focus on three; the call, reaching the lost, and expanding God's glory. I should note upfront that though I will be critiquing these with a view to that which appeals to Generation Z, all of them are potential motivators for missions. There is no reason to narrow God's work in expressing His will for us to reach the lost down to one element, to do so would restrict Him and practice reductionism.

The Call

Perhaps still the most pervasive motivator for someone to engage in any kind of ministry is the idea of being called specifically by God to do that work. George Peter's spends a significant portion of his text, *A Biblical Theology of Missions* expounding on the concept of calling as it is laid out in scripture. He points out first that scripture elucidates to three separate and distinct calls; the call to salvation, the call to discipleship, and the call to the ministry of the Word.[404]

It is the call to ministry which is in reference here as to this prevalent

---

[402] George Peters, *A Biblical Theology of Missions*, (Chicago: Moody Press, 1972).
[403] C. Gordon Olson, *What in the World is God Doing? The Essentials of Global Missions*, 7th ed. (Lynchburg, VA: Global Gospel Publishers, 2013), 11.
[404] Peters, *A Biblical Theology of Missions*, 270.

mindset that there are some believers who are specifically called to missions or the pastorate or other ministries and others are not. The primary evidence that Peters' gives for the concept of calling is the many examples that we have in the Bible of God specifically calling people to a certain ministry. These examples include but are not limited to; the twelve (Mark 3:13-14, John 15:16), Barnabus and Saul (Acts 13:1-4), as well as "Moses, Aaron, Joshua, David, Isaiah, Jeremiah, Jonah and Amos."[405]

The first challenge that we might raise to the issue of calling is the difference between that which is prescriptive and that which is descriptive. Herein lies an important hermeneutical principle that just because something is recorded in the Bible does not mean that it is applicable to all people for all time, nor that it is God's normal practice. Prescriptive, refers to those directly applicable principles that we find in scripture which are timeless and for all people, for all time. An example would be to abstain from sexual immorality in 1 Thess. 4:3. Descriptive, simply means that the Bible is describing an event that took place.[406] To recognize this distinction is to understand that no matter how many times or people God called to a specific task in Scripture does not mean that He will call everyone to a specific task.

A quick study of 1 Timothy 3:1 would also seem to contradict the notion of a special divine call as necessary for ministry in general. "The saying is trustworthy: If anyone <u>aspires</u> to the office of overseer, he <u>desires</u> a noble task" (emphasis mine). Two different Greek words are in view here; ὀρέγεται, translated "aspires" above and can mean, to be eager for, long for, or desire[407]; and ἐπιθυμεῖ, which is a similar but stronger word that in its widest sense can even mean to covet or lust for something.[408] 1 Timothy 3 continues on to give qualifications for elders and then deacons, almost all of which are character traits of the individual in question. The prescriptive principle to be found here then, is not if the person has received a divine call, but rather a simpler do they want to do the work of that ministry and are they qualified for it? J. Herbert Kane says it rather plainly, "The term *missionary call* should never have been coined. It is not Scriptural and therefore can be harmful. Thousands of youths desiring to serve the Lord have waited and waited for some mysterious 'missionary call' that never came."[409]

While I would not challenge the student, who tells me that they feel called

---

[405] Peters, *A Biblical Theology of Missions*, 272-273.

[406] Henry A. Virkler, *Hermeneutics: Principles and Processes of Biblical Interpretation,* (Grand Rapids: Baker Books, 1981), 86.

[407] J. H, Moulton and G. Milligan, *Vocabulary of the Greek New Testament*, 2nd printing, (Peabody: Hendrickson Publishers, 2004), 456.

[408] Moulton and Milligan, *Vocabulary of the Greek New Testament,* 239.

[409] J. Herbert Kane, *Understanding Christian Missions*, 2nd ed. (Grand Rapids: Baker, 1982), 41.

to missions and that is their primary motivator, I would seek for them to explain what they mean by that. Typically, the answer is better described as a pattern of guidance or direction as opposed to a one-time experience. Another challenge to the notion of calling is the reality that all believers are sent on God's mission. The clearest indication of this is in 2 Corinthians 5:18-20, Paul writes,

> All this is from God, who through Christ reconciled us to himself and gave us the ministry of reconciliation; that is, in Christ God was reconciling the world to himself, not counting their trespasses against them and entrusting to us the message of reconciliation. Therefore, we are ambassadors for Christ, God making his appeal through us. We implore you on behalf of Christ, be reconciled to God.

The motivation for spreading the gospel is the reconciled nature of all believers and that all believers who have been thus reconciled have this ministry of reconciliation. While I will not go so far as to say all Christians are "missionaries", we are all "witnesses".[410]

Finally, a study on calling conducted by Jason Pieratt on the *Lived Experiences of American and Majority World Missionaries of Children's Relief International* (CRI) revealed some interesting conclusions on the concept of calling.[411] After an extensive literature review and interviewing missionaries with CRI Pieratt noted that the experience of calling is better described as "progressive experience" instead of a powerful religious one.[412] The concept of calling while being articulated by many both biblically and through interviews was in reality the confluence of numerous life experiences that God used to lead an individual into ministry, missions specifically. Pieratt indicates that one of the most common aspects of this progressive experience is relationships.[413] An interesting conclusion in light of research on Generation Z that highlights the importance of relationships to them.

Reaching the Lost: The Need Constitutes the Call

Another common motivator for missions is the concept that the need constitutes the call. Simply put, the mentality is that those who engage in

---

[410] Terms have meaning and significance in how we use them. The modern over usage of the term "missionary" has led to many misunderstandings of what a missionary is and does. Most common, is that the term is associated with how someone makes their income not their ministry. The term is rooted in the Greek word *apostelo*.

[411] Jason Pieratt, "Calling to the Missionary Vocation: A Study of the Lived Experiences of American and Majority World Missionaries of Children's Relief International," (DIS Dissertation, Western Seminary, Portland, 2018).

[412] Pieratt, "Calling to the Missionary Vocation," 112.

[413] Pieratt, "Calling to the Missionary Vocation," 113.

reaching the lost should focus on those areas of the world where the gospel has the least amount of access. Oswald Smith perfectly captured this line of thought when he said, "Why should anyone have a chance to hear the gospel twice until all have had a chance to hear it once?"[414] This line of thinking has much to commend it. Jesus, himself, told us, "The harvest is plentiful, but the laborers are few; therefore, pray earnestly to the Lord of the harvest to send out laborers into his harvest."[415]

Indeed, the harvest is plentiful, while figures vary the highest estimates put the total number of unreached people in the world today at around 3.2 billion, close to 40% of the global population.[416] Perhaps no figure represents this mentality better than the contrast between two maps created by the Traveling Team. Figure 14 indicates the non-Christian population in millions. Figure 15 indicates where missionaries are going.

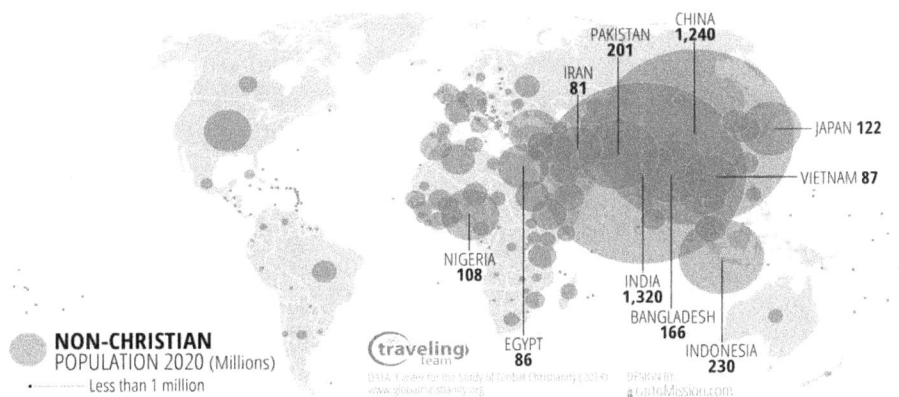

Figure 27. Non-Christian Population in Millions[417]

[414] Oswald J. Smith, quoted in: Olson, *What in the World is God Doing*, 77.
[415] Matthew 9:37b-38 (ESV)
[416] Joshua Project, *Status of World Evangelization*, accessed March 23, 2020, https://joshuaproject.net/assets/media/handouts/status-of-world-evangelization.pdf.
[417] The Traveling Team, *Missions Statistics*, accessed March 23, 2020, http://www.thetravelingteam.org/stats.

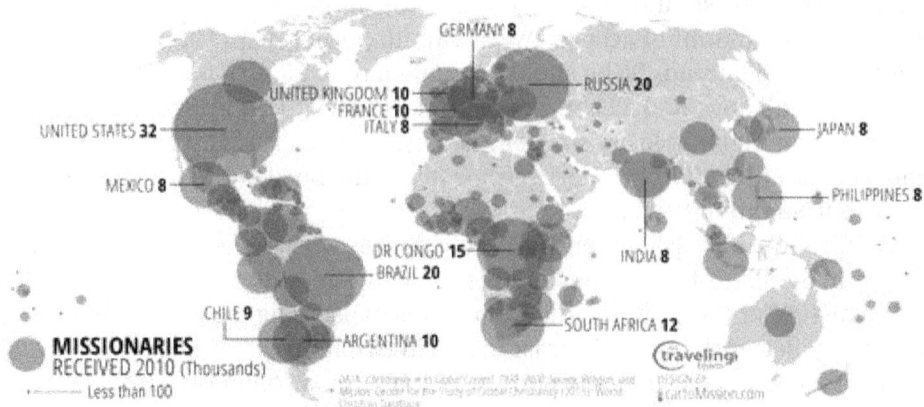

Figure 28. Missionaries Received in Thousands[418]

The difference between these two pictures is staggering. Clearly, there is an imbalance between where the areas of greatest need are and where the missionaries are going. If indeed it is true that the need constitutes the call, then not very many people are listening to that call and going to the areas of greatest need.

Jesus told many parables that emphasized his and the Father's heart for reaching the lost. Luke 15 records the parables of the Lost Sheep, the Lost Coin and the Prodigal Son. Jesus says in Luke 19:10 that part of his reason for coming was to "seek and to save the lost." The Bible presents a clear emphasis on the lostness of mankind and Christ's provision for salvation.[419] While there is a clear emphasis throughout the Bible on the lostness of mankind and God's desire to save us. Does this constitute enough of a motivation to forsake home, family, and career and venture out into the world as a career missionary? While the imbalance between where the gospel is needed most and where missionaries are going is plain to see what arguments can be made against a sole focus on the need as a primary motivator for missions? While the need is clear and desire of our Father to reach the lost is clear this motivation is still very task oriented.

J. Hampton Keathley III, deals with this question of needs and calling in his *ABC's of Christian Growth*. Speaking on the 'stewardship of time' Keathley says, "The fact is there will always be more to do than we can ever accomplish whether we are talking about needs, work, leisure, travel, or you name it. The need does not constitute the call."[420] He continues to make the example of

---

[418] The Traveling Team, *Missions Statistics*.

[419] (Gen 1:26,27, 3; Psalm 51:4, 5; John 3:16-18; Rom. 1:18-32; 3:23, 24; 5:12-30; 6:23; 10:9, 10; 1 Cor. 15:1-5)

[420] J. Hampton Keathley, *The ABC's of Christian Growth: Laying the Foundation*, (Biblical Studies Press, 2013), 361.

Christ Himself, who during His three and half years of ministry could say at the end of it, "I glorified you on Earth, having accomplished the work that you gave me to do."[421] Jesus did not heal everyone, he did not drive out every demon, He did not meet every need. His goal was to do the will of the Father and as such his motivation was based on something much higher than simply meeting needs. "Jesus saw the needs, but he saw them through the Father's will."[422]

The Glory of God

The view that the primary motivator for missions is for the Glory of God was best popularized by John Piper in his well-known work *Let the Nations be Glad*.[423] The now oft quoted and famous line from that book that encapsulates the entire theory is that "missions exists because worship doesn't."[424] Piper spends the next 228 pages of this work expounding on this principle. His basic argument being that God deserves all the glory, however because of the fall he is not receiving the glory that is due to Him and as such we engage in proclaiming his name to the nations in order to bring Him more glory. This view has much to commend it and it is a scripturally accurate reason for engaging in missions work. Piper spends five pages of his book over to quoting verse after verses which clearly speaks to God's glory as a motivating factor for all that he does. The glory of God is a clear motif that spreads throughout all of Scripture so much so that the Westminster Shorter Catechism declares that "man's chief end is to glorify God and enjoy him forever."[425]

As Louis Jacob Cloud discusses in his literature review several other authors have touched on the doxological motivation for missions including, Cotton Mather, Samuel Hopkins, Jonathan Edwards, John Stott and more recently Michael Pocock.[426] However, Cloud contends that his study is the first scholarly treatment of doxological missiology. "There is no research that brings these subjects together (mission motivation, psychological motivation, doxology) in an interdisciplinary approach."[427] Cloud lays a solid scriptural foundation for the glory of God as the chief motivating factor in missions. He takes issue with the modern emphasis on pragmatic approaches that focus on

---

[421] John 17:4, ESV.

[422] Keathley, *The ABC's of Christian Growth*, 362.

[423] John Piper, *Let the Nations be Glad: The Supremacy of God in Missions*. (Grand Rapids: Baker, 1993).

[424] Piper, *Let the Nations be Glad*, 11.

[425] *The Westminster Shorter Catechism*, accessed March 23, 2020, https://www.apuritansmind.com/westminster-standards/shorter-catechism/.

[426] Louis Jacob Cloud, "Doxological Missiology: Theory, Motivation, and Practice," (DIS Dissertation, Western Seminary, Portland, 2020).

[427] Cloud, "Doxological Missiology," 31.

results as determined by number of people or financial support.[428]

To bring glory to God is one aim of all of creation, and it was clearly a motivating factor for Jesus as he declares in John 17:1-5. To bring glory to God should be a reason behind everything that we do as believers in Christ and not limited to being a motivator for missions. Indeed, Cloud applies doxological missiology to several areas, including theological education.[429] The thought that by engaging in missions we can somehow better glorify God than by working a 9-5 job or being a trash collector has only contributed to the mentality that places missionaries on an unnecessary pedestal and sets them up as super saints. As missionaries too are but sinners saved by grace alone through faith alone.[430] While Scripture presents a clear picture of glorifying God, that picture is in the context of everything that we are to be and do as believers. If we eat or drink it is for God's glory (1 Corinthians 10:31); whatever you do, do everything in the name of the Lord Jesus (Colossians 3:17), those who speak and serve should do in a way that glorifies God (1 Peter 4:11). While glorifying God is one clear motivating factor for missions activity, glorifying God should be the reason behind all that we do and should not be limited merely to missions.

The Dangers of Reductionism

The reality for most of these concepts of motivations for missions is not an issue of them being good or bad but rather of focus and emphasis. Other reasons for evangelism, missions and just plain proclaiming the gospel exist: the character of God,[431] the content of Scripture, the command of Christ,[432] the cross of Christ.[433] There are many and even multiple reasons for following the Lord's guidance into proclaiming the gospel to the lost. The primary problem lies in choosing just one. God never has only one thing in mind. It is our human mind's finite capacity which leads us in many situations to try and find the one reason or the best reason behind why something happens the way it does, believing that in doing so we can somehow highlight the problem and then fix the problem. Most motivations, as covered so far, are task oriented. Originating, as they have, primarily from a Western, functionalist mindset they focus on what needs to be accomplished. The tendency then, is to reduce

---

[428] Cloud, "Doxological Missiology," 82.

[429] Cloud, "Doxological Missiology," 82.

[430] Ephesians 2:8, 9

[431] Robert E. Spear during the Duff Lectures in 1910 declared, "It is in the very being and character of God that the deepest ground of the missionary enterprise is to be found."

[432] Typically given as the Great Commission (Matthew 28:18-20; Mark 16:15, Luke 24:46-47; John 20-21; Acts 1:8).

[433] (John 3:16-18; Romans 5:8; 1 John 4:14; John 14:6; Acts 4:12; 1 Cor. 15:1-5; Rom. 10:9-10; 1 Tim. 2:5, 6)

missions down to a task, that once finished will result in the Lord's return.[434] The chief danger that lies in this task-oriented approach is that we once again lose focus on the work that God is doing and place more emphasis on the work that we are doing. Cloud also takes issue with the problem of pragmatism in missions in offering doxological missiology as an alternative.[435] However, as important as the glory of God is, it too can become pragmatic if we lose focus on relationships and try to measure how much glory we are bringing Him.

I will now turn my attention to the research behind Generation Z with a view to what motivates them. While this section seeks to provide a way forward for contextualizing missions for Generation Z, the caution is to do so while still presenting the whole council of God.

Shaping a Generation

James Emery White gives 5 key characteristics that define Generation Z in order to help us understand who we are talking about. It is important to keep in view that both White and Barna focus on the generation "as a whole" while this study is concerned mostly for those who are already Christ followers and engaged in a local Church.

Every generation has its defining moments and Gen Z is no exception. The first characteristic that White gives is that they are recession minded.[436] In contrast to the Millennials (the generation preceding them) who experienced the economic boom and relative peace of the 90's, Gen Z has been marked by the war on terror and the so called Great Recession of 2007-2009.[437] The result of this according to White has been a strong desire for economic security and wanting to make a difference.[438] The study conducted by Barna further supports this view of Gen Z, 43% of whom believe that happiness is defined by financial success.[439] Barna gives this as one of their six trends shaping this generation, "between the financial crisis and perpetual war, they are apt to be distrustful of the future."[440] Barna lists two similar characteristics in this realm, the first is that "safe spaces" are normal and the

---

[434] The eschatological motivation for missions is perfectly captured by such organizations as "call2all", which use Matthew 24:14 as a proof text that Jesus will return once all people groups have heard the gospel. https://www.call2all.org/finish-lines/, (accessed March 23, 2020).

[435] Cloud, "Doxological Missiology," 83.

[436] James Emery White, *Meet Generation Z: Understanding and Reaching the New Post-Christian World*, (Grand Rapids: Baker Books, 2017), 39.

[437] Pamela Paul, "The Playground Gets Even Tougher," *New York Times*, October 8, 2010, https://www.nytimes.com/2010/10/10/fashion/10Cultural.html.

[438] White, *Meet Gen Z*, 40.

[439] Barna, *Gen Z*, 13.

[440] Barna, *Gen Z*, 13.

second that real safety is a myth.[441] Gen Z has been raised in an environment that is highly concerned with the psychological impact of words and actions on the feelings of others. As such they have developed a collective aversion to offense. However, with the financial crises and a post 9-11 world that has constantly been at war they have no illusions of real security. One defining characteristic that was not mentioned in any research, is that Gen Z has grown up in a time of unprecedented school shootings in the United States. Since the Columbine shooting in Colorado there have been a total of 229 school shootings in the United States.[442] Security and safety are major concerns for this generation. Barna further gives another characteristic regarding Gen Z's parents. They summarize it by saying that in many ways Gen Z's parents have been "overinvolved in many of the wrong ways and too detached in others."[443] Barna refers to this as "double-minded parenting" in which Gen Z's parents have in some ways followed the helicopter parenting style of limiting children's independence and freedom to explore on their own but on the other side given them free access and reign when it comes to the internet, technology and entertainment which has exposed them to many adult concepts at a very young age.[444]

The second characteristic is that they are "always on." Generation Z has grown up in a world where the internet has always been available to them. The first smartphone was released in 1992, three years before this generation was born and when the first members of this generation were turning 12 the first iPhone was launched, changing the world of cell phones forever.[445] As of June of 2019, Pew Research Center reports that 96% of Americans now own a cell phone of some kind and 81% of them are smartphones.[446] All of this leads to one startling conclusion, that Gen Z is able to access any information the world has to offer without the help of someone guiding them. Again the Barna study agrees, citing that 57% of Gen Z, use screen media for four or more hours per day.[447] They have been labeled "screenagers," "digital native," and "iGen" for this very reason.[448] This has even led to a new psychological condition known as "nomophobia," described as a feeling of anxiety whenever

---

[441] Barna, *Gen Z*, 27-28.

[442] Gabe Turner, "A Timeline of School Shootings Since Columbine," Security Baron, accessed March 25, 2020, https://securitybaron.com/blog/a-timeline-of-school-shootings-since-columbine/.

[443] Barna, *Gen Z*, 35.

[444] Barna, *Gen Z*, 35.

[445] Text Request, "The History and Evolution of the Smartphone: 1992-2018," accessed March 24, 2020, https://www.textrequest.com/blog/history-evolution-smartphone/.

[446] Pew Research Center, "Mobile Fact Sheet," accessed March 24, 2020, https://www.pewresearch.org/internet/fact-sheet/mobile/.

[447] Barna, *Gen Z*, 13.

[448] Barna, *Gen Z*, 15.

they are separated from the mobile devices.[449] However, an interesting trend has taken place as a result of this incredible connectivity. While on the one hand Gen Z utilizes social media to a high degree and sees it as building a personal brand. This brand is often viewed by them as inauthentic.[450] As a result, White indicates that only 15% of Gen Z prefer to use social media to interact with their friends.[451] All of this points to a reality that while Gen Z is comfortable with technological interaction and tools, they desire real relationships. They are skeptical of how people present themselves on social media and primarily use it to interact with friends. Barna reports that 91% of Gen Z uses social media primarily to "talk" with friends and relatives.[452] According to White, "only 15% prefer to interact with their friends via social media rather than face-to-face.[453] Generation Z is also one of the most diverse generations in history, a trend which is only going to continue, as the demographics of the Barna study indicate. [454]

White further points to the growing trends of multiracial marriages, stating that "when the 2020 census is conducted, it is estimated that more than half of all US children will be part of a minority race or ethnic group."[455] For Generation Z ethnic and cultural diversity is a normal factor of life. However, another type of diversity is also shaping this generation.

White's fourth characteristic of Generation Z is that they are sexually fluid.[456] Leaving out all the potential ramifications of this characteristic that are not the focus of this study. The most relevant is one that White points out, "the greatest value for this generation is nothing less than individual freedom."[457] Closely related, Barna highlights personal achievement as being the most central aspect of Gen Z's identity.[458] The ever-increasing nature of personal freedom, choice, and self-expression has been a hallmark of this generation. A defining moment for them has been the 2015 Supreme Court decision to legalize gay marriage. Barna reports that 12% describe themselves as transgender and 69% believe it is acceptable to be born one gender and feel like another.[459]

While Western culture has prized individualism for a long time, Generation

---

[449] Tim Elmore, "Nomophobia: A Rising Trend in Students," in *Psychology Today*, accessed March 24, 2020, https://www.psychologytoday.com/us/blog/artificial-maturity/201409/nomophobia-rising-trend-in-students.

[450] Barna, *Gen Z*, 20.

[451] White, *Meet Gen Z*, 45.

[452] Barna, *Gen Z*, 18.

[453] White, *Meet Gen Z*, 45.

[454] Barna, *Gen Z*, 30.

[455] White, *Meet Gen Z*, 46.

[456] White, *Meet Gen Z*, 46.

[457] White, *Meet Gen Z*, 48.

[458] Barna, *Gen Z*, 41.

[459] Barna, *Gen Z*, 40.

Z is taking it to new extremes. This has long term repercussions for how they are motivated and how they make decisions on where to spend their time. It remains to be seen what the long-term ramifications will be of the Coronavirus Pandemic. The United States and many other nations were placed on lockdown and many people where quarantined or self-confined to their own homes as we practiced 'social distancing' to stem the tide of this disease. It remains to be seen what impact this event will have on Generation Z's development, but it is already driving more and more people to use electronic means of keeping in touch with one another.

The fifth and final characteristic that White highlights for Generation Z, and that is also supported by Barna and many others, is that Generation Z is the first post-Christian generation.[460] Over the years that Barna has been doing research the percentage of those with a biblical worldview in each succeeding generation has been steadily declining. With Boomers it was 10%; Generation X was 7%; Millennials was 6%; and now Generation Z is a mere 4%.[461] The largest faith group in Generation Z is those who say they have no faith at all. Barna reports that 34% of Generation Z, more than any group before them, when asked about their religious affiliation simply choose "none of the above."[462] James Emery White records this rise of the religiously unaffiliated in his book *The Rise of the Nones*.[463] White refers to this trend as a "second fall," a functional atheism that simply does not result from considering religion and rejecting it but from not considering it at all.[464] In the next section I will examine how these characteristics have contributed to Generation Z's motivations.

---

[460] White, *Meet Gen Z*, 49.
[461] Barna, *Gen Z*, 25.
[462] Barna, *Gen Z*, 26.
[463] James Emery White, *The Rise of the Nones: Understanding and Reaching the Religiously Unaffiliated*, (Grand Rapids: Baker Books, 2014).
[464] White, *Meet Gen Z*, 20.

Table 15. Summary of Generation Z Characteristics

Defining Characteristics of Generation Z	
White[465]	Barna[466]
Recession Marked	Safe Spaces vs. Real Safety
Wi-Fi Enabled	Screenagers
Multiracial	Diverse
Sexually Fluid	
Post-Christian	Post-Christian
	Double-Minded Parents

Motivating Factors

In a very real sense Generation Z has grown up as a generation of children that had the proverbial blinders of childhood violently ripped from their faces. Whether as a result of the economic downturn, school shootings, constant conflict or changing gender norms, they have not had the luxury of ignorant childhood bliss. The chief result of all of this has been an increasing desire for safety and security. "Between the financial crises and perpetual war, they are apt to be distrustful of the future."[467] They desire economic security but also to make a real difference in the world around them. "Two thirds want to finish their education (66%), start a career (66%) and become financially independent (65%) by age 30."[468] One clear motivating factor for this generation is a sense of personal achievement that is also tied into financial security and contributing to the world around them. Research conducted by Sparks and Honey reveals that social entrepreneurship is one of their most popular career choices.[469] While Gen Z wants security, they want to make a difference. This desire for both security and to contribute has unique implications for how churches, schools, and mission agencies engage in mobilizing them for missions.

Generation Z is always on. Using technology, social media and constantly being in touch with friends, family members. They utilize it for everything from relationships to learning. This constant connectivity has many effects on them, some of which are only now being discovered and many more that may yet remain unknown. Two considerations for this study are the impact that

---

465 White, *Meet Gen Z.*
466 Barna, *Gen Z.*
467 Barna, *Gen Z*, 29.
468 Barna, *Gen Z*, 40.
469 "Meet Generation Z: Forget Everything You Learned about Millennials," Sparks and Honey, June 17, 2014, https://www.slideshare.net/sparksandhoney/generation-z-final-june-17.

this connectivity has on their need for guidance and the demonstrated reality of their desire for real relationships.

First, Generation Z has all the collective knowledge of humanity at their fingertips, but they struggle to sift through it all. The recent rise of "fake news" has only served to highlight the double-edged sword effect of this access to information technology. Coupled with the research that suggests that many of Gen Z's parents have given them unfettered access to the internet the result is a clear conclusion that they need guidance and direction. I have earlier mentioned the impact this has on their educational needs and the changing role of teachers. One further implication is the need for mentors to provide them with guidance and direction in filtering out this information and making good life choices. Second, their use of social media highlights a collective desire for relationships. Rather than fulfilling the predictions and concerns of some who felt that social media would result in an increasing disconnect between people, Generation Z uses it to meet new people and to further existing relationships.[470] While positive in some ways it also created the psychological condition referred to as "FOMO" or "fear of missing out." Generation Z wants to be engaged with other people in real relationships. They also recognize the collective inauthenticity of how people present themselves on social media. As I have been engaged with them myself, one clear theme that has arisen and that I frequently pass on to mission mobilizers is that this generation of students does not base their decisions on opportunities but on relationships.

As the most ethnic and culturally diverse generation yet, Gen Z is readily aware of and familiar with both individual and cultural differences. Growing up, as they have, during the rise of increased acceptance of alternate gender and sexual norms has also contributed to their sense of tolerance of differences. Barna reports that among Gen Z only 48% hold that gender is attached to biological sex (76% among engaged Christians) and 69% believe it is acceptable to be born one gender and feel like another (34% among engaged Christians).[471] These trends present both positive and potentially negative implications for engaging Gen Z in missions. One the positive side is a greater awareness of cultural differences and increased global mentality. As these two factors continue to converge, we could see an increasing ability in Generation Z to be culturally adaptable in sharing the gospel. Generation Z has the potential to be one of the most effective missional generations in history. On the negative side is the rise of tolerance as acceptance. "Gen Z's collective aversion to causing offense is the natural product of a pluralistic, inclusive culture that frowns on passing judgement."[472] The potential concern is that as

---

[470] Barna, *Gen Z*, 17.
[471] Barna, *Gen Z*, 47, 48.
[472] Barna, *Gen Z*, 27.

acceptance of cultural and religious differences is increasingly popularized Generation Z Christians will increasingly face opposition to missions from both a pluralistic and tolerant society without and an internal desire to not rock the boat. While they have the potential to be the greatest missions force ever, they may be stalled by a spirit that desires to leave people to themselves and their personal choices.

Finally, the ever-increasing post-Christian context of American society presents multiple challenges for Generation Z. As pluralism and diversity become the norm and the greatest value of all is increasingly tolerance then this generation and the ones following it will increasingly find themselves at odds with the majority culture around them. I will briefly highlight two challenges that have the potential to affect their involvement in missions.

The first challenge is what David Kinnaman, President of the Barna Group refers to as "The Dropout Problem."[473] Barna's research indicates that between the ages of 18-29 there is a 43% drop off in church engagement. "These numbers represent about eight million twenty somethings who were active churchgoers as teenagers but who will no longer be particularly engaged in a church by their thirtieth birthday."[474] (This research was focused on Millennials, however as seen by the Barna study on Gen Z, the issue has not improved.) These ages are the prime ages that mission agencies are looking to mobilize young Christians to be engaged in missions work. The reasons behind this decline vary and many of them may eventually return. However, this drop at a key time for them to be thinking about being a missionary is a significant factor in how many will be mobilized to the field. I have not been able to locate research on the topic, but one aspect of this trend to consider could be that while even among committed and engaged Christians there is a distrust of liberal higher education, parents are still sending, and young Christians are still choosing to attend these schools. The increased secularization of American culture and the ever-declining statistics on subsequent generation's engagement in the church present a bleak picture for mobilizing the next generation of missionaries. Perhaps herein lies one of the key roles of the theological school in the tri-part mobilization puzzle of school, church, agency. Yet, even here the school cannot meet this challenge alone, especially as more private Christian universities close and these schools find themselves at odds with the prevailing culture.[475] If each generation brings forth less and less believers then who will be left to send to the mission field?

---

473 David Kinnaman, *You Lost Me: Why Young Christians Are Leaving Church...And Rethinking Faith,* (Grand Rapids: Baker Books, 2011), 22.

474 Kinnaman, *You Lost Me, 22.*

475 William Anderson, "The Coming Crises for Christian Colleges", *The James G. Martin Center for Academic Renewal,* Jan, 16, 2019, https://www.jamesgmartin.center/2019/01/the-coming-crises-for-christian-colleges/.

Perhaps an even greater question is who will reach the subsequent generation here?

The second challenge relates directly to having a biblical worldview in an age of tolerance. A study conducted by Barna in 2005 found that while most adults in America feel accepted by God, they lack a true biblical worldview.[476] In the Gen Z study the category of engaged Christians consistently rated higher in all areas of morality questions, however the most interesting distinction was the difference between "Engaged Christians" and "Churched Christians".[477] For example, the difference between these two groups on the following questions was staggering; "Lying is morally wrong" (engaged 77%, churched 38%), "Abortion is wrong" (engaged 80%, churched 37%), "Homosexual behavior is morally wrong" (engaged 77%, churched 24%).[478] With this being the environment that Generation Z believers are growing up and coming of age in it is no wonder that the Barna report makes the following statement. "Gen Z, including engaged Christians, are generally opposed to challenging other's beliefs."[479] While the engaged Christians individual views and morality are in stark contrast to their peers in this report, the age of tolerance leaves them unwilling to challenge others. How then can they be called upon to cross cultural barriers or even just walk across the street to confront others with the message of the gospel? A message which is by its very nature confrontational to the core beliefs of anyone who hears it.

Connecting Generation Z to Missions

Considering the characteristics of Generation Z and their motivations is vital to mobilizing them for missions. Sparks & Honey have labeled Generation Z as "the final generation". Their reasoning behind this is that "the very speed of culture will compress the 15-year generation into a .zip file of a few years, months or moments. We'll have to keep up to understand the overlapping influences of not just one generation at a time, but of a constantly in-flux,

---

[476] Research Releases in Faith & Christianity, "Most Adults Feel Accepted by God But Lack a Biblical Worldview," accessed March 30, 2020, https://www.barna.com/research/most-adults-feel-accepted-by-god-but-lack-a-biblical-worldview/.

[477] The Barna study defines these terms as: Churched Christians – "identify as Christians and have attended church within the past six months, but do not qualify as engaged under the definition below." Engaged Christians – "identify as Christian, have attended church within the past six months, and strongly agree with each of the following: The Bible is the inspired word of God and contains truth about the world. I have made a personal commitment to Jesus Christ that is still important to my life today. I engage with my church in more than just attending services. I believe that Jesus Christ was crucified and raised from the dead to conquer sin and death."

[478] Barna, *Gen Z*, 57.

[479] Barna, *Gen Z*, 58.

innovative, wow-inducing global collective."[480] The continued interconnectivity brought on by globalization and technology may yet result in a fundamental shift in how generations are formed and considered as the lines between one generation and the next continue to be blurred by rapid change.[481] Into this changing environment God's Word speaks more than ever in Hebrews 13:8 that, "Jesus Christ is the same yesterday and today and forever." In a world of constant change and flux our God stands strong as ever, a constant unmoving, unchanging, unyielding bulwark and it is to Him that we must always look.

There are many conclusions and a multifaceted approach to mobilizing Generation Z is necessary. David Kinnaman lists 50 ideas for engaging them at the end of *You Lost Me*.[482] However, throughout this research, there has been one consistent theme that stands out from the rest. That theme is a clear emphasis on relationships. Missio Nexus held a virtual conference at the beginning of March 2020 called "On Mission 2020." The theme for this year was on mobilization and many of the presenters spoke on mobilizing Generation Z. Real, authentic, mentoring, guidance and relationships were clear themes among these presenters.[483]

With a traditionally task-oriented approach to the *Missio Dei*, most Western approaches to motivating Generation Z fall flat because they do not originate out of a relational dynamic. Over the past seven years of organizing Calvary University's annual missions conference, I have seen time and again how most students don't care about the opportunities that are presented to them by mission agencies, rather they are motivated by their relationships. The most successful mobilizers are those who visit the campus frequently, invest in the lives of students, share their hearts, and build relationships with them. What biblical basis exists then for a relational motivation for missions?

Contextualizing Mission

Traditional motivations for missions have been based largely on the activity of completing the Great Commission. In chapter two of *Diaspora Mission to International Students*, Enoch Wan provides a fresh understanding of the mission of God from the paradigm of Relational Realism.[484] Wan breaks

---

[480] Sparks & Honey Culture Forecast, "Gen Z 2025: The Final Generation," accessed March 31, 2020, https://www.sparksandhoney.com/reports-list/2018/10/5/generation-z-2025-the-final-generation.

[481] All that considered it remains to be seen what the long-term impact of the 2020 Covid-19 Pandemic will be on the current generation in school who has faced drastic changes in how they are educated and interact with the world as a result of mask wearing and social distancing.

[482] Kinnaman, *You Lost Me,* 213-241.

[483] Rory Bonte and Laney Mills, "Mobilizing Millennials and Generation Z," *On Mission 2020: Mobilization*, accessed March 31, 2020, https://missionexus.org/onmission2020ondemand/.

[484] Wan, *Diaspora Missions to International Students*, 10.

down the prevailing theology of Christian mission as built upon the Great Commission. This programmatic, managerial approach to mission is based specifically in the American cultural mindset that places precedence on activity, 'doing' over 'being.'[485] Using his STARS" approach, Wan calls for a relational understanding of Christian mission,[486] Essentially, the popular pragmatic view of mission is too narrow in focus, as it emphasizes only the activity of mission and gives the impression that "doing" precedes "being".[487] This programmatic approach to not just mission but Christianity in generally, to doing over being, is exactly the claim that many members of Generation Z have leveled against the local church. "Most young Christians are struggling less with their faith in Christ than with their experience of church."[488] The full implications of this for the Western church are beyond the scope of this study. However, its impact on a programmatic approach to missions mobilization among Generation Z is clear, when the focus is on the task to the exclusion of real authentic relationships, they are unwilling to sign up.

Wan defines 'mission' as, "a process by which Christians (individuals) and the Church (institutional) continue on and carry out the *Missio Dei* of the Triune God ("mission") at both individual and institutional levels spiritually (saving souls) and socially (ushering in *shalom)* for redemption, reconciliation, and transformation ("missions")."[489] 'Missions' is defined as the "ways and means of accomplishing, "the mission" which has been entrusted by the Triune God to the Church and Christians."[490]

The reality for Generation Z then is missions requires very little contextualization. Rather it is our long-held understanding that needs to be readjusted to biblical truth. Generation Z may in fact be more ready for missions than previous generations have been. What then are practical steps that can be implemented for motivating and mobilizing Gen Z students for the mission?

Mobilizing Generation Z

Generation Z presents some new realities for educators and yet even in the

---

[485] Wan, *Diaspora Missions to International Students*, 13.

[486] "STARS" stands for an approach to missiological research that is, in order of priority, 1. Scripturally Sound, 2. Theologically Coherent, 3. Analytically Coherent, 4. Relevant Contextual, 5. Strategically Practical. See. Enoch Wan, "Rethinking Missiological Research Methodology: Exploring a New Direction," *Global Missiology*, October 2003, www.GlobalMissiology.org.

[487] Wan, *Diaspora Missions to International Students*, 17.

[488] Kinnaman, *You Lost Me,* 26.

[489] Enoch Wan, "Mission and '*Missio Dei*'; Response to Charles van Engen's 'Mission Defined and Described,'" in *MissionShift: Global Missions Issues in the Third Millennium*, ed. David J. Hesselgrave and Ed Stetzer, (Nashville: B & H Publishing Group, 2010), 42-50.

[490] Enoch Wan, "Rethinking Missiological Research Methodology," www.GlobalMissiology.org.

midst of those new realities the solutions may seem as traditional as ever. Completing our chart with the implications for how we can engage in mobilizing Generation Z for missions within a strong relational framework we arrive at the following table. This gives us four solid areas of focus for the local church, university, and mission agency to consider in mobilizing students from Generation Z, discipleship, guidance, biblical worldview, and mentoring.

Table 16. Implications for Mobilizing Generation Z

White[491]	Barna[492]	Motivating Factors	Implications
Recession Marked	Safe Spaces vs. Real Safety	Security/Contribution	Discipleship
Wi-Fi Enabled	Screenagers	Knowledge/Guidance/ Relationships	Guidance
	Double-Minded Parents		
Multiracial Sexually Fluid	Diverse	Awareness/Tolerance	Biblical Worldview
Post-Christian	Post-Christian	Real Discipleship	Mentoring

First, let us consider the implications for the university. Generation Z needs mentoring. As they have looked at the problems of their age, the recession, war on terror, and now a global pandemic in COVID19, security is a major concern. At the same time, they view themselves as world-changers, desiring to make a real contribution to society and change it for the better. In both areas they need solid mentoring. They need mature believers who will come alongside them and provide wisdom and accountability to produce the kind of character that helps them develop into the world changers they desire to be. Educators can play a unique role in mentoring young believers if they view their role as educators from a relational perspective rather than just doing their job. Program Directors and other faculty members should be seeking to build personal relationships with students. Be free to share your own personal struggles and even faith questions but along with those where you find security and confidence in Christ.

Second, as Generation Z copes with the world of information at their fingertips and the difficulty of deciphering it all, they need guidance. The difficulty for this generation is not a world without options, but rather a world

---

[491] James Emery White, *Meet Generation Z: Understanding and Reaching the New Post-Christian World*, (Grand Rapids: Baker, 2017).

[492] Barna. Gen Z: The Culture, Beliefs and Motivations Shaping the Next Generation. (Ventura, CA: Barna Group, 2018).

with too many options and information overload. How do they wade through it all to find the relevant nuggets for their own lives? Another interesting dynamic in this puzzle is that many of them are already highly motivated for what they want to do. Rather than choosing an already laid out college program they want a designer degree tailored to their interests and educational goals. Two implications for the university can be found here. One is that the teacher is no longer in the role of expert or mere dispenser of knowledge but rather needs to take the role of a guide in guiding the Gen Z student through their own learning process. The second is that colleges and universities need to consider more flexible degree programs. Northeastern University found that 75% of Gen Z students are interested in designing their own major.[493] Universities should take seriously these trends and consider how to utilize surveys and inventories along with interviewing students personally to determine their career goals and designing programs that fit. One direction that Calvary University is increasingly moving is interdisciplinary degrees. These programs which combine any two minors into a single major with plenty of open electives give students the opportunity to design their own program to fit their goals.[494] A combination such as Intercultural Studies/TESOL coupled with Calvary's unique Synergy program provides students interested in teaching English internationally with a fast track to the chosen ministry. Other options could include Intercultural Studies and Business or a new minor in Outdoor Adventure Leadership. Generation Z needs guidance and direction and a pathway to equip them for carrying out their own vision.

With the research that demonstrates the changing religious face of the United States, more than ever, Generation Z needs real discipleship and a biblical worldview. While much of this involves the role of the local church, the university has a part to play as well. An education that is grounded in God's unchanging word during changing times will ground them both personally and professionally.

One of the more telling statistics to come out of Barna's study on Gen Z was conducted on their parents. Parents were asked several questions about their children and rated them as to whether they were very important or somewhat important. To the question, "How important is it to you that your teen develops a faith that lasts into their adulthood?" 82% of respondents answered that it was very important.[495] However, to the question, "How important is it to you that your teen attends a Christian College?" a mere 15%

[493] Karuna Harishanker, "Gen Z: The Future of Higher Education," Altitude Inc., accessed April 1, 2020, https://www.altitudeinc.com/gen-z-the-future-of-higher-education/.

[494] "Warrior's Choice Bachelor's Degrees," Calvary University, accessed April 1, 2020, https://www.calvary.edu/warriors-choice-bachelors-degrees/.

[495] Barna, *Gen Z*, 83.

said this was very important.[496] Given the well documented reality of the current state of liberal higher education as well as the statistic indicated by Kinnaman that the ages of 18-29 are the key ages for those raised in a Christian home to drop out of the church, the difference between these numbers is staggering![497] These statistics indicate a clear disconnect in the understanding of the importance and role of higher education in an individual's development. Is it any wonder that so many young people are leaving the church currently? All of this indicates a great need for discipleship and imparting a biblical worldview. The theological school can do this through dorm devotions, relationships and mentoring with professors and staff members, chapel services, classes, and extracurricular activities. However, it cannot do it alone. While the theological school has a significant role to play in the mobilization of the next generation, the local church and the mission agency are important players as well.

For the local church, this research indicates a real need for true discipleship and imparting a biblical worldview. The local church is the primary place for believers to receive teaching and fellowship, so it must be the starting point in this process of mobilization. Kinnaman lists 50 suggestions for engaging Generation Z at the end of *You Lost Me*.[498] Churches should take the reality of facing a new generation and contextualizing the gospel to reach them. Some ideas are better than others, not all work for every context, but unless local churches make a concerted effort to reach the largest generation in history, called by some the last generation, then Christian universities will be extremely limited or continue to close. A final and very clear implication as seen above, is a renewed commitment on the part of local churches and Christian parents to engage their children with attending a Christian university: a school that will not require them to check their faith at the door but will support and uphold their faith and convictions even as they are challenged by new ideas and concepts.

For the mission agency, it is all about real authentic relationships. You cannot sell them on your programs and your places, your ministries or adventure. For every option that they are given they have one hundred more just as enticing. Mission agencies must make concerted efforts to utilize technology in getting their message to the masses but not rely on it to do the job. Generation Z has option fatigue and anxiety in making choices.[499] They need someone to be their coach, their guide and mentor, to come alongside and not recruit them but tell them the grand story of what God is doing in the world and direct them to participating in it.

---

[496] Barna, *Gen Z*, 83.
[497] Kinnaman, *You Lost Me*, 22.
[498] Kinnaman, *You Lost Me*, 214-249.
[499] Bonte and Mills, "Mobilizing Millennials and Gen Z," 3.

Another recent work conducted by Barna is also extremely relevant for this study. Barna sought to answer 10 questions related to how the next generation will approach missions.[500] Their conclusions for mobilizing the next generation were; "bridge the gap; deal with the past; pray and teach prayer; preach the whole gospel; talk about money; connect with missionaries; use your imagination; discern, equip and release; disciple parents; and involve everybody."[501] Several of these conclusions have implications for this study and the design of Synergy .

Relational Partnerships

Partnership Within the Trinity

Enoch Wan, writing with several others, has released a series of papers on partnership which examines the Trinity as a "model for work and relationships in Christian mission today."[502] These papers draw principles from the Trinity that can be applied to partnership. Wan and Penman demonstrate the participation of the Persons of the Trinity in different historical events.[503]

---

[500] Barna, *The Future of Missions: 10 Questions About Global Ministry the Church Must Answer with the Next Generation*, (Ventura, CA: Barna Group, 2020).

[501] Barna, *The Future of Missions, 96-100*.

[502] Enoch Wan and Kevin P. Penman, "The Trinity: A Model for Partnership in Christian Missions," *GlobalMissiology.org*. April 1, 2010, http://ojs.globalmissiology.org/index.php/english/article/view/102/295.

[503] Wan and Penman, "The Trinity: A Model for Partnership in Christian Missions."

Table 17. Participation of the Persons in the Godhead[504]

WORK	VERSE	PERSON
Creation	Gen. 1:2; Ps. 33:6b; Job 33:4	Spirit
	John 1:3; Col. 1:15ff, Heb 1:1-4	Jesus
	1 Cor. 8:6	Jesus & Father
	Gen. 1:1	God
	Gen 1:26	Trinity
Salvation	Ex. 15:2; Ps. 13:5; John 3:16-17; Acts 28:28	Father
	Heb. 9:14	Jesus & Spirit
	Acts 4:12; Eph. 1:13; 1 Thess. 5:9; 2 Tim. 2:10	Jesus
Redemption	Isa. 43:1; 44:22; Luke 1:68	Father
	Rom 3:24; Gal. 3:13; 4:5	Jesus
	Rom 8:23; Eph. 4:30	Spirit
	1 Cor. 1:30; Eph. 1:7	Father & Jesus
Sanctification	Eph. 3:14-19	Trinity
	Rom. 15:16; 2 Thess. 2:13	Spirit
	1 Cor. 6:11	Jesus & Spirit
	John 17:19; 1 Cor. 1:2	Jesus
	1 Thess. 4:3	Father
Mission	Matt. 28:18f	Trinity
	John 20:21	Father& Jesus
	Acts 1:8	Spirit
Indwelling	John 14:13	Father & Son
	Rom. 8:9; John 3:6	Spirit

Wan and Penman continue to list seven key principles for partnership in missions that can be derived from the Trinity. "These principles, in the context of the Universal Church and the Missio Dei, are love, diversity, unity, humility, interdependence, relationship, and peace and joy."[505]

Just as the Trinity is a demonstration of the love between the Father, Son, and Spirit so should ministry partners demonstrate love for one another. This is that agape love which chooses the good of the other over itself (1 Cor. 13; Php. 2:1-4). This sacrificial love and looking out for the interests of others, especially the interests of our partners, should be a characteristic of all

---

504 Wan and Penman, "The Trinity: A Model for Partnership in Christian Missions."
505 Wan and Penman, "The Trinity: A Model for Partnership in Christian Missions."

relationships between believers (John 13:35; 1 John 3:11-18). Partnership based on the Trinity will have love between the partners as a defining characteristic as they are bound together not primarily through contracts but by their shared fellowship with Christ and one another.

The Trinity is the prime example of unity amid diversity. While all three members are equally God, they also have distinct personalities, roles, and participation in history, as demonstrated above. Partnership based on the Trinity will be characterized not by competition but cooperation and unity as each partner understands its role and performs its function. Diversity and specialization are not something to be shunned but embraced as each recognizes the role they have to play and the necessity of the other members. Indeed, within the Church we are given a similar illustration by Paul on the functions of the Body (1 Cor. 12:27). Both characteristics of unity and diversity are held in dynamic tension. This tension creates interdependence, just as every part of the body needs every other part of the body. If any member of the Trinity could be proven to not be divine, then God's entire nature is called into question. Just as each member is interdependent on the others, so also in partnerships between Christians and ministries should there be this sense of interdependency.

Humility is a missing component in many relationships today and especially a struggle for those in a Western individualistic society. Western culture teaches us to look out for ourselves and consider our own interests above others. Yet the pattern we see in the Trinity and especially the character of Christ is one of self-sacrifice for the good of others. Philippians 2 clearly sets forth this principle of humility as Christ willingly underwent the shame and scorn of the cross, placing our need for salvation ahead of His need for safety and comfort.

Finally, relationships characterized by peace and joy find their full expression in the Trinity and are an example for our human partnerships. Just as the persons of the Trinity do not need to fret about the motivations of the others, so too our partnerships, especially when marked by unity in Christ, should be founded on the joy we have of fellowship with one another and peace without worry of ulterior motives. Phill Butler writes that, "all durable, effective partnerships are built on trust and whole relationships."[506] He further divides this into three areas of trust; in the members, in the process, and in the partnership's vision, objectives, and plan.[507]

Enoch Wan and Johnny Yee-chong Wan also incorporate a study of

---

[506] Phill Butler, *Well Connected: Releasing Power, Restoring Hope Through Kingdom Partnerships*, (Colorado Springs, CO: Authentic, 2006), 50.
[507] Butler, *Well Connected*, 50.

Trinitarian partnership in the Epistle to the Philippians.[508] They are not the only ones to examine Philippians as a basis for partnership. Luis Bush and Lorry Lutz also draw out several principles for partnership from Paul's letter to the Philippians. They include love and fellowship, partnering in the gospel (Phil. 1:5), partnering in the Spirit (Phil. 2:1), unity (Phil. 2:2), helping others grow (Phil. 2:4-8, 3:20, 4:21), suffering (Phil. 3:10), finances (Phil. 4:16), and prayer (Phil. 4:1, 6).[509] As Wan and Wan state, "Thus, the Apostle Paul and the Philippians, amongst whom he ministered, followed a most excellent model of human-human partnership in mission."[510] From their study they develop the following two tables to describe partnership within the Trinity and the partnership of the Trinity in Mission.

---

[508] Enoch Wan and Johnny Yee-chong Wan, "A Relational Study of the Trinity and the Epistle to the Philippians," *GlobalMissiology.org*, April 1, 2010, http://ojs.globalmissiology.org/index.php/english/article/view/102/295.

[509] Lois Bush and Lorry Lutz, *Partnering in Ministry: The Direction of World Evangelism.* (Downers Grove, IL: Intervarsity Press, 1990), 22-31..

[510] Wan and Wan, "A Relational Study of the Trinity and the Epistle to the Philippians," 3.

Table 18. Partnership within the Triune God[511]

GOD	THE FATHER	THE SON	HOLY SPIRIT
THE FATHER	N/A	- Obeys the Father's will (perfect obedience) - Intercedes to the Father on behalf of believers; - Mediates the Father's blessings - Mutual counsel	- The Father's agent of creation - Agent of Revelation - Is the agent of God's wisdom, power and knowledge - Proceeds from the Father - Mutual Counsel Gen 1:26
THE SON	- Sends the Son - Gives him Power - Mutual love - Mutual Glorification - Mutual Counsel	N/A	- Came upon Mary and Jesus was conceived (agent of virginal conception) - Filled the Son from his birth; and in baptismal and after baptism (authenticates Jesus' Messiahship) - Empowered Jesus to serve - Mutual Counsel
HOLY SPIRIT	- In OT, Holy Spirit sent to authenticate the anointing of the king - The Father sends the Holy Spirit as a helper to Christ's disciples to al believers in conversion	- The Son sends the Holy Spirit - Jesus Baptizes with the Holy Spirit (agent of regeneration) - Mutual counsel	N/A

511 Wan and Wan, "A Relational Study of the Trinity and the Epistle to the Philippians," 4.

Table 19. Partnership of the Trinity in Mission[512]

AREA	RE: TRIUNE GOD	DESCRIPTION	THE TRIUNE GOD			HUMAN CULTURE	
			FATHER	SON	H.S.	Christian	Non-XN
MESSEN-GER / MES-SAGE	from	- divine missions of the Son & H.S. - Gospel of salvation from the Trinity - Gospel of salvation from the Trinity	- sends the Son - loves the world -elects the saved	-sent by the Father -Incarnation, Atonement, the Way, the Truth, the Life	- sent by the Father & Son - Illumination, regeneration	-sent by Christ & guided by H.S. - beneficiary / bearer of the Gospel	-receive / reject the Messengers - receive / reject the Gospel
MOTIVE / MODE	for	- unity of the Trinity in love	-love: sent the Son & H.S. -grace: general for all: especial for saints	-submits to Father & incarnated: love -Immanuel, incarnation, identification	-pours forth God's love in believer's heart -habitation, guidance	-love of God -compassion for the lost	-receive / reject God's love through Christians -saved & incorporated or judged
MANIFE-STATION / MEANS	with	- Kingdom (already but not yet) - access to the Father through Christ in the Spirit	-sent H.S as gift of the risen Christ -in Christ through the H.S	-in words & deeds, by miracles, etc. -by Christ's authority & in His name	-individually: fruit of Spirit; institutionally: gifts of Spirit -endowment & empower-ment	-Xn. Unity & love as in the Trinity -the Church: God's children, X's body & Spirit's temple	-rebellion against God or receive the Gospel

It is noteworthy, as outlined in table 19 that the Trinity does not operate alone in missions. In developing the Relational Paradigm, Wan encourages us to return to a scriptural basis for reality on the foundation of relationship first within the Trinity, then God to us, and finally humanity with each other.[513] Applied to partnership for missions, the Trinity becomes the model for human-human partnerships in reaching the lost. Second Corinthians outlines well the progression of how God operated first to reconcile us to Himself (in Trinitarian partnership) and then gave us the ministry of reconciliation. In that ministry, commonly referred to as missions, we ought to follow trinitarian principles for partnership.

Other Scriptural Encouragements for Partnership

In examining the Trinity as a model for partnership, several other scriptural principles have found their way into the discussion that are worthy of being noted as well. The first is Christ's call to unity in John 17:20-23.[514]

---

[512] Wan and Wan, "A Relational Study of the Trinity and the Epistle to the Philippians," 5.
[513] Wan, "The Paradigm of 'Relational Realism,'" 1.
[514] Calls to unity should not be mistaken as "unity for unity's sake" apart from relevant doctrinal distinctions.

Unity was briefly mentioned already as one of the seven principles derived from Wan and Penman's study of the Trinity. It is also mentioned by several authors in discussing biblical precedents for partnership. Enoch Wan and Geoff Baggett reference Christ's prayer as a foundation for partnership, "to refuse all efforts at Christian unity is a direct rejection of the prayer of the Lord."[515] Phill Butler mentions it along with wholeness and diversity in discussing God's design for relationships.[516] Bush references unity as a key component of Paul's partnership with the Philippians (Phil. 2:2).[517] Addicott writes to the importance of unity in the midst of diversity as well, saying, "God's trademark is to make absolutely everything different, and yet he delights in *unity*."[518] Unity is well attested to in the literature on partnerships of all kinds, but why? Christ's prayer gives as a specific reason with a specific ramification for missions. "I do not ask for these only, but also for those who will believe in me through their word, that they may all be one, just as you, Father, are in me, and I in you, that they also may be in us, *so that the world may believe that you have sent me*."[519] Christ's prayer for unity is based on the unity that exists within the Trinity itself. The reason He gives for such unity is missional, as confirmation to the world of who Christ is. Organizations must clearly retain their doctrinal distinctiveness and make decisions on who they partner with based on those distinctives. However, Christians working together is a demonstration to the world of who Christ is and the veracity of the Gospel.

Another frequently used scriptural encouragement for partnership is the example of the body given by Paul in Romans 12:4-8 and 1 Corinthians 12. This is the chief scriptural framework for Addicott's *Body Matters* in which he states, "a re-emphasis on the Body of Christ – the *Person* with whom the gospel began. An emphasis on the Body also means an emphasis on the importance of members of the Body working together to fulfill the Great Commission."[520] In context, both passages indicate the importance of each member of the body, individually using their gifts, skills and abilities for the benefit of the whole body. In both contexts Paul is writing to the churches of Rome and Corinth regarding the use of spiritual gifts and the necessity of all gifts/members of the body for the health and growth of the church. The question is whether this analogy can be applied equally to the Universal Church as it is to the local church. Wan and Baggett, in agreement with

---

[515] Enoch Wan and Geoff Baggett, "A Theology of Partnership: Implications for Implementation by a Local Church," *GlobalMissiology.org*, April 1, 2010, http://ojs.globalmissiology.org/index.php/english/article/view/102/295.

[516] Butler, *Well Connected*, 47.

[517] Bush and Lutz, *Partnering in Ministry*, 26.

[518] Addicott, *Body Matters*, 7.

[519] John 17:20-21, emphasis mine.

[520] Addicott, *Body Matters*, 3.

Douglas Moo,[521] state that indeed these same principles apply equally to the Universal Church as "the local church is an expression of the Universal Church."[522] How this dynamic of the body-life of partnerships between local churches, theological school, and missions agencies operates is explored further in another part of the dissertation.

Finally, frequently referenced throughout the literature is the scriptural foundation for partnership based on an understanding of the Greek word *koinonia*. *Koinonia* is most often translated as "fellowship"; however, "partnership" is also referenced as a meaning behind the word.[523] Louw and Nida specifically reference a form of the word *koinoneo* as bearing the meaning, "to join with others in some activity."[524] Evelyn and James Whitehead reference the Jerusalem Bible's use of "partnership" to translate *koinonia* in Galatians 2:9.[525] Wan and Baggett point out the use of "partnership" to translate *koinonia* in Philippians 1:3-5 in the New International Version (NIV): "I thank my God every time I remember you, In all my prayers for all of you, I always pray with joy because of your *partnership* in the gospel from the first day until now."[526] The English Standard Version (ESV) also uses "partnership" to translate this instance of the word. The parallel demonstrated of the biblical concept of *koinonia* and relational partnerships between believers and their organizations is significant. Partnerships that the world creates are based on what each member can get from the partnership; the focus is often selfish. When the partnership ceases to be of benefit to one member, they have no reason to continue it, and the partnership often breaks down. However, the connection between believers is stronger than mere contracts and memos of understanding. It is a connection brought by our fellowship with God (first vertically) and then one another (horizontally). These relational connections provide not only a stronger foundation but even a mandate for believers to work together. As Wan and Baggett conclude, "The principle of *koinonia* is an important element of our missions efforts and strategies. As such, we cannot ignore the biblical mandate to serve in partnership with other believers, even across great geographic and cultural distances, within the mission of God."[527]

---

[521] Douglas J. Moo, "Romans," in *The NIV Application Commentary*. Edited by Terry Muck, (Grand Rapids: Zondervan, 2000).

[522] Wan and Baggett, "A Theology of Partnership."

[523] J. H. Moulton and G. Milligan, *Vocabulary of the Greek Testament*, (Peabody, MA: Hendrickson Pub., 2004), 351.

[524] Johannes P. Louw and Eugene A. Nida, *Greek-English Lexicon of the New Testament Based on Semantic* Domains, vol. 1, (New York: United Bible Societies, 1989), 512.

[525] Evelyn Eaton Whitehead and James D. Whitehead, *The Promise of Partnership: A Model for Collaborative Ministry*, (Lincoln, iUniverse.com Inc., 2000), 7.

[526] Wan and Baggett, "A Theology of Partnership."

[527] Wan and Baggett, "A Theology of Partnership."

Partnership Theories

Theories on partnership abound, the literature review has turned up many biblically based ideas surrounding what it means for Christians to partner together. Much of the literature regarding partnerships in missions is focused on partnerships that cross cultural barriers and deal with Western agencies partnering with national churches. There are similarities and differences to partnerships that are focused on primarily same culture partners working together to mobilize missionaries from within their own culture. Similarities include many of the blessings and the problems that partnership brings, the key difference being the lack of significant cross-cultural hurdles to partnership. However, organizational cultures can also present problems even within a same culture background and similar theological circles.

Daniel Rickett has written two works devoted to partnership between Western and Non-western agencies and churches for missions. In the first he defines partnership as, "a complementary relationship driven by a common purpose and sustained by a willingness to learn and grow together in obedience to God."[528] His focus is on establishing partnerships that contribute to the mutual development of the members. These kinds of partnerships have three characteristics: results (the partnership accomplishes a tangible outcome), relationship (is the foundation of the partnership), and vision (what the partnership could achieve and how to do it).[529] Rickett further outlines three guiding principles for a partnership to be complementary: the autonomy of each partnering organization, compatibility in doctrine and values, and complementary strengths and resources.[530]

Rickett's other work, *Making Your Partnership Work*, focused specifically on the one-to-one relationship building aspect of partnership. While it was written again for cross-cultural partnerships, he indicated that the principles were applicable across all types of partnership.[531] Specifically related to partnership theory, Rickett began this work with a helpful discussion of the different levels of partnership including associations, service alliance, multilateral alliance, joint venture, complementary partnership, and merger.[532] Table 13 summarizes the distinctions between these different partnership forms.

---

[528] Daniel Rickett, *Building Strategic Relationships: A Practical Guide to Partnering with Non-Western Missions*, (Minneapolis: STEM Press, 2008), 13.

[529] Rickett, *Building Strategic Relationships*, 16-18.

[530] Rickett, *Building Strategic Relationships*, 19.

[531] Daniel Rickett, *Making Your Partnership Work*, 3rd ed., (Roswell, GA: Daniel Rickett, 2014), Kindle version, Preface, Kindle location 308.

[532] Rickett, *Making Your Partnership Work*, Kindle location 319.

Table 20. Different Partnership Levels[533]

Association	affiliation of independent ministries with a common interest in mutual encouragement and a limited exchange of resources
Service Alliance	association of independent organizations in which one supplies resources or services to the other
Multilateral Alliance	association of independent ministries that correlate separate action toward a common purpose
Joint Venture	short-term alliance of independent ministries for a limited or specified purpose
Complementary Partnership	long-term alliance of two or more organizations that share complimentary gifts and abilities to achieve a common purpose (Synergy)
Merger	incorporation of one ministry into another whereby personnel, finances, and programs are integrated into one organization

Rickett's differentiation is helpful for understanding the type of partnership that one is aiming for. He further places them on a scale on involvement vs. interdependence, moving from the top down with associations requiring the least of both and mergers the most.[534] Rickett's focus in his work is on the relationships that exist within joint ventures and complementary partnerships. Synergy fits well within the realm of his description of a complimentary partnership. Once again, he focuses on the three primary aspects of vision, relationships, and results. A helpful table summarizes his argument, all these questions being important ones for new partners to answer.

---

[533] Adapted from Rickett, *Making Your Partnership Work*, location 319-340.
[534] Rickett, *Making Your Partnership Work*, Kindle location 319.

Table 21. Rickett's Imperatives of Partnership Design[535]

Vision	Shared Vision	What has God invited us to do together?
	Compatibility	What binds us together? What could tear us apart?
	Ground Rules	How do we work together?
Relationship	Alliance Champions	Who is responsible to make it work?
	Cross-Cultural Understanding	What cultural differences may help or hinder the relationship?
	Mutual Trust	What gives us confidence in each other?
Results	Meaningful Results	What difference will it really make in the work of the gospel?
	Documentation	How do we keep track of agreements, contributions, and outcomes?
	Learning and Change	How do we handle changes, opportunities, and disappointments?

Building on the theological foundation already established above, Ernie Addicott addresses the goal of partnership as synergy.[536] Utilizing the illustration of the body, he speaks of synergy as, "combined energy, united action, parts working together as a whole...this speaks straight into the biblical image of *bodywork*, when the parts are properly relating to each other."[537] He places a strong emphasis on what the partnership is to accomplish, that it must be active and intentional and seen as a process.[538] Addicott defines partnership as, "Partnership is when two or more individuals or organizations, having different assets to bring to the table agree to share resources, plan, pray and work together to fulfill a common purpose."[539] His theory of partnership is compared to a wedding cake with multiple layers built upon one another.

---

[535] Rickett, *Making Your Partnership Work,* Kindle location 372.
[536] The irony that the name Synergy was chosen for Calvary's partnership program long before this author picked up Addicott's book is not lost on him!
[537] Addicott, *Body Matters*, 11.
[538] Addicott, *Body Matters*, 14.
[539] Addicott, *Body Matters*, 20.

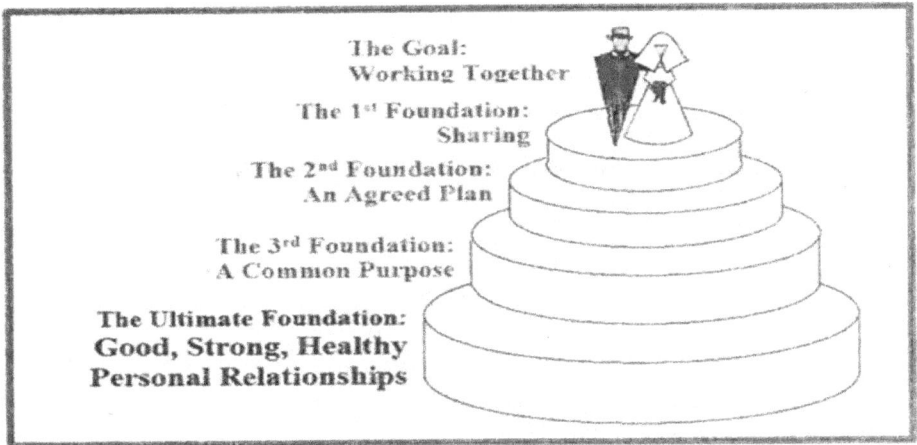

Figure 29. Addicott's Partnership Principles[540]

Immediately noticeable in Addicott's theory of partnership are the similarities to Rickett. Both emphasize the vision/purpose, goal/results, and the relationships. Addicott is perhaps even stronger in emphasizing the importance of relationships, quoting one of his colleagues, John Rogers, "There are three things that are important in Partnership: *Relationships, Relationships, Relationships!*"[541] Finally, and consistent with a Trinitarian perspective, he describes the will, the word, and the work of God as the "bedrock" of partnership.[542]

Luis Bush, well known for his work with Partners International, would also agree with both Rickett and Addicott. He begins *Partnering in Ministry* with the statement, "The heart of Christian partnership is fellowship."[543] In his study of partnership, he moves from the Trinity to an emphasis on Paul's partnership with the Philippians. Three key principles that he draws out of Philippians are the following:

1. Look out for your own interests so that you will grow, but also look out for the interests of your partner (2:4).
2. Develop a servant attitude (2:5-9).
3. Continually give of yourself to meet the legitimate needs of your partner (2:8).[544]

Bush continues with his description to define partnership as, "an association of two or more autonomous bodies who have formed a trusting

---

[540] Addicott, *Body Matters*, 29.
[541] Addicott, *Body Matters*, 31.
[542] Addicott, *Body Matters*, 32.
[543] Bush and Lutz, *Partnering in Ministry*, 9.
[544] Bush and Lutz, *Partnering in Ministry*, 27.

relationship and fulfill agreed upon expectations by sharing complementary strengths and resources to reach their mutual goal."[545] There are many similarities between Bush's understanding of partnership and others already mentioned. Table 6 summarizes his ingredients for success.

Table 22. Bush's Ingredients for Successful Partnership[546]

1. Partners agree on doctrine and ethical behavior.
2. Partners share a common goal.
3. Partners must develop an attitude of equality.
4. Partnership avoids dominance of one over the other.
5. Partnership requires open communication.
6. Partners demonstrate trust and accountability.
7. Partners must have clear financial policies.
8. True partnership demands the sharing of complementary gifts.
9. Partnership demands sacrificial commitment.
10. Partners Pray for each other.

While many of Bush's "ingredients" stray out of the realm of theory and into the realm of practice, they are helpful for once again supporting the research and writing of other authors. Relationship, intentionality, purpose/goal, and sharing are clear themes throughout these principles.

Evelyn and James Whitehead, writing from a Catholic perspective, focus heavily on partnership in contrast to paternalism. While the focus of *The Promise of Partnership* is on the role of women in the church, especially the Catholic Church, they present some interesting principles for consideration. One of their chief points is recognizing the importance of shared power in partnership relationships.[547] Paternalistic attitudes in missions have a long history of causing problems, especially dependency; Jonathan Barnes writes specifically on this issue in *Power and Partnership*.[548] While paternalism is not directly a concern in same-culture partnerships, the reality of authority and power is.

The Whiteheads continue, emphasizing the importance of recognizing mutual gifts and bringing them to the relationship. "In a mutual relationship each party brings something of value; each receives something of worth. Partnership thrives when we recognize and respect this mutual exchange of

---

[545] Bush and Lutz, *Partnering in Ministry*, 46.

[546] Bush and Lutz, *Partnering in Ministry*, 46-56.

[547] Whitehead and Whitehead, *The Promise of Partnership*, 8.

[548] Jonathan S. Barnes, *Power and Partnership: A History of the Protestant Missions Movement*, (Eugene, OR: Pickwick Publications, 2013).

gifts."[549] They contrast three models of collaboration in the staff, team, and community.

Table 23. Whiteheads' Staff/Team/Community Models of Partnership[550]

Character Type	Style	Strengths	Challenges
Staff	Distinct responsibility; vertical accountability	Order and efficiency	Encourage connections; keep structure flexible
Team	Interdependent action and accountability	Complementary strengths: flexibility and spontaneity	Befriend structure; establish workable patterns for ongoing activities
Community	Strong value components; explicit concern for task, vision, and support	Group witness to values; commitment to mutual support.	Move values beyond rhetoric; develop structures that hold belonging in tension with effectiveness

Of the three models presented by the Whiteheads, the community model is held up as ideal and most fits the context of this study on relational partnerships through Synergy. "Community can be used more precisely, to describe a way of collaborating in ministry. A community is a ministry group in which *shared values* lead to *common action* undertaken in a spirit of *mutual concern*."[551] Three specific areas are highlighted where a ministering community needs to focus: common vision, mutual concern, and effective action. Common vision means that the community has some agreement on their values, which again highlights the importance of trust, time, and relationships.[552] Communities must get to know each other and build relationships beyond just a staff or team working level. In a ministering community having mutual concern means genuinely looking out for the

---

[549] Whitehead and Whitehead, *The Promise of Partnership*, 8.
[550] Whitehead and Whitehead, *The Promise of Partnership*, 55.
[551] Whitehead and Whitehead, *The Promise of Partnership*, 57.
[552] Whitehead and Whitehead, *The Promise of Partnership*, 59.

interests of all partners, not just oneself. The community is marked by prayer and support for all partners involved.[553] A ministering community is not just about what my organization stands to gain from the partnership but also how we can serve and bless each other (Phil. 2:1-4). Finally, the community leads to effective action. While relationships are important and take center stage, the community does have something to accomplish, and in this they must work together, hold each other accountable, and support one another to complete their assigned tasks.[554]

David Pickard with OMF International has concluded that while there are many different models and theories of partnership, four basic principles are common to all. First, partnerships are dynamic, not static, "partnerships are always in a process of development."[555] While a partnership may begin with either a relationship or a formal agreement, they grow, change, and develop over time. This maturation of the relationship should be welcomed. Second, partnerships require integrity. Here Pickard focuses on two aspects that have already been mentioned, that of trust and service (1 Cor. 10:24).[556] Next, partnership requires long-term thinking. It takes time to build the relationship; in the immediate the results might not be what you desire, but it takes time and commitment to aim for long-term results.[557] Pickard's fourth common principle is that partnerships require clarity, both in purpose and communication.[558] All of the partners must be aware of the goals and direction for the partnership. What is this partnership trying to achieve and how will it get there? Clear communication is essential to creating this shared understanding, avoiding misunderstandings and the pitfalls that can come from ambiguity in the relationship.

One of the most well-known names in mission partnership is Phil Butler, founder, and senior strategic advisor of *visionSynergy*. Butler defines partnership simply as, "two or more people or ministries who agree to work together to accomplish a common vision."[559] However, while the definition is simple, as the rest of *Well Connected* expounds upon, the creation of partnerships is clearly not. Before exploring it in more depth and with much agreement to what has already been covered, Butler lays out 15 principles for partnership.

---

[553] Whitehead and Whitehead, *The Promise of Partnership,* 60.
[554] Whitehead and Whitehead, *The Promise of Partnership,* 60.
[555] David Pickard, "Partnership in Mission: OMF in a Unique China Partnership," in *Kingdom Partnerships for Synergy in Missions*, William Taylor, ed. (Pasadena: William Carey Library, 1994), 189.
[556] Pickard, "Partnership in Mission," 189-190.
[557] Pickard, "Partnership in Mission," 190.
[558] Pickard, "Partnership in Mission," 191.
[559] Butler, *Well Connected,* 2.

1. All effective strategic partnerships are driven by energizing challenging vision.
2. Trust, openness, and mutual concern are vital ingredients.
3. Effective lasting partnerships need a committed facilitator.
4. Effective, durable partnerships are a process, not an event.
5. Effective, durable partnerships have limited, achievable objectives – in the beginning.
6. Effective partnerships require substantial, ongoing prayer.
7. High participation and ownership is vital.
8. Start by identifying priority felt needs among the people being served.
9. Partnerships composed of churches, ministries, or other organizations need a partnership champion in each of those groups.
10. As effective partnerships become more complex, they serve at least four constituencies: the people we are trying to reach or serve; the partner agencies/ministries; the funding and praying constituencies behind each of these ministries; and, eventually, the partnership itself.
11. Partners with clear identity and vision are the best.
12. Acknowledging, even celebrating, differences are important.
13. Effective partnerships do not come free.
14. Effective partnerships are even more challenging to maintain than to start.
15. Expect problems and proactively deal with them.[560]

Whether related to cross-cultural partnerships or those within a Western framework as the topic of this study, several key principles have been noted. Chief among all the theories and principles is the importance of relationships. Numerous authors noted that relationships are the foundation of a strong partnership, not just formal agreements. This is not surprising as it follows a Trinitarian understanding of partnership as well and is reflected throughout Scripture in the context of the body-life of the Church. Phil Butler established his philosophy of partnerships on God's design for relationships. "Ministry partnerships are only effective and durable as they build trust, work actively at restoring relationships, and celebrate diversity within unity."[561] Much of the discussion then centered on how those relationships should be formed and maintained. Also important are shared values (including doctrine), common goals, recognition of each organization's role, understanding of cultural differences (including organizational), and well communicated plans and expectations. However, partnership must be done, it is not enough to just talk about being partners, partnership must be intentionally put into practice.

---

[560] Butler, *Well Connected*, 16-18.
[561] Butler, *Well Connected*, 47.

Next, the review will examine practical steps to creating relational partnerships.

Steps Toward Building Relational Partnerships

Before getting into the details of practical steps toward building relational partnerships, Phil Butler highlights three very important realities to keep in mind. The first is that the partnership is driven by vision, "great vision motivates effective partnerships."[562] The greatest of partnerships are motivated by the greatest of visions, provided not by man but by God in His Word and what He wishes to see accomplished. Butler traces many instances of God giving someone a vision in scripture, from Abraham going to a land He has never seen (Gen. 12:1) to Jesus completing the Father's work (John 17:4).[563] While much could be and has been said of the Great Commission (Matt. 28:18-20; Mark 16:15; Luke 24:47; John 20:21; Acts 1:8), perhaps the greatest "vision" for Christian partnership in missions is actually that given by Revelation 7:9-10.

> After this I looked, and behold, a great multitude that no one could number, from every nation, from all tribes and peoples and languages, standing before the throne and before the Lamb, clothed in white robes, with palm branches in their hands, and crying out with a loud voice, "Salvation belongs to our God who sits on the throne, and to the Lamb!"

The second essential that Butler highlights is prayer.[564] Prayer, once again, demonstrates the importance of the relationship in the partnership. If even Jesus being God himself took time to step aside from His ministry to communicate in prayer with His heavenly Father, how much more is it essential to our own relationships? In prayer we see the importance of the impact of relational realism. As noted before, relationship is first vertically with God the Father and then horizontally with one another.[565] Meeting together with our partners on a regular basis to emphasize our mutual dependence on God and our relational connection to Him also contributes to the maturity of the relationship between partners. Butler concludes by saying,

- Intentional, concerted prayer is vital to defeating Satan's offensive to divide and, thereby, neutralize the church's witness.
- Intentional, concerted prayer is vital to the development of trusting, open, restored relationships - the basis for all cooperative Kingdom efforts.

---

562 Butler, *Well Connected*, 93.
563 Butler, *Well Connected*, 99.
564 Butler, *Well Connected*, 101.
565 Wan, "The Paradigm of 'Relational Realism,'" 1.

- Intentional, concerted prayer is vital to bringing about consensus and developing action plans that empower lasting Kingdom cooperation.
- Intentional, concerted prayer is too frequently considered an "add-on" rather than the center of each step in planning, preparing, executing, and sustaining, partnership-based ministry.
- Intentional, concerted prayer is vital if the church seeks the power and refreshment offered as God's gift in Psalm 133.[566]

Prayer transforms us and draws us relationally closer to God, and as it does so, it draws us closer to each other and strengthens the bonds of fellowship and partnership we have with other members of the Body. Finally, Butler reminds us that partnership is a process, not an event.[567] This is a good reminder as we move on to the more practical elements of partnership development, that any steps should be viewed as an overall process. Partnerships formed too quickly on the basis of contracts with little relational connection also fall apart quickly when misunderstanding and conflicts arise.

Ernie Addicott and Phill Butler provide the most practical outlines for building relational partnerships. Both put forth a three-step process of Exploration, Formation, and Operation as phases in the development of a partnership.[568] Butler also adds a fourth step in the Maturation of the partnership.[569] Both authors, as demonstrated above, also lay a solid foundation for partnership that is rooted in the Trinity and demonstrates a relational approach.

Exploration

Addicott defines the exploration phase simply as someone taking the initiative to explore the feasibility of the partnership.[570] Butler adds a little more clarity to the phase, contributing that it is the partners who are involved in "exploring their vision, interest, and readiness to at least prayerfully talk about partnership."[571] The exploration phase could begin where there is already an established relationship between partners. For example, Crossworld and Calvary University had been connected through individuals, missions conferences, Calvary students serving with the organization, missionaries in residence, and many other informal ways long before the formal aspect of Synergy was entertained. In this case the relationship already existed. Another example would be the story of Avant's partnership with

---

[566] Butler, *Well Connected*, 109.
[567] Butler, *Well Connected*, 111.
[568] Addicott, *Body Matters*, 60., Butler, *Well Connected*, 121-200.
[569] Butler, *Well Connected*, 114.
[570] Addicott, *Body Matters*, 60.
[571] Butler, *Well Connected*, 113.

Crossworld through their Shared Services organization. In this case while there was very little prior relationship, a mutual problem (the finances involved in the back office of running a missions agency) created the situation for the relationship to begin and be explored further.

Addicott likens the exploration phase to the concrete foundation of a house.[572] If the foundation is strong, much like Jesus' parable in Matthew 7:24-27, then the house/partnership will be able to weather the storms. The two main objectives for Addicott are research and relationships, and he also includes reconciliation as a potential third if there is a bad history between the partners.[573]

Research – a reasonable understanding of 'the field'; what the needs are, who is doing what, and where they're doing it.

Relationships – a relationship of trust with each of the key players in the field and a consensus that there would be value in meeting to discuss the possibility of working together.

Reconciliation – a knowledge of any sensitivities or conflicts between key players and, if possible, some resolution of them.

Butler provides four main steps for the exploration phase.

1. Be knowledgeable about your topic.
2. Find out who is already involved.
3. Based on your initial informational gathering, decide which individuals, organizations, or ministries are your first personal interview priorities.
4. Once your exploration interviews are complete, use the information you gather to make a decision about moving on to the next phase.[574]

Formation

The second phase is the actual formation of the partnership. Simply put, it is when the partners agree to work together.[575] Butler calls it the "go/no-go" phase in which the partners agree that the only way they can accomplish their shared vision is by working together.[576] Addicott focuses mostly on the particulars of the formation meeting and how it should be arranged, from prayer and worship to identifying needs and prioritizing tasks.[577] While Butler

---

[572] Addicott, *Body Matters,* 60.
[573] Addicott, *Body Matters,* 63.
[574] Butler, *Well Connected,* 140.
[575] Addicott, *Body Matters,* 60.
[576] Butler, *Well Connected,* 141.
[577] Addicott, *Body Matters,* 73.

also goes into detail on meeting arrangements, he also explores several topics that are good for the overall formation stage of the partnership. Butler provides a checklist of essential success factors for the formation stage.

- Enough of the "influentials" are going to be in these initial working meetings to lend the meetings credibility. You do not need everyone, but you do need a number of people or ministries with recognized effectiveness to bring their credibility into the Formation process.
- Everyone clearly understands the objectives and expectations for the first round of discussions. If everyone knows the agenda and has had a chance to give input, the trust factor goes up, along with your likelihood of success.
- Your initial meeting discussion time is long enough to allow you to develop a base of common information and relationships among participants. Trying to cut corners for busy people will come back to haunt you!
- You make a point of building trust. Building "equity" in your "trust account" will greatly strengthen your ability to serve and facilitate the process. Word will spread that the partnership and its leadership have integrity.
- You have pursued careful planning and facilitating of this initial face-to-face meeting. Do not leave the plans or execution to chance or the last minute. Careful, detailed planning pays off – big!
- Before you get to the vital "go/no-go" question, you make sure your participants have at least general agreement on the points outlined in the section later in this chapter on building trust.[578]

As mentioned in the last point above, Butler spends a great deal of time in this stage of partnership formation talking about the importance of trust. It goes without saying that in the Trinity there is a high degree of trust between the Father, Son, and Spirit. So also do partnerships based on the Trinity need a highly trusting relationship. Butler gives 6 key elements for developing and sustaining trust between partners.

1. *Common vision*: Vision is the *what* of our dream. What major outcome are we hoping for in the area, among the people, or in the project for which we plan to build the partnership?
2. *Common values*: Values determine *how* we will realize our vision. They help us define the strategy, tactics, and qualities of the initiative that we feel are vital to realizing the dream.

---

[578] Butler, *Well Connected*, 142.

3. *Holding each other's best interests at heart*: Are we committed to each other's organizational and personal success and health? Is each member's relationship with the partnership going to result in a genuine "win-win" situation? Or is the relationship only based on convenience and selfish motivation?
4. *Competence*: Can you perform the task, fulfill the promise, or provide the resources you have committed to provide? We have all been disappointed by individuals who made promises without the ability to follow through on them.
5. *Reliability*: You may have the capacity to fulfill your promise, but *will* you? Possibly more disappointing than promises that *cannot* be kept are those that *could be* met but for a variety of reasons *simply aren't*.
6. *Faithfulness*: It is commendable to fulfill your promise once. But in a partnership, long-term reliability has a huge impact on trust. Will you *continue* to provide resources, show up for planned meetings, meet your commitments, perform on time, or demonstrate other aspects of long-term commitment to both the vision and your colleagues in the partnership?[579]

The formation of a partnership is not altogether different from two people dating. It takes time, commitment, and shared relationship to determine if they are right for one another and have common interests and mutual goals. Butler demonstrates this with the following diagram on the building blocks of trust. This provides important questions that the partners should be asking of one another during this stage.

---

[579] Butler, *Well Connected*, 147.

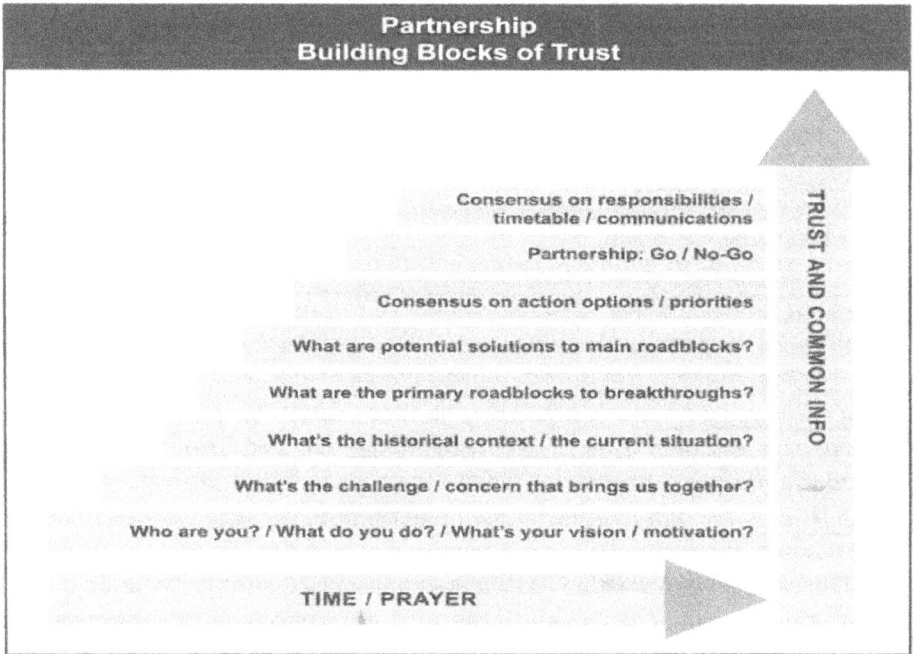

Figure 30. Butler's Building Blocks of Trust[580]

As the group affirms their desire to work together, the formation stage concludes with several important actions for developing consensus among the partners. All the partners should have buy-in in the partnership. "Participants should contribute input on resources, contacts, strategic ideas, and other items that could be relevant to action priorities the group has agreed to."[581] Several authors in this study have pointed out the importance of "buy-in" and ownership of the partnership by all partners, especially, in cross-cultural situations. It is important that no one partner is seen as having more or less authority or ownership than any other. In some cases, it may be necessary to form a smaller task force to handle practical next steps rather than involving everyone in the overall organization.[582] In Synergy, while the whole local church, the entire school body, and the mission agency are involved in the partnership, it only takes a few key people to make the partnership happen and others step in to fulfill their roles when necessary. That said, Butler indicates that there are several items the larger group needs to be aware of: the actions of the task force, what feedback they can expect, no action steps will be taken without the larger group's knowledge, who is responsible for

---

[580] Butler, *Well Connected*, 148.
[581] Butler, *Well Connected*, 163.
[582] Butler, *Well Connected*, 163.

communication, how success is to be measured, and when the large group needs to meet.[583] The smaller task force also needs to agree on who will do what, who will coordinate the group's efforts, their timetable, and who is responsible for reporting back to the larger group.[584]

Three final important issues need to also be addressed before moving on to the operation stage: how will decisions be made and who will make them, what kind of financial commitment will be involved from each partner, and will the partners be able to maintain their own organizational identity?[585] Having agreement on these three key issues will prevent a lot of unnecessary headaches down the line as the partnership begins to bear fruit.

Operation

As the partnership enters the operation stage, the focus now shifts from the formation of the partnership itself to the actual work to be accomplished.[586] It is in the operation stage that the importance of a relational foundation for the partnership really comes to the front. Through strong relationships, connections and ties can be maintained and potential issues averted thanks to the mutual commitment of the partners. Addicott especially highlights the role of the partnership facilitator. This is an individual who ensures that the working groups of the partnership are being successful and that communication is consistently flowing with the partners.[587] In Synergy there are really three partnership facilitators: the local church's pastor, the school's professor, and the mission agency's mobilizer. Each of these individuals work closely together to ensure that the partnership's tasks are being completed.

Two key issues that must be dealt with in this stage are security and sharing credit.[588] While cross-cultural partnerships or even partnerships directly involving workers in restricted access countries must be concerned with security, so too is this an issue in partnerships involving students. For the theological school that is accredited, Title 4 and Title 9 statutes require the student's privacy, so academic files can only be made available to those to whom the student has given permission. Practically, this means that the professor cannot divulge academic information to the pastor or agency mobilizer without the student's expressed written consent. While sharing credit is not as significant from a legal standing, it is still important to the overall health of the partnership. The reality is that a student may have many

---

583 Butler, *Well Connected*, 163.
584 Butler, *Well Connected*, 164.
585 Butler, *Well Connected*, 164.
586 Addicott, *Body Matters*, 76.
587 Addicott, *Body Matters*, 77.
588 Addicott, *Body Matters*, 77.

influences towards missions by the time they arrive at the theological school, and as such no one partner can ever fully take credit for mobilizing the student to the mission field. It is important that everyone celebrates the successes and the contributions of all partners to the overall goal, lest hurt feelings drive a rift between partners.

Every partnership needs a way to determine its success in achieving the goals it was created for. Butler highlights the importance of recognizing the difference between those aspects of the partnership that are part of the process and those that are a program.[589] This discussion is in the context of how to evaluate if the partnership is meeting its objectives. One way to do this is to create a road map of near and long-term objectives. This helps the partners outline the process for achieving those objectives as well as who is responsible and a time frame for when they should be completed.[590]

All partnerships will have both quantitative elements that can be counted or measured as well as qualitative issues and outcomes.[591] As an example, quantitative elements in the Synergy process at Calvary could include: the number of students in the pipeline, the number of students who have completed it, students successfully on the mission field, and the number of church and agency partners. More qualitative elements would be such things as the content of classes, relationships between school/church/agency, and contributions of the program to the overall culture of the school or local church. All of these are measurable elements which can be included in an evaluation of the program and partnerships to provide direction for changes or where resources need to be allocated. An early estimation regarding Synergy is that more resources need to be allocated towards marketing and building local church relationships.

Three more key elements are important throughout the operation stage of the partnership. The first of these is communication.[592] Butler indicates that four major groups need to be in view regarding communication of the partnership and its outcomes: the focus group or the group you are trying to reach (students), the leadership of the organizations, the stakeholders (prayer warriors, financial investors), and the people in the partnership itself (church, agency, school). A collectively understood system for handling finances needs to be in place as well as a means for handling conflict.[593]

Taken together, these practical steps provide an excellent foundation for exploring and reviewing the current state of Calvary's Synergy process and partnerships with local churches and mission agencies. Numerous excellent

---

[589] Butler, *Well Connected*, 180.
[590] Butler, *Well Connected*, 181-183.
[591] Butler, *Well Connected*, 183.
[592] Butler, *Well Connected*, 189.
[593] Butler, *Well Connected*, 190-194.

questions have come out of this literature review for use in the research and personal interviews for the action research study of relational partnerships through Synergy.

John Flinn in his dissertation study for Western Seminary defined "Mission Partnership" as,

> Mission partnerships are relationships of two or more people or organizations, who possess complimentary resources and skills, who have a common vision for Christian mission, and who, orchestrated by the Triune God, join forces to participate holistically in God's mission. The relationship of the partners to one another mimics that of the relationship of the Trinity through their unity with one another, their mutual love and respect for one another, and their mutual submission.[594]

It would be difficult, in the least, to find a more appropriate summary for this literature review. John Flinn's dissertation serves as an excellent example of a case study of relational partnership for mission. Utilizing the same principles that have been outlined here, he describes the partnership between Total Health (a U.S. medical mission) and La Ceiba church in Honduras.[595] His research findings discovered four key principles in this partnership.

1. Having a common vision.
2. The authentic nature of the relationships between partner members.
3. An interdependent and mutual relationship.
4. The ability to work through cultural issues with sensitivity, patience, grace.[596]

All four are principles which have been echoed by other authors above. Flinn's research serves as an example that this kind of partnership can be effective in multiplying the ministry of the partners and leading to transformation of both the ministry partners and those being served.

---

[594] John Jay Flinn, "Achieving Holistic Mission Through Mission Partnership: An Instrumental Case Study of a Mission Partnership in La Ceiba, Honduras," (DIS Dissertation, Western Seminary, Portland, 2020), 8.

[595] Flinn, "Achieving Holistic Mission Through Mission Partnership," viii.

[596] Flinn, "Achieving Holistic Mission Through Mission Partnership," 124.

William Taylor in summarizing the contributions of many authors in 1994 gave four next steps in the partnership conversation.

1. We must see partnerships as God sees them.
2. We must see the great benefits of partnerships.
3. Recognize there are frustrated and failed partnerships (seek to do better).
4. Church and mission leadership must take deliberate steps to commit to and enter careful partnerships.[597]

The years since these next steps were written have seen significant strides in partnership development between churches and missions agencies across the globe. However, more remains to be done. Taylor identifies the major partnership players as the local church, mission agencies, and national and regional mission associations.[598] He briefly mentions the contributions of "formal Bible/theology/missions schools"; however, they are not included as one of the major players but rather as a useful tool. It is time for the partnership discussion to begin including all aspects of the Body of Christ, including the university. Much more could also be said about the contributions of numerous Christian owned businesses around the world that provide both resources and platforms for the continued expansion of the Gospel. However, that is beyond the scope of this study. The task of mobilizing believers to take the gospel to the nations can only be improved through relational partnerships between local churches, theological schools, and mission agencies with the intent to mobilize the next generation of missionaries.

---

[597] Taylor, *Kingdom Partnerships for Synergy in Missions*, 238.
[598] Taylor, *Kingdom Partnerships for Synergy in Missions*, 238.

APPENDIX III
Research Findings

Interview Findings (Look)

Introduction

Synergy has been in operation at Calvary for five years now. In that time, while there has been interest in the process only three students have taken advantage of it and none of those three finished the program. To gain a better understanding of why that might be the case 12 people were interviewed to determine what strengths and weaknesses there are in the existing process and where improvements could be made. Interview questions also focused broadly on issues related to partnership, mobilizing Generation Z and the roles of local churches, universities, and mission agencies to establish each partner's understanding of these components in the process and support the findings from the literature review. Following the interviews, the broad findings were presented to focus groups to determine the most immediate areas of improvement for this research cycle.

Synergy Students

The three students who have had experience with Synergy were interviewed to gauge their perspective of the program, potential reasons they didn't finish it as well as any recommendations that they had. These three students include 2 males and 1 female. One of the students has graduated from Calvary and the other two are currently in their senior year. They represent a wide variety of backgrounds and interests. All three have different majors. All three also have some level of cross-cultural experience. The three students also completed over half of the Synergy process, with one of them doing all but the final class. Their responses will be broken into three categories, their overall impression of the experience, support that they did or did not receive including why they did not finish it, and recommendations based on their experience of the process. The specific interview questions are given in Appendix V.

Overall Impression of Synergy

All three students expressed a positive impression of Synergy and that while they didn't finish for various reasons, they were still very happy for the experience and what they learned. Their reasons for considering the program in their education included its structure and the ability to progress to the mission field quickly. For all three of them, missionary service was a part of their plan after graduating and Synergy fit well with that plan. The ability to gain practical experience and be trained by the agency were also mentioned as reason for choosing Synergy.

The students gave several benefits that they gained from their time with Synergy. The process was challenging but beneficial. Highlights included the classes themselves and learning more about culture and its inner workings, being able talk to and build relationships with missionaries, and getting practical experience including taking a vision trip with the Agency. For one student the biggest highlight was the counseling sessions which were conducted by the agency as part of the process. This is a normal component of the training for many mission organizations where candidates take several personality assessments and then work through them with mentors. Another student mentioned that this process was beneficial as well and served as a wakeup call for personal issues and a lack of faithfulness on his part. Students also mentioned that the dual aspect of going through the training coupled with a class at Calvary that required assignments served to reinforce many of the things they were learning.

Support They Received/Why They Didn't Finish

The next set of questions focused on what support they received throughout the program from Calvary, the mission agency, and their local church. All three students indicated that the support they received from Calvary was good. Calvary was the main driving force for them in their involvement in Synergy and support through follow up meetings or weekly meetings was good. For one student the support received from Calvary was what helped him to keep going.

Support from the mission agency was good as well. The personal involvement of a couple missions mobilizers on Calvary's campus was specifically mentioned. Although I could not verify it, one student indicated receiving a scholarship from the agency for the cost of the training. Another student indicated the agency could have done better from a mentoring standpoint. This student was assigned a mentor to work with, however, the mentor did not really follow up and expressed that their meetings could wait until the student was further along in the process, they only met once. Another difficulty was that as a college student he was in a very different place in life from many of the other missionary candidates.

Surprisingly and somewhat disheartening, although there could be various reasons for it was the lack of support that students received from their local church. All three students indicated little to no support from the local church.

A portion of that lack could be on the part of the student. One student indicated that they really didn't communicate the program with the local church and when they tried the pastor didn't understand it because it didn't match his experience. For another student there was a degree of church hopping as this student was looking for ministry opportunities while at Calvary so never really set down roots in a local church. Finally, for the last student their home church was several states away, so they never really got connected with him while at Calvary. The local church expressed interest, but both the student and the church were not sure of the next steps, so it fizzled out.

Multiple conclusions could be drawn from the disconnect that these students experienced with their local churches. Part of it could be the student's involvement with the church, part of it could be interest on the part of the pastor, and an equal part could be a lack of communication between Calvary or the agency to the local churches.

In the end the students identified that their reasons for not completing Synergy were largely personal. One student indicated that it was their own personality and indecisiveness. This student changed their major multiple times and was just never sure that missions was the end goal. For another student, it was maturity issues and a need to be discipled and have stronger roots in a local church. In the end, this student found those roots and a spiritual family in a local church in Kansas City. For the final student, missions was a focus primarily because of family members who had gone into it. However, the Synergy experience as well as a field visit and another ministry opportunity helped the student to solidify what their real strengths, weaknesses and interests are. In the end, this student chose to focus on an area more in keeping with their gifts and the direction they felt lead by the Lord.

Recommendations for Improvement

While none of the interviews with the students brought to light significant issues with the Synergy process, the students did have several recommendations. Those recommendations included pushing decisions back, while the process is designed to equip students and get them to the field it would also be beneficial for pastoral students or students with other majors to give them a grasp of what missions really involves. A key component here was how the process is communicated and it's intended goal. While yes, it is designed to mobilize missionaries, there are other benefits as well. Other students indicated the need to ensure that students who enter the process have missions as their goal. Another frequently mentioned subject was the commitment required. Students indicated that it is just hard to commit to a program like Synergy that early on in their college career. Perhaps if the process could be designed in a commitment-free way where can take advantage of the opportunity to expand their education with the option of joining the agency at the end.

Throughout the interviews with students the involvement of the local church was frequently referenced. For two students this was a major reason why they didn't continue. No specific fault could be leveled at either the students or their churches as there are various reasons why this took place. However, it does serve to highlight the importance of the local church in the process and the need for intentionality in creating relationships with the local church. Some specific recommendations involved coaching the student on how to get involved in their local church and its ministries as well as how to have the conversation with them about missions. Another recommendation was to ensure that students understand that Calvary is not a replacement for the local church.

Mission Agency Leaders

Three individuals were interviewed from each of the current Synergy partners. Each of the interviewees is a recognized leader in their organization. Two of them are directly involved in their agencies training and education departments and the third was also the co-creator of the Synergy program along with myself. They have anywhere from 6 to 33 years of experience with their organization.

The agency leaders were asked four questions specifically related to their views on partnership, four questions directed at how to mobilize Generation Z for Christian missions and the roles of the (church/agency/university) in doing so, and two questions regarding their experience of Synergy and potential recommendations to the program. The specific interview guide is given in Appendix B.

Partnership

Specific to partnership, all three reflected a shared understanding of partnership that is consistent with the findings in Chapter 2. Each organization has multiple partnerships at different levels. As mentioned earlier, Crossworld has a partnership with Avant Ministries that called Shared Services in which these two organizations share many of the back office, financial management and information technology of their organizations to save on paying staff. The have also formed an alliance with three other organizations, partnering on different projects, training, and encouraging their missionaries. Biblical Ministries Worldwide has begun partnering with multiple schools for training students, including Bob Jones University, the

Institute for Biblical Leadership, Veritas, and the Bible Training Center for Pastors. Partnership is an important element to all three organizations.

One specific question asked who the most important partners are for carrying out missions? All three of the individuals interviewed answered that the local church, mission agency, and university are vital partners in the process. They also reflected on the importance being connected in partnership with the Trinity. One interviewee also highlighted the role of the national church on the mission field. Another interviewee stated that for their organization the education partners are currently their most important from a mobilization perspective as they are building educational and training partnerships with multiple schools.

All three were asked specifically about what they would like to see in partnerships between their agency and churches as well as between their agency and schools like Calvary. In response to the question regarding partnerships with local churches three very specific items were highlighted. First, the interviews revealed concern that while recognizing that the primary pool for mission recruits is the local church, that pool is shrinking. If the local churches collapse, then the agency will too. On the other hand, was the recognition that many larger local churches have begun to do mission on their own apart from the agency. The church lone ranger mentality was seen as a big negative as the agency typically has years of experience, infrastructure and resources that would benefit the local church through partnerships. The third item that these agency leaders would like to see is encouraging more responsibility on the part of the sending church and specifically the pastor. One agency has even created a program of sending pastors to visit their missionaries on the field, the goal being to encourage the local church to share responsibility and not just outsource to the agency.

Asked what they would like to see in partnerships between the agency and the school there were several responses, one of which has already had a practical outcome. Biblical Ministries Worldwide reflected that they would like to see more intentional pathways to the mission field, of which Synergy is a prime example. This agency is also actively working on similar partnerships with other schools. The interview itself resulted in the immediate creation of an event at Calvary for the Fall of 2021 and continuing each year. This Explore Event bring several representatives from BMW on campus for an initial training module, conducted over a day and a half. This module can be attended by students as an introduction to the Synergy process and also by local churches who are interested in learning more about how to be Sending churches.

Another idea put forth in the interviews was to have agency mobilizers on campus as professors in the Intercultural Studies or Missions program. Consistent with Generation Z's desire for relationships and mentoring this would allow the mobilizer to naturally create relationships with students. I have already had a desire to add to the Burnham Center for Global Engagement at Calvary a space for mobilizers with the credentials to serve as adjunct professors in courses specific to the area of expertise and then potentially lead students on summer short-term missions trips. This serves as another affirmation of the relational nature of missions mobilization.

Roles of the Local Church, University, and Mission Agency

The next set of interview questions focused on the roles of the local church, university, and mission agency in mobilizing Generation Z for Christian Missions. Several themes emerged from these interviews regarding both issues and recommendations to how the local church mobilizes the next generation for missions, they are presented in the table below.

Table 24. Mobilization Issues and Recommendations

Organization	Issues	Recommendations
Local Church	- When we look at the church in Antioch (Acts 13) who sent the first missionaries we don't see the same kind of radical living out the gospel in community today as we do then. - There is a tension between witnessing locally and witnessing globally.	- Make missions accessible and attractive in how you communicate it. - Provide an intentional pathway from interest to deployment. - The church needs to help people fall in love with Jesus, if we have people who love the Lord, we will have people who step out to serve Him.

Organization	Issues	Recommendations
University	- Historical education is very compartmentalized. - A focus on head knowledge without experience-based education.	- Provide experiential learning activities to complement the classroom. - Consider changing what you call it, the term 'missions' is an obstacle to many people. - Providing vocational training accompanied by biblical/theological and cultural training can set students up for careers that can be used overseas.
Mission Agency	- Historically agencies have struggled with having a controlling attitude. - Agencies have not traditionally appealed to the calling of all students especially vocationally.	- Agencies need to be actively reaching into the local church and school, creating intentional pathways. - Providing overseas, experiential learning opportunities. - Creating intentional relationships and providing training.

In addition to the items mentioned above the three agency leaders also responded to the question, what is the most important issue in mobilizing Generation Z? One responded that it is commitment. Generation Z makes commitments differently than previous generations did. While still committed their commitments are not to organizations or business but rather to relationships. Again, this corroborates with research from Chapter 2, which highlights the importance of relationships in reaching and mobilizing this generation. Another interviewee highlighted the importance of presenting alternatives to the traditional missionary model. We should focus on a more holistic approach of communicating how they can use their career on the mission field and viewing missions as a lifestyle more than a vocational choice. The third highlighted the importance of relationships and especially community and going together on mission rather than being so individually focused.

Strengths, Weaknesses and Recommendations for Synergy

The final two questions that were asked of the agency leaders invited them to give insight into the Synergy process based on their experience thus far. For two of the interviewees their experience has been very limited. Only Crossworld has yet to see students come through the process. One of the interviewees has also only been in his current position for a little under a year and was not fully aware of the process. All of them are encouraged and excited to be involved in Synergy with their organization and recognize the importance of this type of partnership-based mobilization and equipping program.

Biblical Ministries Worldwide has had a difficult time in implementing the Synergy process. While they are strongly moving in a similar direction and actively engaged in building partnerships of the same kind or similar with Bob Jones University, Veritas and others there is little fruit to report as of yet. The Synergy partnership with BMW is three years old and, in that time, they have experienced both a transition in their President as well as the impact of the Covid-19 pandemic along with everyone else. The individual interviewed expressed that while implementation of the process has been slow, they are very encouraged by the partnership and there is a lot of excitement to see it happen. That said, as mentioned previously regarding the choice of participatory action research for this study, the interview itself served to spark greater opportunities for partnership through an Explore Missions Event hosted on Calvary's campus Fall 2021.

Ethnos 360 finds itself in a similar situation to BMW as there have not yet been students go through the Synergy process with them. Yet, the interviewee expressed the same excitement about the partnership and desire to see it come to fruition. An inherent difficulty for students considering Ethnos 360 is the timing of the process. While both Crossworld and BMW can be completed in the context of the student's four-year degree, completing Synergy with Ethnos 360 automatically adds a year. However, it does still save the student time in the normal process would involve six years. He believes that reason for not seeing students yet is the two-year commitment to training with them and that Synergy is simply not well known at this point. His recommendations were similar to those of BMW in that they need more mobilizer presence on campus, talking about the process and building relationships with students. Other suggestions included trips for students to their Missionary Training Center in southern Missouri, the Wayumi church planting course in Jersey Shore, Pennsylvania, and short-term overseas trips.

Crossworld, as the first Synergy partner and co-creator of the process and having three students try it has the most experience to offer. The interviewee reflecting on this experience mentioned the importance of screening participants, 2 of the 3 students who tried it were simply not prepared to follow through with it. He also noted the importance of the role of the student's home church. He also highlighted the importance of building relationships with the students early in the process.

One final insight came from interviewing the mission agency leaders. All three reflected that the program has simply not been marketed enough. It remains largely unknown among the local church community and even on Calvary's campus many students would not be able to accurately answer the question, "What is Synergy?" This marketing component hints at a weakness for the school's side where there is a lack of commitment from the entire school to the program. Much like BMW, Calvary has also faced challenges in the past couple years with Covid and a Presidential transition. It is encouraging that there is renewed commitment on the part of administration to make Synergy a part of Calvary's culture and market it better.

Local Church Pastors

The three pastors interviewed represent churches that are consistent with Calvary's constituency. All three churches are affiliated with the IFCA (Independent Fundamental Church's of America) an organization that Calvary has historical ties to and is consistent with Calvary's doctrinal statement. Two of the three pastors have served on Calvary's board and all three collectively represent 106 years of pastoral experience. All three are also very involved in the missions' programs of their churches and have relational connections to at least two of the mission agencies in this study either personally or through missionaries their church supports. They were asked to respond to 14 questions, the interview guide is found in Appendix B. Although the exact wording of the questions varied slightly, they were broken into similar categories as the mission agency questions.

Partnership

All three pastors expressed that partnership was incredibly important to them, much as it was for the agencies as well. They were also able to give me specific examples of partnerships they have with particular mission agencies and Calvary. Two of the pastors reflected specifically on their experience with Biblical Ministries Worldwide and what a blessing it was to participate in the opportunity to visit their missionaries on the field. The relational characteristic of partnerships was highlighted as well as the influence that Calvary has had on these pastors, through training, classes, speakers, and conferences they have attended.

All three pastors also reflected a similar mindset to that of the agency leaders regarding the most important partners in missions. They named, God, the local church, the university (specifically Calvary), and the mission agency.

Also named were other local churches, mission agency and university presidents, and key faculty members.

Roles of the Local Church, University, and Mission Agency

The pastors were also asked specifically on the benefits that they saw to partnering with both universities, like Calvary, and mission agencies. Those findings are summarized in the table below and are consistent with the literature review in Chapter 2.

Table 25. Benefits of Partnership as Recognized by Pastors

Role of the Local Church	Partnership Benefits with Universities (Calvary)	Partnership Benefits with Agencies
- The local church can give opportunities for ministry, internships, missions committee service, hands on ministry training.	- Calvary can provide academic, theological, and biblical training in a concentrated way that is difficult for the local church. - Faculty members can come and speak at the church on specific topics related to their area of expertise. -Offer extension courses, ongoing training for pastors or just church members who want to learn more. - For one church in particular the church is full of Calvary graduates, elders, deacons, Sunday school teachers etc. the pastor felt the church was strong because many of the leaders were well grounded in the Bible and theology from having attended Calvary.	- The agency can help involve other churches in the deputation process, it fills the gap with handling finances, taxes, insurance, benefits, retirement... things the local church would struggle with. - The agency is vital for administrative tasks and maintaining relationships with missionaries. - The agency can educate the local church on matters pertaining to missions. - They provide on-field oversight and support that the local church can't do.

The three pastors interviewed for this study clearly demonstrate an understanding of the importance of partnership. They also recognize the vital role that the local church, university and mission agency play in the preparation of missionary candidates. The following table gives the pastors responses to the same questions of the roles and responsibilities of each partner in mobilizing Generation Z. Once again, I have divided their comments into areas of issues and recommendations.

Table 26. Mobilization Issues and Recommendations from Pastors

Organization	Issues	Recommendations
Local Church	- "The church can't equip them for how to approach cross-cultural ministry without the help of the school and agency." - Not having the agency would limit the church's effectiveness in world outreach.	- Have a missions emphasis in the church that they can catch. Emphasis for the children and youth to see that emphasis. - Have missionaries visiting the church. - People personally challenged to consider missions through Sunday school, sermons. - Encourage Gen Z to go to Bible College - Educate the whole church on their identity in Christ, focus on discipleship. - Make sure their people are prepared, having partnerships with universities and agencies for specialized training. - There was a great deal of emphasis in all three interviews on educating the whole church congregation regarding missions. - The church should be proactive in helping the school and agency.
University	- The potential for 'mission drift' – moving away from a missions focus and a strong foundation in the Scriptures. - The school needs to have a culture of missions. - The classroom education environment is different.	- Challenge those with business majors, education, non-traditional ministry degrees to consider using their vocation in missions. - Continue to be doctrinally and theologically sound. - Make use of technology, be open to alternative education methods. - Create experiential learning opportunities.
Mission Agency	- The need to work with the church and school because this is where they are going to get the missionaries.	- Build strong relationships with the church, sending pastors, workshops, training. - Realize the local church is still dependent on them. - Get Gen Z out on the field where they can see missions firsthand. - Partner with pastors to work together, connect the pastor's interests to the mission field. - Be more pointed towards helping Gen Z find the right place, right people, right ministry, support raising, helping with the practical aspects of being a missionary.

Like the agency leaders the pastors were also asked to identify the most important issue in mobilizing Generation Z for Christian Missions. While echoing the same importance of relationships and especially mentoring they highlighted several other factors as well. There are the negative aspects such as the loss of innocence due to over exposure to negative influences via social media and their access to the internet. However, this was also seen in a positive light as Generation Z has been exposed to the needs of the world in a way previous generations were not, and they are motivated to help meet those needs. Another challenge that was mentioned was the generation gap. As the first generation to grow up completely immersed in the internet and technology older generations have a harder time relating to them. While this isn't a new phenomenon the extent of technology use might make it more challenging than ever before. Finally, one pastor expressed that this generation needs to be challenged. Compared with previous generations theirs has been a relatively easy life and they need to be challenged towards considering missions and making an impact for Christ.

Strengths, Weaknesses and Recommendations for Synergy

Like the agency representative the pastors were also asked to give insight into the Synergy process thus far and what strengths and weaknesses they see as well as recommendations for improving it. The pastors were given the opportunity to read the literature review for the study as background before the interview. All three pastors reported that the were encouraged by the strong biblical and theological foundation for the program. They all recognized the importance of partnership and what Synergy was trying to accomplish through its partnership design.

The greatest weakness that all three highlighted in the current Synergy design was the connection to the local church. This was not surprising as Synergy began as a partnership between the school and agency and only later was the local church considered. Taking intentional steps to include the local church as a full partner in the process without making them feel inferior was also mentioned. Another potential weakness that was mentioned was simply the practical outworking of Synergy. While it looks great on paper it will take commitment from all three sides to make it work. There were also specific comments made on the necessity of having commitment and buy-in from the whole church (elders, mission board, congregation) in order for the partnership to truly work.

Finally, the pastors did indicate several recommendations. One pastor recommended adding more agencies to the process. Adding more partners at this point is something that has been halted because of the few numbers of students involved. However, this pastor felt that more partners would result in greater marketing for the program and the school. Another recommendation was to specifically target marketing Synergy to IFCA[599] churches as Calvary is in their constituency as an IFCA friendly school. The learning contract was highlighted as a step in the right direction, it just needs full implementation. One pastor indicated that he would be thrilled to receive one and sign it.

Two recommendations stood out from among the rest as being real focus areas for the immediate future. The first was marketing. It has already been noted that one of the primary reasons for Synergy getting a slow start and low participation is that the program remains a relative unknown. Two of the interviews are members of Calvary's board of trustees and even they were largely unfamiliar with the program. A comprehensive marketing plan needs to be developed, focusing specifically on IFCA and other churches in Calvary's constituency. The second was reaching out to the churches in a helpful way. Calvary could offer church-based missions' courses, special events involving our agency partners, and conferences that seek to improve the local churches understanding of missions and increase their involvement. Two such events were held during the 2022-23 school year.

Alumni Missionaries

One final group that was interviewed for this study was three of Calvary's alumni missionaries. This group was included specifically to ask them to reflect on their time at Calvary and some of the influences that lead them towards missions as well as to present Synergy to them and ask them to think about if it would have been beneficial for them in their preparation for the mission field. Again, the specific interview questions are in the appendices, in this review I will focus on these three primary areas of their time at Calvary, what factors were essential in mobilizing them, and their thoughts on Synergy. This group has 37 years of missions experience collectively, with the shortest being 9 years. They are involved primarily in Aviation and Church Planting with other ministries being represented as well.

Preparation at Calvary

The responses from all three missionaries to the question of what best prepared them at Calvary were incredibly varied, as was their background. Two of them came to the school with an interest in missions. Of those one of them lost all interest in it as a result of a poor missions professor at the school during that time. The third was not interested in missions at all and only came to study the Bible, not to get a degree.

Preparation for missions during their time at Calvary included a spouse, relationships, on-campus activities, missions conferences and prayer groups.

---

[599] Independent Fundamental Churches of America

The most common element that each of them mentioned were the Bible courses. courses in Bible, theology, and biblical languages were all important factors for them and mentioned as some of the best aspects of what they received from Calvary.

A related question was asked regarding what they didn't receive but would have liked to, given their experience in missions. While none of them felt that their education was truly lacking, there were a couple areas that stood out that would have been helpful to their ministry. Those areas included courses on conflict resolution, and an emphasis on service. However, far and away the answer that every missionary named they wished they had received more of was practical ministry experience. Two of them mentioned that while Calvary has a Christian Ministry requirement for students every semester, it was too easy to fill with things that were in their comfort zone. The Christian Ministry requirement needs to be more focused on getting students involved in ministries that will contribute to their long-term ministry goals. Another missionary highlighted involving local churches by encouraging them to really invest in students by providing ministry opportunities.

Essential Mobilizing Factors for Alumni

The student who lost interest due to the missions professor while he was here indicated that what really helped him was being on the field and seeing it firsthand. The involvement of other Calvary faculty who had been missionaries was also instrumental for this interviewee. Other essential mobilizing factors included relationships with other students, upbringing, advice from the missions professor,[600] a spouse, internships, ministry opportunities through their local church, and the missionary in residence. The most common element that they all mentioned was again real practical ministry experience. Getting out on the field, taking short-term missions trips, and seeing missions first-hand for themselves was the top motivating factor.

Alumni Reflections on Synergy

The Synergy process was presented to the alumni missionaries, and they were asked to reflect on its strengths, weakness, and potential improvements. They were also asked to consider if had it been available when they were in school would they have taken advantage of it? All three indicated that had it been in place then they would have at least checked it out and two said they likely would have done it. The table below summarizes their responses on Synergy's strengths, weaknesses, and areas of improvement.

---

[600] Two of the interviewees studied under one missions professor, the same professor who influenced the author of this book, who is noted as having a big impact on mobilizing many students.

Table 27. Summary of Alumni Responses to Synergy

Strengths/Benefits	Potential Weaknesses	Recommendations
- For non-missions majors could provide a helpful perspective they would not have received from their education. - Understanding culture and cross-cultural ministry is extremely helpful. - Helpful to have specific mission training. - The agencies training and screening process, training in finances, home office staff, church-planting training. - Training from the agency reinforces education at Calvary. - Also, helpful to have the broader education from Calvary as most missions training is very specific and might not be applicable if the missionary changes ministries or needs to be flexible in their approach. - Bridging the gaps between church/agency/school - Getting to the field quicker - The local church being more involved and proactive in sending, Synergy provides a tool that is available to churches to get missionaries there. - Gets the student involved in the fundraising process sooner, building those relationships. - Helps the local church gain a vision for sending their people.	- Getting the local church on board with the process. - Student debt, the process needs a way to reduce the student's college debt. - The world needs more than just trained missionaries but other vocations/professionals as well who do ministry as part of their job. - Needs to incorporate an internship. - The next generation views missions differently, how to train them according to how they view it – he would go as a tentmaker if he did it over. - Needs emphasis on practical opportunities. - An issue that needs to be addressed is a competitive attitude on the missions field. Missionaries competing against one another instead of supporting each other. - A strong need for a discipleship focus for the student. Building strong relationships and cultivating an attitude of service and humility. - Potential issues where a student starts Synergy with one organization and then wants to switch to a different one. - Cost of training on top of cost of school.	- One missionary did not have any recommendations. - There needs to be more thought given to how the program is marketed, how would a music student learn about it? - Needs a strong emphasis on practical ministry experience, using the Christian Ministry requirement to its fullest. - Don't forget that the church is the sender, be intentional to maintain that spirit of the local church as sender. - A 1–2-year evaluation period for the student after they deploy to the field. - Perhaps a specific ministry assignment following graduation that the student can step into for a couple years and get supervised experience.

Summary

At the conclusion of the interviews, it was clear the Synergy has great potential to establish relational connections between the church, school, and agency for mobilizing Gen Z missionaries. Like all new initiatives it has strengths, weaknesses, and areas for improvement. The action research process has identified several areas of improvement. Having worked through these results from the interviews they were then presented to three focus groups of the interview participants to narrow down some specific areas that the director could focus on improving for this research cycle.

Focus Groups for Synergy Improvements (Think)

Three focus groups were created from the interview participants with one representative from each area (pastor, mission rep, student, missionary). They were conducted via zoom just like the interviews. The participants were given the opportunity to read a summary of the interview findings and then asked to reflect on three questions, potential areas for improving Synergy, how partnerships can be created, and first steps for this research cycle. While many ideas were discussed several key themes emerged across all three focus groups. These are summarized in the table below followed by a brief discussion of the key next steps that were highlighted by all three groups.

Table 28. Focus Group Findings

Areas of Improvement	Creating Partnerships	First Steps
- Marketing (nobody knows about it, communication to churches, students). - Students who felt disconnected from the church. - Extenuating circumstances (covid/organizational transitions). - Students being asked to commit too early (sophomore year) this may be a communication issue though. - Students who don't finish because they realize it isn't for them is a good thing. - Include experiential opportunities (overseas trips, trips to agency headquarters, on campus events with agencies/missionaries). - Learning Contracts – make them yearly rather than whole program. -Missions agencies need a presence on campus. - Educating the local church on what missions is. - Emphasize the relational aspect of going with someone, working alongside them (Paul/Timothy). - Process for screening students to ensure their commitment and success. - Broaden the idea of cross-cultural missions to include other programs.	- Marketing Director meeting personally with pastors to explain it. Going to regional IFCA meetings. - Church consortium or network, using the school as an opportunity to connect local churches in a network. - Explore Events – Agency led events on campus, include students, pastors, others, advertise as professional development. - Calvary/Agency led missions trips that are offered to students but also the broader constituency. - Directing new students to churches that are missions minded. - Think Tank - Offer Professional Development courses to pastors and churches.	- Marketing (specifically to IFCA). - Missions Conference/Think Tank as an avenue for building partnerships and sharing the concept. - Offering Agency led conferences on campus. - Semi-permanent mission rep presence on campus. - Include more agencies in the partnership, more options for students and more awareness in the community. - Vision Casting - Culture building

The focus groups highlighted several important areas for improvement in the Synergy process. Very few of them were related to the structure of the process itself and most involve extra areas of emphasis or concern. The lack of specific improvements to the process at this point is likely due to the few number of students and a general lack of awareness about it. Across the board, in every focus group marketing was mentioned repeatedly as a chief concern. The very simple reality for where Synergy is at right now is that very few people know about the program. There were several contributing factors to this including the Covid-19 pandemic and organizational changes at both Calvary and with the missions agencies. In addition, having a consistent marking plan is something that Calvary has traditionally struggled with, however, the new administration is making practical steps to better market the school and its programs.

Some specific areas that were brought up concerning students included their connection with the local church, the timing of the commitment being asked of them, and the screening and application process. It was noted that based on the students' comments from the interview the fact that they did not complete Synergy should be viewed as a positive as they were not ready and pushing them through the program and onto the field could have led to more complicated issues, including their failure and return. There also seemed to be a miscommunication issue related to the commitment of the students. The participants felt like students were being asked to commit to the process too soon. However, further explanation was needed, that in participating in this process the student is not making the decision to commit to serve with this organization following graduation. Both the student and the agency enter the Synergy process with the understanding that at the end of it either one could decide that either the student is not a good fit for this agency, or they have decided not to serve in mission long term. Synergy should be communicated as an opportunity not a contract. Clarity is needed in how it is communicated to students. Two other consistent factors across all three focus groups were educating the local church and relational connections with the missions agency. Several steps are already being taken in these areas and will be discussed nest.

Proposed Synergy Process Changes (Act)

Closing the loop on action research means choosing those areas that present the most opportunity for improvement in the current research cycle. It was encouraging that very few of the noted action steps involve changing the process itself. While there is room for improvement in several areas, those areas are outside the actual program of Synergy.

General Improvements

One of the clear improvements, if Synergy is going to be successful in both creating partnerships and mobilizing students, is marketing. Almost every interview candidate and each focus group mentioned marketing as one of the number one areas for improvement. Two of the interview participants are members of Calvary's board and even they expressed that they had no idea this process was in place. One of the clear first steps forward is to do a better job in marketing the program. Several practical ideas were put forth by the focus groups for starting to market Synergy better.

Calvary has a close connection with the IFCA (Independent Fundamental Churches of America). This network of churches has both regional meetings and a national convention. One clear first step is for the Synergy Director to attend these meetings to present Synergy before churches and engage in the process of building relationships with the churches. Those relationships could be further explored through the creation of a network of churches associated with Calvary that collaborate on the sending and supporting of their missionaries, including Calvary graduates.

Throughout the research, the church was noted, even by the pastors, as being the weakest link in the process. While the literature review and supporting research clearly lay a foundation for missions as the responsibility of the local church, local church involvement in missions can vary greatly. This again highlights the importance of relational partnerships for the local church with the school and mission agency. As noted in the interviews the mission agencies in this report all have processes for helping the local church with their missions program. Calvary is also in a position to bless the local churches and assist them in improving their approach to missions. To that end, three practical improvements to the operation of the Burnham Center for Global Engagement (which oversees Synergy) have come from this study.

First, Calvary has begun working in partnership with these agencies to host on-campus events specifically for our local church constituency. The first of these was held October 28-29th, 2021 and was cohosted by the Burnham Center and Village Missions. Village Missions is one of Calvary's national focused Synergy partners with an emphasis on rural church planting and revitalization.[601] Representatives from Village Missions joined Calvary to host the "So, This is Rural" Conference. The conference brought together students, pastors, teachers, and agency leaders around the topic of rural ministry. During the conference Synergy was presented as an opportunity for students as well as an opportunity for local churches to join in an intentional preparation program for their members to "On Ramp" directly to rural ministry.[602] The second event was held immediately after on November 4-5, 2021. This two day "Explore Missions" conference brought representative from Biblical Ministries Worldwide (including one of the interview participants) on campus to share with students and pastors. Several local church representatives were present. These mini conferences present an opportunity for churches to learn about both Calvary and the mission agency

---

[601] Village Missions, accessed 10/18/2021, https://villagemissions.org/.
[602] The national focused Synergy Programs are referred to as On Ramp.

as well as serve to foster the relationship between all three.

The second area involves our regular missions conference. Calvary's Conference on Global Engagement, held annually, the last week of January, regularly brings together 35-40 missions reps from 30+ missions organizations. Two years ago (2020) we hosted our first Partnership Think Tank. This event brought together pastors and missions leaders from 10 churches, while the missions reps were still on campus for a time of discussing how we can partner better together for mobilizing the next generation. Covid-19 and some organizational changes then conspired to prevent any follow-up from this initial meeting. While it was intended to be annual it was not possible to hold it in 2021 due to ongoing concerns from the Covid-19 pandemic. However, the Partnership Think Tank will be relaunched in 2022 with a focus on building practical areas of partnership between local churches, Calvary, and missions agencies. The focus of the 2022 conference will be the creation of a local church consortium for collaboration on sending and supporting missionaries.

This leads me to the third area which is the church consortium itself. Not much can be said at this point as it currently remains a future prospect. However, all three pastors included in this study indicated a desire to see this type of local church network come together around the Burnham Center for Global Engagement at Calvary. Calvary occupies a unique position, in that while it seeks to serve both the local church and the mission agency, its practical involvement is focused on the student. Calvary is not in a position of competition with either the local church or the missions agency, as such it can serve both without an agenda. This makes it the ideal location for beginning this type of church network where the interests of the local churches and the agencies can be heard and shared equally. The details of this consortium remain to be worked out at the January 2022 Partnership Think Tank.

Specific Synergy Areas

For the current research cycle there were some areas that were identified as potential improvements in Synergy itself. The first has already been mentioned in the way the process is communicated to students. Greater care needs to be taken in contextualizing Synergy for the current generation such that a vision is cast for Synergy being and opportunity for the student to build a relationship with a missions organization and their local church while being trained and prepared for missions. However, it needs to be emphasized that the student is not being asked to decide their long-term career goals so early in their college career. While Synergy represents a significant commitment by the local church, the school and the mission agency in the student. It must be an open-ended commitment. On the one hand none of us want missionaries on the field who will cause more harm than good. On the other, even a student who does not finish the program is not a loss as they will now enter their local church better prepared to support and raise awareness for the reality of missions.

The second next step was including more agencies in the Synergy Process. This was recommended from the standpoint that more agencies participating would lead to a greater awareness and marketing of the program. However, this is an area that should be handled with caution. At this point the decision was made to not add any more partners until there are more students taking advantage of Synergy. While several other agencies have expressed an interest in Synergy, having too many agencies and not enough students is a difficult balance.

Finally, throughout this study there has been a constant and consistent focus on the importance of relationships. Whether it is relationships between the partners themselves of with the student or each one's relationship with the Triune God, relationships form the backbone of the entire Synergy process. Any attempt to improve, build, or sustain relationships between the three organizations is a step in the right direction. To that end a dream has emerged which sees each of the missions agencies having a permeant representation on campus. Calvary, like many similar schools and Bible colleges has a tradition of having a missionary-in-residence on campus each school year. However, that tradition has waned in recent years and Calvary has less to offer the missionary and missionaries are less likely to spend an entire year off the field and away from their ministry. At the same time, recognizing the importance and impact that these individuals have had in the past on mobilizing students as well as the importance of relationships an idea has developed. The idea, which was shared among each focus group and met with a good reception is to offer each partner agency permanent office space on Calvary's campus. The goal would be to see mobilizers from each agency present on campus full-time, in classes, possibly teaching and leading local outreach events where they can naturally build relationships with students and serve as mentors outside the classroom. This would be the true goal for what the Burnham Center for Global Engagement is to look like on Calvary's campus.

Summary

This chapter focused on the results of the participatory action research that was conducted via interviews and focus groups. Twelve individuals were interviewed representing local churches, mission agencies, students, and graduates serving in missions. The results of those interviews were then shared with three focus groups of the same participants. Overall, the research indicated several general areas for improvement in Calvary's process that could benefit the Synergy process. Some specific areas of improvement for

Synergy were also noted. Synergy was noted as being a solid basis for partnership between the local church, Calvary, and mission organizations. Its current lack of student involvement was noted as mostly being a marketing issue with some focus on how the process is understood and its goal. This research cycle ended with some specific areas for improvement, some of which have already begun to be implemented. The next chapter will highlight both missiological and educational implications that have come from this study.

APPENDIX IV
Synergy Learning Contract

Student: _____

Program/Ministry Focus: _____

Mentor Contact Info:

Name: _____

Occupation: _____

Phone Number: _____

Address: _____

_____

E-mail: _____

Home Church: _____

Pastor Contact Info:

Name: _____

Phone Number: _____

Address: _____

_____

E-mail: _____

Local Church: _____

Pastor Contact Info:

Name: _____

Phone Number: _____

Address: _____

_____

E-mail: _____

Christian Ministries:

Freshman:

Fall _____

Spring _____

Sophomore:

Fall _____

Spring _____

Junior:

Fall _____

Spring _____

Senior

Fall _____

Spring _____

Internship: _____

Contact: _____

Phone: _____

Address: _____

E-mail: _____

Signatures

Student: _____ Date: _____

Program Director: _____ Date: _____

Mentor: _____ Date: _____

Pastor: _____ Date: _____

Anticipated Graduation Date: _____

Planned Schedule of Completion[576]

---

[576] Specific Courses will vary depending on the student's actual program.

Professional Courses	Credit	Course Title	Semester/Year
IC111	3	Introduction to Christian Missions	
CO244	3	Introduction to Biblical Counseling	
MS237	3	Teaching the Bible	
MS322	3	Administrative Process	
MS340	3	Theological Foundations for Ministry	
RP339	2	Introduction to Philosophy	
CO247	3	Counseling Cross-Culturally	
IC303	3	Theology of Missions	
IC336	3	Intercultural Communication & Evangelism	
IC346	3	Contemporary Issues in Missions	
IC434	3	Intercultural Church Planting	
IC446	3	Practical Relations in Intercultural Studies	
IC453	3	Intercultural Studies Internship	
IC459	3	Senior Seminar - Intercultural Studies	
SS337	3	Cultural Anthropology	
Pick `1			
BI238	2	Acts	
IC320	2	History of Missions	
Open Electives			
	3		
	3		
	3		
	3		
	3		

My current understanding of my learning goals is:

_____
_____
_____
_____
_____
_____
_____
_____
_____
_____

APPENDIX V
Interview Guide for Participatory Action Research
Study of Synergy

* This is a guide for beginning the interviews with each set of participants. The actual direction of the conversation and interview could change depending on the interviewee and the initial responses. The goal of this qualitative study is to discover themes in the context of the interview relevant to the Synergy process not to develop quantitative data based on each question.

3 Agency Leaders from Synergy partners
Questions for Agency Leaders
1. How important is partnership to your organization?
2. How would you define partnership?
3. Who would you consider to be the most important partners necessary for carrying out missions?
4. What would you like to see in partnerships between your agency and local churches?
5. What would you like to see in partnerships between your agency and schools like Calvary?
6. What, in your opinion, is the most important issue in mobilizing Generation Z for Christian Missions?
7. What is the role and responsibilities of the local church in mobilizing Generation Z for Christian Missions?
8. What is the role and responsibilities of universities, like Calvary, in mobilizing Generation Z for Christian Missions?
9. What is the role and responsibilities of mission agencies like your own in mobilizing Generation Z for Christian Missions?
10. What has been your experience of Calvary's Synergy process thus far? Has it been explained to you?
11. As you have been involved in Calvary's Synergy process for the past couple years what recommendations do you have for improvements?

3 Pastors from constituency churches
Questions for Pastors
1. How important is partnership to your church?
2. How would you define partnership?

3. Who would you consider the most important partners necessary for carrying out missions?
4. What benefits do you see to your church partnering with schools like Calvary?
5. What benefit do you see to your church partnering with mission agencies?
6. What, in your opinion, is the most important issue in mobilizing Generation Z for Christian Missions?
7. What is the role and responsibilities of the local church in mobilizing Generation Z for Christian Missions?
8. What is the role and responsibilities of universities, like Calvary, in mobilizing Generation Z for Christian Missions?
9. What is the role and responsibilities of mission agencies like your own in mobilizing Generation Z for Christian Missions?
10. What has been your experience of Calvary's Synergy process thus far? Has it been explained to you?
11. As Synergy has been explained to you more, what recommendations/concerns do you have?
12. How do you think Synergy could be improved?
13. How can Calvary be of even greater benefit to your church?
14. What would your dream be for partnerships between local churches, mission agencies, and schools?

3 Missionaries on the field
Questions for Missionaries
1. When did you graduate from Calvary and with what degree?
2. How long have you been on the mission field and what is your primary ministry?
3. What did you receive from Calvary that best prepared you for your current ministry?
4. What do you most wish Calvary would have given you that you did not receive?
5. As Synergy has been explained to you what do you see as the benefits of this process?
6. What, in your opinion, are the greatest potential weaknesses in the Synergy process?
7. Do you think you would have personally benefitted from a program like Synergy in your preparation for the mission field? How?
8. What recommendations or changes would you have for how Synergy has been presented?
9. What concerns, if any, would you have for a student going through Synergy?
10. If you could say anything to a college student preparing for missions, what would it be?

3 Students who have been in the program

<u>Questions for Students</u>

1. Why did you elect to do Synergy as part of your education at Calvary?
2. What is the greatest benefit your received from being involved in Synergy?
3. What was your overall impression of the process?
4. What support or lack of did you receive from your local church?
5. What support or lack of did you receive from Calvary and or the Director of Synergy?
6. What support or lack of did you receive from the mission agency?
7. Was Synergy a help or hindrance to your education?
8. Did you complete Synergy?
9. If you did not complete it, what factors led to your decision and how might you have been encouraged to continue?
10. What recommendations would you have for improvements to Synergy?
11. What would you most like incoming students who are considering Synergy to know?
12. What final thoughts do you have on already proposed changes to Synergy?

BIBLIOGRAPHY

Abbe, Allison. "Building Cultural Capability for Full-Spectrum Operations." Study Report 2008-04. U.S. Army Research Institute. 2008.

Abbe, Allison, Lisa M.V. Gulick and Jeffery L. Herman. *Cross-Cultural Competence in Army Leaders: A Conceptual and Empirical Foundation.* Arlington, VA: United States Army Research Institute for the Behavioral and Social Sciences, 2007.

Adair, Wendi L., Ivona Hideg and Jeffery R. Spence. "The Culturally Intelligent Team: The Impact of Team Cultural Intelligence and Cultural Heterogeneity on Team Shared Values." *Journal of Cross-Cultural Psychology* 44.941 (2013): 941-962.

Addicott, Ernie. *Body Matters: A Guide for Partnership in Christian Mission.* Edmonds, WA: Interdev Partnership Associates, 2005.

Anderson, Dan. *Missiological implications of Biblical Mentoring for Mentoring Duna Youth* Paper submitted in Partial Requirements for course DIS 780. Western Seminary. Portland, 2014.

Anderson, Ray S. *The Shape of Practical Theology.* Downers Grove, IL: InterVarsity Press, 2001.

Anderson, William. "The Coming Crises for Christian Colleges." accessed October 4, 2019. *The James G. Martin Center for Academic Renewal.* https://www.jamesgmartin.center/2019/01/the-coming-crises-for-christian-colleges/.

Anthony, Michael J., ed. *Evangelical Dictionary of Christian Education.* Grand Rapids, MI: Baker Academics, 2001.

Ardiwardana, Margaretha. "Formal and Non-Formal Pre-Field Training, Perspective of the New Sending Countries." In *Too Valuable to Lose.* Taylor, William B. ed. Pasadena, CA: William Carey Library, 1995.

Argyis, C, and D.A. Schon. "Increasing Professional Effectiveness." In *Theory into Practice.* San Francisco: Jossey-Bass, 1974.

Armstrong, Ruth M. "A Christian Approach to Learning Theory." In *Christian Approaches to Learning Theory, A Symposium.* De Jung, Norman, ed. Lanham, MD: University of America Press, 1984.

Banks, Robert. *Reenvisioning Theological Education. Exploring a Missional Alternative to Current Models.* Grand Rapids, MI: William B. Eerdmans Publishing Company, 1999.

Barna. *The Future of Missions: 10 Questions About Global Ministry the Church Must Answer with the Next Generation.* Ventura, CA: Barna Group, 2020.

Barna. *Gen Z: The Culture, Beliefs and Motivations Shaping the Next Generation.* Ventura, CA: Barna Group, 2018.

Barnes, Jonathan S. *Power and Partnership: A History of the Protestant Mission Movement.* Eugene, OR: Pickwick Publications, 2013.

_____. "Whither Partnership? Reflections on the History of Mutuality in Mission." *Review and Expositor.* Vol. 113 (1) (2016): 32-45.

Barnes & Noble College. *Getting to Know Gen Z: Exploring Middle and High Schoolers' Expectations for Higher Education.* accessed February 25, 2019, https://next.bncollege.com/wp-content/uploads/2015/10/Gen-Z-Research-Report-Final.pdf.

Bavinck, J.H. *An Introduction to the Science of Missions.* Philadelphia, PA: Presbyterian and Reformed Pub. Co., 1960.

Beals, Paul A. *A People for His Name: A Church-based Missions Strategy.* Revised ed. Pasadena: William Carey, 1995.

Bennett, Milton J. "Becoming Interculturally Competent," in J. Wurzel (ed). *Towards Multiculturalism: A Reader in Multicultural Education.* 2nd ed. Newton, MA: Intercultural Resources Corp., 2004.

Berardo, Kate and Darla Deardorff, *Building Cultural Competence; Innovative activities and Models.* Sterling, VA: Stylus Publishing, LLC, 2012.

Biblical Ministries Worldwide. "Senders Think Tank." Atlanta: Biblical Ministries Worldwide, unpublished handout. 2019.

Bloecher, Detlef. "Missionary Training Makes Missionaries Resilient – Lessons From ReMAP II," 18 Oct 2003, 1-14. accessed June 5, 2020, http://www.wearesources.org.

Bloom, Benjamin S. *Taxonomy of Educational Objectives. Book One: Cognitive Domain.* New York: Longman Inc., 1954.

Boff, Leonard. *Holy Trinity, Perfect Community.* Translated by Phillip Berryman, Maryknoll, NY: Orbis Books, 1991. Originally published in Portuguese *Santisima Trindade e a Melhor Communidade,* 1988.

Bowman, Joshua Stephen. *Cross-Cultural Mission Partnership: Mediating Relational, Cultural, and Hermeneutical Tensions for Mutual, Faithful*

Missional Engagement. PhD Thesis, Southeastern Baptist Theological Seminary, September 2019.

Boyd, Robert D., and J. Gordon Myers. "Transformative Education." *International Journal of Lifelong Education* 7, no. 4, October-December 1988: 261-284.

Brinkman, Ursula and van Weerdenburg, Oscar. *Intercultural Readiness. Four Competences for working across cultures.* New York: Palagrave Macmillan, 2014.

Brookfield, N. C. and R. Berk (1999) "Critical Thinking and Critical Pedagogy: Relations, Differences, and Limits." In Thomas S. Popkewitz and Lynn Fendler, eds.: *Critical Theories in Education.* New York: Routledge, Available at http://faculty.ed.uiuc.edu/burbules/ncb/papers/critical.html.

Broucek, Dave. "An In-Service Training Idea for Church Planters." *Occasional Bulletin of the Evangelical Missiological Society*, Vol 10, no. 2, Spring, 1998.

_____. "Best Practice Standards for Missionary Training," paper presented at IFMA/EFMA Personnel Conference, International Missions Board of the Southern Baptist Convention Missionary Learning Center, Rockville, VA: Dec 4-6, 2003.

Bruce, A B. *The Training of the Twelve.* New Canaan, CT.: Keats Publishing, 1979.

Bryan, C. Doug. *Relationship Learning. A Primer in Christian Education.* Nashville, TN: Broadman Press, 1990.

Brynjolison, Rob. "Effective Equipping of the Cross-Cultural Worker." *The Journal of WEA Missions Commission,* Jan-April, 2004, 72-79. www.globalmission.org.

Bush, Luis and Lorry Lutz, *Partnering in Ministry: The Direction of World Evangelism.* Downers Grove, IL: Intervarsity Press, 1990.

Butler, Phill. *Well Connected: Releasing Power, Restoring Hope Through Kingdom Partnerships.* Colorado Springs, CO: Authentic, 2006.

Calvary University Catalog 2017-2019. Kansas City, MO: Calvary University, 2017.

Carroll, James B. "Social Action and Evangelism: Envisioning a New Relational Paradigm for 21st Century American Christianity." July 2012. www.globalmissiology.org.

Caswell, Hollis L. and Doak S. Campbell. *Curriculum Development.* New York: American Book Co., 1935.

Center for Church Based Training. *Elders and Leaders, Field Guide*. Richardson, TX: CCBT, 2003.

Chang, Peter. "Steak, Potato, Peas and Chopsuey: Linear and Non-linear Thinking in Theological Education." *Evangelical Review of Theology*. Vol. V, no. 2, Oct. 1981.

Chafer, Lewis Sperry. "Ecclesiology." *Systematic Theology Vols. 7 & 8*. Grand Rapids: Kregel Publications, 1976.

Chafer, Lewis Sperry. *Systematic Theology Vols. 1 & 2*. Grand Rapids: Kregel Publications, 1976.

Chittum, Matthew. *Unmasking Consumerism for the Practice of Relational Discipleship within the Contemporary American Cultural Context*. DIS Dissertation. Western Seminary, 2014.

Cloud, Louis Jacob. *Doxological Missiology: Theory, Motivation, and Practice*. DIS Dissertation. Western Seminary, 2020.

Cobb, John B. Jr. and David Ray Griffin. *Process Theology. An Introductory Exposition*. Philadelphia, PA: Westminster Press, 1976.

Cohen, Norman H. *Mentoring Adult Learners – A Guide for Educators and Trainers*. Malabar, FL: Krieger Publishing Company, 1995.

Coombs, Philip H. with Marzoor Ahmed. *Attacking Rural Poverty – How Nonformal Education Can Help*. Baltimore, M.D.: Johns Hopkins Univ. Press, 1974.

Corwin, Gary. "Reinventing Missionary Training." *Evangelical Missions Quarterly*, Vol 32: no. 2, April 1996, 144-145.

Cragg, C.E., Plotnikoff, R.C., Hugo, K. and A. Casey (2001) "Perspective transformation in RN-to-BSN distance education." *Journal of nursing education*, 40(7).

Cranton, Patricia. *Understanding and Promoting Transformative Learning: A Guide for Educators of Adults*. San Francisco, CA: Jossey-Bass, 1994.

_____. *Professional Development as Transformative Learning: New Perspectives for Teachers of Adults*. San Francisco, CA: Jossey-Bass Inc., 1996.

_____, ed. *Transformative Learning in Action: Insights from Practice. New Directions for Adult Continuing Education*. No. 74. San Francisco, CA: Jossey-Bass, Summer 1997.

_____. *Understanding and Promoting Transformative Learning: A Guide for Educators of Adults*, 2nd ed. San Francisco, CA: John Wiley & Sons, Inc. 2006.

Cranton, Patricia. And K.P. King. "Transformative learning as a professional development goal." *New Directions for Adult and Continuing Education*, no. 98 (2003), 31-37.

Creswell, John W. and Cheryl N. Poth. *Qualitative Inquiry & Research Design: Choosing Among Five Approaches*, 4th ed. Los Angeles: SAGE, 2018.

Cone, Christopher. "Why Biblical Foundations for Education Still Matter." *Christopher Cone.* November 2018. http://www.drcone.com. Accessed November 5, 2018.

Cummings, William K. "Evaluation and Examinations: Why and How Are Educational Outcomes Assessed." In *International Comparative Education – Practices, Issues And Prospects.* Thomas, R. Murray, ed. New York: Pergamon Press, 1990.

Cunningham, David. *These Three Are One. The Practice of Trinitarian Theology.* Malden, MA: Blackwell Publishers, 1998.

Dahms, John V. "Biblical Ecclesiology." *Global Missiology*, January 2005, www.globalmissiology.net.

_____. "Biblical Feelings and Emotions." *Global Missiology*, January 2005, www.globalmissiology.net.

Deardorff, Darla K. "Theory Reflections: Intercultural Competence Framework/Model." https://www.nafsa.org/_/File/_/theory_connections_intercultural_competence.pdf 2006.

_____. "Identification and Assessment of Intercultural Competence as a Student Outcome of Internationalization." *Journal of Studies in International Education* 10.241 (2006): 241-266.

DeJung, Norman, ed. *Christian Approaches to Learning Theory, A Symposium.* Latham, MD: University of America Press, 1984.

_____, ed. *Christian Approaches to Learning Theory, Vol 2. The Nature of the Learner.* Latham, MD: University of America Press, 1985.

DeYoung, Kevin and Greg Gilbert. *What Is the Mission of the Church? Making Sense of Social Justice, Shalom, and the Great Commission.* Wheaton: Crossway, 2011.

Dirks, J.M., Mezirow, J., and Patricia Cranton. "Musings and reflections on the meaning, context, and process of transformational learning: A dialogue between John M. Dirkx and Jack Mezirow." *Journal of Transformative Education,* 4(2), (2006), 123-139.

Driel, Marius van, and William K. Jr. Gabrenya. "Organizational Cross-Cultural Competence: Approaches to Measurement." *Journal of Cross-Cultural Psychology* 44, no. 874 (2013).

Elias, D. "It's time to change our minds: An introduction to transformative learning." *Revision*, 20(1), 1997.

Elias, John L and Sharan B. Merriam, *Philosophical Foundations of Adult Education, 3rd Ed.* Malabar, FL: Krieger Publishing Company, 2005.

Elmer, Muriel I. and Duane H. *The Learning Cycle: Insights for Faithful Teaching from Neuroscience and the Social Sciences.* Downers Grove: IVP Academic, 2020.

Enns, Paul. *The Moody Handbook of Theology.* Chicago: Moody Press, 1989.

Escobar, Samuel. *The New Global Mission: The Gospel From Everywhere to Everyone.* Downers Grove, IL: InterVarsity Press, 2003.

_____. "The Training for Missiologists for a Latin American Context." In *Missiological Education for the 21st Century*, 105, n.d.

Farley, Edward. The Fragility of Knowledge, Theological Education in the Church And the University. Philadelphia, PA: Fortress Press, 1988.

_____. *Theologia*: *The Fragmentation And Unity of Theological Education.* Philadelphia, PA: Fortress Press, 1983.

Feenestra, Ronald J., and Cornelius Plantiga Jr., eds. *Trinity, Incarnation, and Atonement.* Notre Dame, IN: University of Notre Dame Press, 1989.

Fernando, Ajith. "Grounding Our Reflections in Scripture: Biblical Trinitarianism and Mission." In *Global Missiology for the 21st Century: The Iguassu Dialogue.* Taylor, William B., ed. Pasadena, CA: William Carey Library, 1999.

Ferris, Robert W., ed. *Establishing Ministry Training.* Pasadena, CA: William Carey Library, 1995.

_____. "Standards of Excellence in Missionary Training Centers, "1-7, <www.wearesources.org> 2005. First published in *Training for Cross-Cultural Ministries*, Vol 2000: no 1, January 2000.

Fletcher, S. "Mentoring Adult Learners: Realizing possible selves." In M. Rossiter (Ed.), *Possible selves and adult learning: Perspectives and potential. New Directions for adult and continuing education.* no. 114, 2007, 75-86.

Flinn, John Jay. *Achieving Holistic Mission Through Mission Partnership: An Instrumental Case Study of a Mission Partnership in La Ceiba, Honduras.* DIS Dissertation, Western Seminary, 2020.

Ford, Leroy. *Curriculum Design Manual for Theological Education: A Learning Outcomes Focus.* Nashville, TN: Broadman Press, 1991.

Gagnon, Jr., G.W. & M. Collay. *Constructivist Learning Design.* http://web.wnlsd.ca/rocketry/resources/Gagnon_Collay_ConstructivistLearningDesign.pdf. (Accessed February 25, 2019).

Gilbert, Marvin, Alan R. Johnson, and Paul W. Lewsi, eds. *Missiological Research: Interdisciplinary Foundations, Methods, and Integration.* Pasadena: William Carey Library, 2018.

Grabove, Valerie. "The Many Facets of Transformative Learning Theory and Practice." In: *Transformative Learning in Action: Insights from Practice. New Directions for Adult and Continuing Education.* no. 74, edited by P. Cranton, 89-96. San Francisco, CA: Jossey Bass, Summer 1997.

Grudem, Wayne. *Bible Doctrine: Essential Teachings of the Christian Faith.* Grand Rapids: Zondervan, 1999.

Gunton, Colin E. *The One, The Three and the Many. God, Creation and the Culture of Modernity.* New York: Cambridge University Press, 1993.

_____. *The Promise of Trinitarian Theology*, 2nd Edition, New York: T & T Clark, 1997.

Hall, Edward T. *Beyond Culture.* New York: Anchor Books, 1997, 1989.

Harley, David. *Preparing to Serve. Training for Cross-Cultural Mission.* Pasadena, CA: William Carey Library, 1995.

Hassel, Stefanie and Nathan Ridout. "An Investigation of Frist-Year Student's and Lecturers' Expectations of University Education." *Frontiers in Psychology*, January 2018. https://www.frontiersin.org/articles/10.3389/fpsyg.2017.02218/full. (Accessed February 25, 2019).

Hedinger, Mark R. *Towards a Paradigm of Integrated Missionary Training.* D. Miss. Dissertation, Western Seminary, 2006.

Hesselgrave, David J. *Communicating Christ Cross-Culturally: An Introduction to Missionary Communication.* Grand Rapids: Zondervan, 1991.

Hiebert, Paul G. *Anthropological Insights for Missionaries.* Grand Rapids, MI: Baker Book House, 1985.

_____. *Cultural Anthropology.* Grand Rapids: Baker Book House, 1983.

_____. *Missiological Implications of Epistemological Shifts.* Harrisburg, PA: Trinity Press International, 1999.

Hoke, Steve. "Missionary Training." *Connections*. August 2007. www.initialmedia.com.

Hoke, Steve and Bill Taylor. *Send Me! Your Journey to the Nations*. Pasadena, CA: William Carey Library, 1999.

Horrell, J. Scott. "In The Name of the Father, Son and Holy Spirit: Constructing a Trinitarian Worldview," http://www.bible.org. (Accessed January 4, 2022).

_____. "Toward Clarifying a Biblical Model of the Social Trinity: Avoiding Equivocation of Nature And Order," *Global Missiology*, January 2004. http://www.globalmissiology.net.

Hyman, Ronald and Barbara Rosoff. "Matching Learning and Teaching Styles: the Jug and What's in it." *Theory into Practice* 23.1 (1984): 35-43.

Illeris, Knud. *Transformative Learning and Identity*. New York: Routledge, 2014.

James, E. Alana, Tracesea Slater, and Alan Bucknam. *Action Research for Business, Nonprofit, and Public Administration: A Tool for Complex Times*. Los Angeles: Sage Publications, 2012.

Jarvis, Peter, ed. *Twentieth Century Thinkers in Adult and Continuing Education*, 2nd edition. Sterling, VA: Stylus Publishing Inc., 2001.

Jenkins, Philip. *The Next Christendom. The Coming of Global Christianity*. New York: Oxford Univ. Press, 2002.

Johnson, R. Burke and Larry Christensen. *Educational Research: Quantitative, Qualitative, and Mixed Approaches*, 6th ed. Los Angeles: Sage, 2017.

Kane, J. Herbert. *Understanding Christian Missions*: Grand Rapids: Baker Book House, 1974.

Kaplan, Robert. "Cultural Thought Patterns in Intercultural Education." *Language Learning* 16 (1966).

Kemmis, Stephen and Robin McTaggart. "Participatory Action Research." *The Handbook of Qualitative Research*, 2nd ed. Thousand Oaks, CA: Sage Publications, 2000.

King, Kathleen P. *Bringing transformative learning to life*. Malabar, FL: Krieger, 2005.

Kinnaman, David. *You Lost Me: Why Young Christians Are Leaving Church...And Rethinking Faith*. Grand Rapids: Baker Books, 2011.

Kligyte, G. "Transformational narratives in academic practice. "*International Journal for Academic Development*, 16(3), 2011, 201-213.

Kohls, L. Robert with Herbert L. Brussow. *Training Know-How for Cross Cultural and Diversity Trainers*. Duncanville, TX: Adult Learning Systems, Inc., 1995.

Kohls, L. Robert and John M. Knight. *Developing Intercultural Awareness. A Cross-Cultural Training Handbook* 2nd ed. Yarmouth, ME: Intercultural Press. 1994.

Kolb, David A. *Experimental Learning: Experience as the Source of Learning and Development*. Englewood Cliffs; London: Prentice-Hall, 1984.

Kolb, David and Simy Joy. "Are There Cultural Differences in Learning Styles?" Weatherhead School of Management, Case Western University, Dept of Organizational Research., n.d.

Konieczny, Richard J. and Enoch Wan. "An Old Testament Theory of Multiculturalism." *Global Missiology*, July, 2004. www.globalmissiology.net.

Landis, Dan and Rabi S. Bhagat, *Handbook of Intercultural Training, 2nd Ed.* Thousand Oaks, CA: SAGE Publications, Inc, 1996.

Lederleitner, Mary T. *Cross-Cultural Partnerships: Navigating the Complexities of Money and Mission*. Downers Grove, IL: Intervarsity, 2010.

Lewis, Jonathan, "International Missionary Training Fellowship: What the Army Needs," *The Journal of the WEA Missions Commission*, February 2003, 46-48. http://www.globalmission.org.

_____. "Internet Based Missionary Training." *Journal of the WEA Missions Commission*, October 2004 – January 2005, 60-61. http://globalmission.org.

_____. "Teaching, Technology And Transformation," *Evangelical Missions Quarterly*, Vol 36 no 4, Oct. 2000. 490-496.

Lindsell, Harold. *The World, the Flesh, and the Devil.* Canon Press. 1973.

Lister, J. Ryan. *The Presence of God: Its Place in the Storyline of Scripture and the Story of Our Lives*. Wheaton, IL: Crossway, 2015.

Loughlin, Kathleen A. *A Woman's Perceptions of Transformative Learning Experiences Within Consciousness-Raising*. San Francisco, CA: Mellen Research University Press, 1993.

Louw, Johannes P. & Eugene A. Nida, ed. *Greek-English Lexicon of the New Testament Based on Semantic Domains*. New York: United Bible Societies, 1989.

Lowe, Stephen D. and Mary E. *Ecologies of Faith in a Digital Age: Spiritual Growth Through Online Education*. Downers Grove: IVP Academic, 2018.

Lulee, Su-Tuan, et. al. "Transformative Learning" Created for EDDE 801, Ed D at Athabasca University, Canada on August, 2009. http://www.slideshare.net/susanlulee/introduction-to-transformative-learning.

Lysaker, J. & S. Furness. "Space for transformation: Relational, dialogic pedagogy." *Journal of Transformative Education*, 9(3), 2011, 183-187.

Maffet, Gregory J. "A Scriptural Model of the Learner – A Van Tillian Perspective." In *Christian Approaches to Learning Theory. Vol Two, The Nature of the Learner*. De Jung, Norman ed. Lanham, MD: University of America Press, 1984.

Matsumoto, David and Hyisung C. Hwang. "Assessing Cross-Cultural Competence: A Review of Available Tests." *Journal of Cross-Cultural Psychology* 44 (2013): 849-873. 16 September 2014. http://jcc.sagepub.com/content/44/6/849.refs.html.

McKinney, Lois. "Contextualizing Instruction: Contributions to Missiology From the Field of Education," *Missiology*. Vol XII, no. 3, July 1984.

_____. "Missionaries in the Twenty-First Century. Their Nature, Their Nurture, Their Mission, " *Missiology*. Vol. XXI, no 1, Jan. 1993.

_____. "New Directions in Missionary Education." In *Internationalizing Missionary Training: A Global Perspective*. William David Taylor, ed. Grand Rapids, MI: Baker Books, 1991.

McKinney-Douglas, Lois. "Learning Theories." In *Evangelical Dictionary of World Missions*. A Scott Moreau, ed. Grand Rapids, MI: Baker Book House, 2000.

Mertler, Craig A. *Action Research: Improving School and Empowering Educators* 3rd ed. Thousand Oaks, CA: SAGE, 2012.

Mezirow, J. *Education for Perspective Transformation: Women's Reentry Programs in Community College*. New York: Center for Adult Education Teachers College, Columbia University, 1975.

_____. "Perspective Transformation." *Adult Education*, 1978, 100-110.

_____. "A Critical Theory of Adult Learning and Education." *Adult Education*, no. 32. 1981, 3-23.

_____. *Transformative Dimensions of Adult Learning*. San Francisco, CA: Jossey-Boss, 1991.

_____. "Transformative Theory of Adult Learning." In: *In Defense of the Lifeworld*, edited by M.R. Welton, New York: SUNY Press, 1995. 39-70.

_____. "Transformative Learning: Theory to Practice." *New Directions for Adult and Continuing Education*, no. 74, 1997. 5-12.

_____. *Learning as Transformation: Critical Perspectives on a Theory in Progress*. San Francisco: John Wiley and Sons, 2000.

Miller, J.P. & W. Seller. *Curriculum: perspectives and practice*. Toronto: Copp Clark-Pitnam, 1990.

Moltmann, Jurgen. *The Trinity And the Kingdom*. Minneapolis, MN: Fortress Press, 1993.

Moreland, J.P. and William Lane Craig. *Philosophical Foundations for a Christian Worldview*. Downers Grove: Intervarsity Press, 2003.

Moreau, A., ed. *Evangelical Dictionary of World Missions*. Grand Rapids, MI: Carlisle, Cumbria, UK: Baker Academic, 2000.

Morgan, Lem. *Missions in the Local Church*. Calvary Bible College: unpublished course notes, 2002.

Müller, Roland. *The Messenger, The Message and the Community, 2nd Ed.* Canada: CanBooks, 2010.

Newell, Marvin J. "Who Sent the First Missionaries? A Critical Examination of Acts 13:1-4," (MA Thesis. Grace Theological Seminary, May 1977).

O'Sullivan, E. *Transformative Learning: Educational vision for the 21st century*. Toronto, Canada: University of Toronto Press Inc, 1999.

_____. "Bringing a perspective of transformative learning to globalized consumption." *International Journal of Consumer Studies*, 27(4), 2003, 326-330.

Olsen, C. Gordon. *What in the World is God Doing? The Essentials of Global Missions*. 7th updated ed. Lynchburg: Global Gospel Publishers, 2013.

Paige, R. Michael, *Education for the Intercultural Experience*. 2nd Edition. Yarmouth, ME: Intercultural Press, 1993.

"Partnership and Collaboration: Lausanne Occasional Paper No. 38." *Lausanne Movement*. Pattaya, Thailand, 2004. https://lausanne.org/content/lop/partnership-collaboration-lop-38. (Accessed 6/1/2021).

Patterson, George, with Galen Currah and Enoch Wan. "Classroom Instruction and Mentoring Compared." *Global Missiology*, Sept 2003, http://www.globalmissiology.net.

Paxton, Joshua. "Synergy Handbook." Calvary University: unpublished, 2019.

Pazmino, Robert W. *Foundational Issues in Christian Education*, 2nd edition. Grand Rapids, MI: Baker Books, 1997.

_____. *God Our Teacher, Theological Basics in Christian Education*. Grand Rapids, MI: Baker Academic, 2001.

_____. *Principles and Practices of Christian Education. An Evangelical Perspective*. Eugene, OR: Wipf and Stock Publishers, 2002.

Pearcey, Nancy. *Total Truth. Liberating Christianity from its Cultural Captivity*. Wheaton, IL: Crossway Books, 2004.

Pearson. "Beyond Millennials: The Next Generation of Learners." in *Global Research & Insights*. August 2018. https://www.pearson.com/content/dam/one-dot-com/one-dot-com/global/Files/news/news-annoucements/2018/The-Next-Generation-of-Learners_final.pdf. (Accessed February 25, 2019).

Peter, Jarvis. Ed. *20th Century Thinkers in Adult & Continuing Education*. 2nd Revised ed. London: Routledge, 2001.

Peters, George W. *A Biblical Theology of Missions*. Chicago: Moody, 1972.

Peters, Ted. *God As Trinity. Relationality And Temporality in Divine Life*. Louisville, KY: Westminster Knox Press, 1993.

Pierson, Paul Everett, John Dudley Woodberry, Charles Edward van Engen, and Edgar J. Elliston. *Missiological Education for the Twenty-first Century: The Book, the Circle, and the Sandals: Essays in Honor of Paul E. Pierson*. Maryknoll, NY: Orbis Books, 1996.

Pieratt, Jason. *Calling to the Missionary Vocation: A Study of the Lived Experience of American and Majority World Missionaries of Children's Relief International*. DIS Dissertation. Western Seminary, 2018.

Plueddemann, James E. "Culture, Learning and Missionary Training." In *Internationalizing Missionary Training*. Taylor, William B. ed. Grand Rapids: Baker Book House, 1991.

Poythress, Vern S. "Reforming Ontology and Logic in the Light of the Trinity: An Application of Van Til's Idea of Analogy." *Westminster Theological Journal*, vol 57:1 Spring 1995, 187-219.

Prensky, Mark. "Digital Natives, Digital Immigrants," *On the Horizon* 9, no. 5. (October 2001). https://www.marcprensky.com/writing/Prensky%20-%20Digital%20Natives,%20Digital%20Immigrants%20-%20Part1.pdf. (Accessed July 13, 2020).

Qureshi, Nabeel. *Seeking Allah, Finding Jesus: A Devout Muslim Encounters Christianity*. Grand Rapids: Zondervan, 2014.

Ramirez, Alonzo and Enoch Wan. "A Biblical Theology of Multi-Ethnicity and Multi-Culturality. Diversity in Unity And God's Ultimate Purpose for Humanity." *Global Missiology,* July 2004. www.globalmissiology.net.

Reed, Jeff. "Church Based Missions: Creating a New Paradigm." Paper presented at 3rd Annual Conference, BILD International, Oct 1992. www.BILD.org.

_____. "Church Based Theological Education: Creating a New Paradigm." Paper presented to North American Professors of Christian Education, 1992. www.BILD.org.

Rhodes, Matt. *No Shortcut to Success: A Manifesto for Modern Missions*. Wheaton: Crossway, 2022.

Rickett, Daniel. *Building Strategic Relationships: A Practical Guide to Partnering with Non-Western Missions*. Third Edition. Minneapolis, MN: Stem Press, 2008.

_____. *Making Your Partnership Work*. Third edition. Roswell, GA: Daniel Rickett, 2014.

Ryrie, Charles C. *Basic Theology*: *A Popular Systematic Guide to Understanding Biblical Truth*. Chicago: Moody Press, 1999.

Seemiller, Corey and Meghan Grace. *Generation Z Goes to College*. San Francisco: Jossey Bass, 2010.

Schultz, George. "The BEST Missionary Training Model?" *Evangelical Missions Quarterly*, vol 39: no. 1, January 2003, 90-95.

Scollon, Ron, Suzanne Wong Scollon and Rodney H. Jones. *Intercultural Communication A Discourse Approach*, *3rd Ed.,* West Sussex, UK: John Wiley & Sons, Inc., 2012.

Scott, Sue M. "The Grieving Soul in the Transformation Process." In: *Transformative Learning in Action: Insights from Practice. New Directions for Adult and Continuing Education*. no. 74, edited by P. Cranton, San Francisco, CA: Jossey-Bass, Summer 1997.

Sharp, Larry W. "A Mission Agency Director's Perspective on the Changing Relationship Between UFM, the Church, Training Institutions and the Mobilizers of Mission." Presented at the Evangelical Missiological Society Meeting. March 19-20, 1999, Lancaster, PA.

Shaules, Joseph. *The Intercultural Mind: Connecting Culture, Cognition, and Global Living.* Boston: Intercultural Press, 2015.

Sills, Michael David. "Training Leaders for the Majority World Church in the 21st Century," *Global Missiology*, April, 2004. http://www.globalmissiology.org.

Slimy, Joy and David A Kolb. *Are There Cultural Differences in Learning Styles?* Paper. Case Western Reserve University. Cleveland, OH: n.d.

Smallman, William H. *Able To Teach Others Also. Nationalizing Global Ministry Training.* Pasadena, CA: Mandate Press, 2001.

Smith, Donald K. *Creating Understanding. A Handbook for Christian Communication Across Cultural Landscapes.* Grand Rapids, MI: Zondervan Publishing House, 1992.

Smith, Ralph. *Paradox And Truth. Rethinking Van Till on the Trinity.* Moscow, ID: Canon Press, 2002.

_____. "The Trinitarian Covenant in John 17." *Global Missiology.* January 2005. http://www.globalmissiology.net.

_____. *Trinity And Reality. An Introduction to the Christian Faith.* Moscow, ID: Canon Press, 2004.

_____. "Van Til's Insights on the Trinity." *Global Missiology,* January 2005, http://www.globalmissiology.net.

Smith, Mark K. "Kurt Lewin: groups, experiential learning and action research." *infed.org: education, community-building and change*, 2001. https://infed.org/mobi/kurt-lewin-groups-experiential-learning-and-action-research/. (Accessed October 27, 2020).

Stanley, Paul D. and J. Robert Clinton. *Connecting: The Mentoring Relationships You Need to Succeed in Life.* Colorado Springs, CO: NavPress, 1992.

Steffen, Tom. "Missiological Education for the 21st Century." *Evangelical Missions Quarterly.* April, 1993, 178-183.

Stringer, Ernest T. *Action Research*, 4th ed. Los Angeles: Sage, 2014.

Swanson, K.W. "Constructing a learning partnership in transformative teacher development." *Reflective Practice*, 11(2), 2010, 259-269.

Taylor, Edward W. *The Theory and Practice of Transformative Learning: A Critical Review,* Information Series no. 374. Columbus: ERIC Clearinghouse on Adult, Career, and Vocational Education, Center on Education and Training for Employment, College of Education, the Ohio State University, 1998. http://www.calpro-online.org/eric/docs/taylor/taylor_02.pdf.

Taylor, William David, ed., *Global Missiology for the 21st Century. The Iguassu Dialogue.* Grand Rapids, MI: Baker Academic, 2000.

_____. ed. *Internationalizing Missionary Training, A Global Perspective.* Grand Rapids, MI: Baker Book House, 1991.

_____. ed. *Kingdom Partnerships for Synergy in Missions.* Pasadena, CA: William Carey Library 1994.

_____. ed. *Too Valuable to Lose.* Pasadena, CA: William Carey Library, 1997.

Thiessen, Henry C. *Lectures in Systematic Theology.* revised by Vernon D. Doerksen. Grand Rapids: Eerdmans, 1979.

Thomas, R. Murray, ed. *International Comparative Education – Practices, Issues And Prospect.* New York: Pergamon Press, 1990.

Ting-Toomey, Stella. *Communicating Across Cultures.* New York, NY: The Guilford Press, 1999.

Tira, Sadiri Joy and Enoch Wan, *Missions in Action in the 21st Century.* Quezon City: Lifechange Publishing Inc and Global Diaspora Network, 2012.

Tisdell, Elizabeth J. *Exploring Spirituality and Culture in Adult and Higher Education.* San Francisco, CA: Jossey-Bass. 2003.

Torosyan, Roben. *Teaching for Transformation: Integrative Learning, Consciousness Development and Critical Reflection.* Unpublished manuscript. http://faculty.fairfield.edu/rtorosyan/. (Accessed January 4, 2022).

"Trinity Knot, The History of Triquetra." *Ireland Travel Guides.* https://irelandtravelguides.com/trinity-knot-triquetra/. (Accessed February 15, 2021).

Moo, Douglas J. "Romans," in *The NIV Application Commentary.* Edited by Terry Muck. Grand Rapids: Zondervan, 2000.

Moulton, J. H. and G. Milligan. *Vocabulary of the Greek New Testament.* 2nd printing. Peabody: Hendrickson Publishers, 2004.

Vella, Jane. *Learning to Listen, Learning to Teach: The Power of Dialogue in Educating Adults.* Rev. Ed. San Francisco: Jossey-Bass, 2002.

Warren, Max. *Partnership: The Study of an Idea*. London: SCM Press LTD, 1956.

Wan, Enoch. "A Critique of Charles Kraft's Use/Misuse of Communication and Social Sciences in Biblical Interpretation and Missiological Formulation." *Global Missiology*, October 2004. www.globalmissiology.org.

_____. "Ethnohermeneutics: Its Necessity and Difficulty for All Christians of All Times." *Global Missiology*, January 2004. http://www.globalmissiology.net. (Accessed October 24, 2018).

_____. "Inter-Disciplinary and Integrative Missiological Research: The 'What,' 'Why,' and 'How.'" www.GlobalMissiology.org. (Accessed July 1, 2017).

_____. "A Missio-Relational Reading of Romans." *Enochwan.com*. http:///www.enochwan.com. (Accessed October 24, 2018).

_____. "Mission and '*Missio Dei*'; Response to Charles van Engen's 'Mission Defined and Described.'" in *MissionShift: Global Missions Issues in the Third Millennium*, ed. David J. Hesselgrave and Ed Stetzer. Nashville: B & H Publishing Group, 2010.

_____. "The Paradigm of Relational Realism." *Enochwan.com*. http:///www.enochwan.com. (Accessed October 24, 2018).

_____. "Relational Theology and Relational Missiology." *Enochwan.com*. http:///www.enochwan.com. (Accessed October 24, 2018).

_____. "Rethinking Missiological Research Methodology: Exploring A New Direction." *Global Missiology*. http://www.globalmissiology.net. (Accessed October 24, 2018).

Wan, Enoch, ed. *Diaspora Missions to International Students*. Portland: Western Seminary Press, 2019.

Wan, Enoch and Geoff Baggett. "A Theology of Partnership: Implications for Implementation by a Local Church." *Global Missiology*. April 2010. www.GlobalMissiology.org. (Accessed November 5, 2020).

Wan, Enoch and Johnny Yee-chong Wan. "Partnership in Action - #1: A Relational Study of the Trinity and The Epistle to the Philippians." *Global Missiology*, April 2010. www.GlobalMissiology.org. (Accessed November 5, 2020).

Wan, Enoch and Jon Raibley, *Transformational Change in Christian Ministry*, Portland: Western Seminary Press, 2022.

Wan, Enoch and Kevin P. Penman. "The Trinity: A Model for Partnership in Christian Missions". *Global Missiology*, April 2010. www.GlobalMissiology.org. (Accessed November 5, 2020).

Wan, Enoch and Mark Hedinger, "Missionary Training for the Twenty First Century: Biblical Foundations." *Global Missiology.* July 2011. http://www.globalmissiology.net. (Accessed November 28, 2018).

_____. *Relational Missionary Training.* Urban Ministry in the 21st Century. Skyforest, CA: Urban Lost Publishers, 2017.

_____, "Understanding 'Relationality' From a Trinitarian Perspective." *Enochwan.com.* www.enochwan.com. (Accessed October 24, 2018).

_____. "Transformative Ministry for the Majority World Context: Applying Relational Approaches," *Occasional Bulletin of EMS.* Vol. 32. No. 1. Summer 2018.

Wan, Enoch and Michael Pocock, ed. *Missions from the Majority World: Progress, Challenges, and Case Studies.* Evangelical Missiological Society Series. No. 17. Pasadena: William Carey, 2009.

Wan, Enoch and Tin V. Nguyen. "Toward a Theology of Relational Mission Training – an Application of the Relational Paradigm." *Global Missiology* no. 11. http://ojs.globalmissiology.org/index.php/english/article/view/1626/35 99. (Accessed February 26, 2021).

Ware, Bruce A. *Father, Son & Holy Spirit, Relationships, Roles, & Relevance.* Wheaton, IL: Crossway, 2005.

Welsh, Claude. In This Name. *The Doctrine of the Trinity in Contemporary Theology.* New York: Charles Scribner's Sons, 1952.

White, James Emery. *Meet Generation Z: Understanding and Reaching the New Post-Christian World.* Grand Rapids: Baker, 2017.

Whitehead, Evelyn Eaton and James D. Whitehead. *The Promise of Partnership: A Model for Collaborative Ministry.* Lincoln, iUniverse.com Inc., 2000.

Whiteman, Darnell L. "Integral Training Today for Cross-Cultural Mission." *Missiology and International Review* 36.1 (2008): 5-16.

Wilson, David and Lorene. eds. *Pipeline: Engaging the Church in Missionary Mobilization.* Littleton, CO: William Carey Press, 2018.

Wilson, Jessie, Colleen Ward and Ronald Fischer. "Beyond Culture Learning Theory: What can Personality Tell us about Cultural Competence?" *Journal of Cross-Cultural Psychology* 44 (2013): 900-927.

Woodberry, Dudley J. *Missiological Education for the 21st Century, The Book, The Circle, and the Sandals.* Maryknoll, NY: Orbis Books, 1996.

Wright, Christopher J.H. *The Mission of God.* Downers Grove, IL: Intervarsity Press, 2006.

Yount, William R. and Mike Barnett. *Called to Reach: Equipping Cross-Cultural Disciplers.* Nashville: B&H Academic, 2007.

Zachary, Lois J. *The Mentor's Handbook: Facilitating Effective Learning Relationships* 2nd ed. San Francisco: Jossey-Bass, 2012.

www.ingramcontent.com/pod-product-compliance
Lightning Source LLC
Chambersburg PA
CBHW060206070426
42447CB00035B/2716